German Military Vehicles
of World War II

D1604680

# German Military Vehicles of World War II

*An Illustrated Guide to Cars, Trucks, Half-Tracks, Motorcycles, Amphibious Vehicles and Others*

JEAN-DENIS G.G. LEPAGE

McFarland & Company, Inc., Publishers

*Jefferson, North Carolina, and London*

LIBRARY OF CONGRESS CATALOGUING-IN-PUBLICATION DATA

Lepage, Jean-Denis.
German military vehicles of World War II :
an illustrated guide to cars, trucks, half-tracks, motorcycles,
amphibious vehicles and others / Jean-Denis G.G. Lepage.
p.     cm.
Includes bibliographical references and index.

ISBN-13: 978-0-7864-2898-4
(softcover : 50# alkaline paper) ∞

1. Vehicles, Military—Germany—History—20th century.
2. Germany. Heer—Equipment.   3. World War, 1939–1945—
Germany—Equipment and supplies.   I. Title.
UG620.G3L69 2007     623.7'47094309044—dc22     2007002638

British Library cataloguing data are available

*On the cover:* German SdKfz 8s with 150 mm guns in tow (*World War II in Color*)

Manufactured in the United States of America

*McFarland & Company, Inc., Publishers
Box 611, Jefferson, North Carolina 28640
www.mcfarlandpub.com*

# Contents

# Introduction

Unlike the First World War (1914–1918), World War II (1939–1945) was characterized from the start by quick and vast offensives with tanks and variations of armored vehicles. The main campaigns on land were fought on wheels and tracks, and motor vehicles became a common feature of World War II armies. The industries of all major belligerents were geared up for production of mechanized units.

A lot has been published about World War II German forces, and books dealing with the "glamorous" self-propelled guns and spectacular tanks are plentiful. Much less known and taken for granted are the auxiliary vehicles that made it possible for troops and armored vehicles to keep moving. Indeed, "soft skins" tend to be less covered in modeling and publishing form, but this book is intended to fill that void by covering the motor vehicles used by the German forces during the Second World War. Behind each soldier who fired a bullet, drove a tank or took off on a bomber mission stood a chain of helpers without whom no bullets could have been fired and no victories could have been won. In World War II more victories were won by properly functioning supplies and more defeats suffered from lack of materiel and fuel than could ever have

been believed. This book's emphasis is thus on "soft skins," the unarmored or lightly armored vehicles, cars, motorcycles, vans, ambulances, trucks and tractors that operated behind the front line, on the supply routes at home bases, dumps, airfields and similar areas and locations. They transported soldiers, fuel, ammunition, food and stores to keep the fighting units in actions, and many campaigns were lost by failure of supply lines. In this book, tanks and self-propelled guns have been thus deliberately omitted, but the last two chapters are devoted to combat vehicles: half-tracks and armored cars.

A thorough discussion of the history, development and technical features of every transport vehicle used in World War II by the Germans would need several volumes, as the *Wehrmacht* had indeed many cars and trucks. The reader will meet in this book a good cross-section of the most usual transport vehicles that the Germans produced, such as the *Kübelwagen* light car and the notorious *Opel Blitz* truck, but also less well known designs, civilian-type cars, rarities, and experimental vehicles. It should be noted that many foreign-made vehicles are also listed in this work as the Germans pressed into service many captured vehicles from the European nations that they had annexed or occupied by force. Another fact worthy of mention is the number of pre-war vehicle types that were designed in the second half of the 1930s and that were either continued in production after the outbreak of World War II or were used in large quantities throughout the duration of the conflict. Standardization was a common fact well before the war. In the early 1930s, the *Reichswehr* (German army) ordered vast numbers of specialized types of vehicles, but in an effort to prevent the maintenance problems that were already looming, the so-called *Schell-Programme* of 1938 made a clean sweep of old models and introduced a complete new series of standardized designs. The German armies had well-designed, high-quality military vehicles, but these were always in limited number and allocated with priority to the elite *Panzer* and *Waffen SS* divisions. Motorization of the normal regular infantry divisions—even at the victorious beginning of World War II—was much less modern and abundant than the propaganda asserted. In fact, horses were used in enormous quantities throughout the war, mainly behind but also at the front line. As it was German, army motorization started off very professionally with high hopes and grandiose ideals during the 1930s, but it ended in complete shambles.

From the military automotive history point of view, the period 1933–1945 in Germany is an extremely interesting time, which on purely technical and historical grounds ought to be given more attention. Unfortunately only relatively few specimens of genuine *Wehrmacht* vehicles remain, usually in museums or in the hands of firms which specialize in letting them out on hire to the film industry.

The subject of this book—in comparison with other aspects of World War II—has been so far rather neglected, resulting in scarce documentation and few sources of information. A work of this kind can never be wholly complete in every detail. It has been necessary in certain cases to limit technical data, to approximate information and to omit certain details and particularities. Output was truly enormous, and the entries given here represent only a portion of the models produced from the early 1930s to 1945.

The illustrations, drawn after existing photographs gleaned here and there, are made by myself in an attempt to reveal details that may be unclear on a photograph and with the intention of showing the readers the essential points of the vehicles.

This book is not intended to be a comprehensive survey of every facet of World War II. Its aim is clear, simple and humble. It is hoped that the present volume will be of use and interest—not only to modelers, students and specialists but also to that nebulous class, the "intelligent general reader"—the curious reader with an interest but little specific knowledge in this subject—the technical and historical development of World War II German transport vehicles.

Naturally, the author should like to invite readers to call to his attention (by contacting the publisher) any inaccuracies and factual errors they may detect. Constructive criticisms, suggestions and additional information will always be welcomed.

*Jean-Denis G.G. Lepage*
*Spring 2007*
*Groningen, The Netherlands*

# Glossary

**Allradantrieb** (A): all-wheel drive
**Ausführung** (Ausf): model or variant or mark
**Autobahn**: motorway
**Befehlswagen** (Bef.Wg.): command vehicle
**Beobachtungswagen** (Beob.Wg.): observation vehicle
**deutsch** (d): German
**dreiling** (D.): triple (for gun mount)
**Einheit** (E. or Einh.): standardized design
**Fahrgestell** (Fgst): chassis
**Fernsprecher** (Fe): telephone
**Fliegerabwehrkanone** (Flak): anti-aircraft gun
**französisch** (f): French
**Funk** (Fu.): radio or wireless
**Funkwagen**: radio car
**geländefähig** (gf.): suitable for off-road operation
**geländegängig** (gl.): designed for off-road operation
**gepanzert(er)** (Gp. or gep.): armored
**Halb Ketten** (HK): half-tracked vehicle
**handelsüblich** (o): commercially available
**Heck** (H): rear (for place of engine)
**Hitler Jugend** (HJ): Hitler Youth movement
**(Kaliber)länge** (L/-): caliber length of gun (e.g., L/48: gun barrel length 48 times caliber)
**Kamfpwagenkanone** (KwK): tank gun
**Kanone** (K): gun or cannon
**Kettenkrad**: half-tracked motorcycle
**Kettenschlepper** (Kett.Schlp.): tracked tractor
**Kraftfahrzeug** (Kfz.): motor vehicle, used as prefix to ordnance designation
**Kraftomnibus** (Kom.): motor bus
**Kraftrad** or **Motorrad** (Krad.): motorcycle
**Kraftwagen** (Kw.): motor vehicle, car or truck

**Krankenkraftwagen** (KrKw.): ambulance
**Lastkraftwagen** (LkW.): van or truck
**leicht** (1. or le.): light
**Mannschaftstransportwagen** (MTW): troop carrier
**Maschinegewehr** (MG): machine gun
**mittler** (m. or mittl.): medium
**Motor-SA**: motorized units of the SA
**Nationalsozialistisches Kraftfahrkorps** (NSKK): National-Socialist Drivers Corps
**Nebelwerfer** (Nb.W): smoke mortar, or rocket
**Panzer** (Pz): armor, tank
**Panzerabwehrkanone** (Pak): anti-tank gun
**Panzerbüchse** (Pz.B.): anti-tank rifle or anti-tank light gun
**Panzerjäger** (Pz.Jäg.): self-propelled anti-tank gun (literally "tank hunter")
**Panzerkampfwagen** (Pz.Kpfw.): tank
**Panzerspähwagen** (Pz.Spähw., Pz-Sp-Wg): armored reconnaissance car
**Personenkraftwagen** (PkW): passenger car
**Radschlepper** (Rd.Schlp.): wheeled tractor
**Sanitärkraftwagen** (Sanka): ambulance
**schienengängig** (schg.): for use on railroad
**Schlepper** (Schlp.): tractor
**Schützenpanzerwagen** (Schtz.Pz.Wg. or SPW): armored infantry carrier
**schwer** (s. or schw.): heavy
**schwimmfähig** (schwf.): (literally, capable of floating) amphibious
**Selbstfahrlafette** (Sfl.): self-propelled gun
**Sonderkraftfahrzeug** (SdKfz): special motor vehicle (including tanks), used as prefix to ordnance designation

**Sturmabteilung** (SA): private uniformed militia of the Nazi party created in 1922 and purged in 1934

**Sturmgeschütz** (StuG): assault tank

**Tonne** (-t, -to): metric ton

**tschechisch** (t): Czech

**Vierling**: quadruple (for gun mount)

**Vol Ketten** (VK): fully tracked

**Volkssturm**: German popular militia (Home Guard) created in 1944

**Waffen SS**: armed units of the Schutzstaffel (SS) originally Hitler's body guards, officially created in 1940

**Wagen** (Wg.): vehicle, car

**wasserfähig** (Wg.): amphibious

**Wehrmacht** (WH): German Army comprising Heer (ground forces), Kriegsmarine (navy) and Luftwaffe (air force)

**Zugkraftwagen** (Zgkw.): prime mover, half-track

**Zwilling**: dual or double (twin for gun mount)

# A Note on
# Weights and Measures

All measurements in this book are given in metric units.

1 millimeter (mm) = 0.039 in.
1 centimeter (cm) = 0.393 in.
1 meter (m) = 0.328 ft. or 1.094 yd.
1 kilometer (km) = 0.612 mi.
1 liter (L) = 0.22 Imperial gallon or 0.26 U.S. gallon
1 cubic centimeter (cm³) = 0.061 cubic in.
1 cubic meter (m³) = 1.308 cubic yd.
1 kilogram (kg) = 2.205 lb.
1 tonne (t) = 1.102 U.S. ton (= 2000 lb.) or 0.984 British ton (= 2240 lb.)

# 1

# World War II
# German Vehicles:  General

## Development of military vehicles

The first self-driven military road vehicle appeared in 1769. It was a cumbersome steam-powered tricycle invented by a Frenchman named Nicholas-Joseph Cugnot (1725–1804). Cugnot's *fardier* (lorry) was intended to be a military gun tractor, and during a test, ran for twenty minutes at a speed of 2.25 mph with four passengers. This machine can be seen today in the Conservatoire des Arts et Métiers in Paris, France. In 1832 a certain Samuel Brown invented a primitive gas vacuum engine, which was improved in 1837 by William Barnett. A free-piston engine was invented in Italy in 1859, and the essential theoretical requirements for an efficient gas engine were laid down in 1862 by the French engineer Alphonse Beau de Rochas. The internal combustion engine, destined to revolutionize first transport in war and then the

*Light truck Praga RV*

*NAG 4-ton truck (1910). The Neue Automobil Gesellschaft (NAG) 4-ton truck was one of the first combustion/gasoline engine vehicles to see service in the German army. It was basically a civilian commercial model with an engine developing up to 60 hp. Large numbers of this type were built and saw service during World War I as troop or cargo carriers.*

*Daimler CB truck (c. 1914). The blockade of Germany by the Allies led to a major shortage of vital materials such as rubber needed for tires. To overcome this shortage, many German vehicles in the latter half of the war had all-steel sprung resilient wheels.*

implements of war—the tank and the airplane—showed leisurely development through the 19th century with tremendous acceleration in the final decade. The first satisfactory gas engine was built by Dr. A. Otto in 1874. This was greatly improved in 1882 by Gottlieb Daimler (1834–1900) who produced a lightweight gasoline engine suitable for the development of the automobile. The first commercial production of petroleum began in Romania in 1857 and in the United States in 1859. The development of rubber was also indispensable for the production of automobiles. In 1839 Charles Goodyear discovered the process of vulcan-

ization, and the technique was improved in 1906 by George Oenslager of Akron, Ohio. Important developments in the production of automobile tires were made by the brothers André and Edouard Michelin from Clermont-Ferrand, France.

At the end of the 19th century, military transportation still largely depended upon the horse. However, mechanical traction had begun to make itself felt in military circles. Commercial gasoline vehicles appeared in numbers in the early 1900s, and military authorities in Europe and America were quick to see their value as supply and troop carriers. Vehicles moved

*Landaulette type German staff car (1916). This vehicle was a commercial type purchased for military service.*

*Opel 35 PS Stabwagen (1917)*

by the internal combustion engine soon complemented trains for light and short-haul transportation, extended the range of action, and avoided the care of horses as well as the constraints of railroads.

It was appreciated in the early 1900s, when motor vehicles became a practical military proposition, that any large-scale conflict in the future would necessitate the massive acquisition of cars and trucks at short notice. But peacetime financial stringency did not permit large funds to be spent on expensive transport fleets for which there would be little employ. A subvention scheme was the answer, and the German War Department introduced a subvention to finance a reserve of road vehicles that could be taken over quickly by the army in the event of a war. In this scheme, owners of motor vehicles meeting military requirements received an annual subsidy for a given period from the military authorities in return for which they maintained the vehicles in good working condition and surrendered them to the government for a fixed sum of money in time of war. By 1907 some 158 assorted trucks had been registered for

subsidies, and a year later regulations were laid down for vehicles qualifying for subventions. To qualify for a subsidy, the vehicles had to meet complex and rigid specifications laid down by the military authorities. The salient points were the maximum permitted weight, which was 4,000 kg, and the maximum gross weight of 8,000 kg. Power was not to be less than 35 hp, and a load of up to 4,000 kg was desirable. Interchangeable radiators, four-speed gearbox, transmission by live axle via bevel drive, canvas weather protection for driver and cargo, towing hooks at front and rear, and standardized lighting, wheels and tires were required. The subsidy vehicles underwent exhaustive acceptance trials and technical tests, and the result had a major effect on vehicle design, generally raising the standard considerably, not only in Germany but also in France, Great Britain and Austria as well, where similar subvention schemes were operated. Several companies were involved in the subsidy scheme in Germany, among them Daimler, Ehrhardt, Büssing and Neue Automobil Gesellschaft (NAG). When World War I broke out, other manufacturers joined the war effort and received approval to built subsidy types.

Large numbers of these trucks saw service during the First World War (1914–1918). This conflict saw the emergence of the mechanized age and the introduction of special military purpose vehicles such as ambulance, repair truck, cargo and troop carrier, and staff car, to mention just a few. The railroad was primarily responsible for making it possible to keep large armies in contact for long periods of time. It could bring up more men, supplies, and food from greater distances than ever had been possible for the largest wagon trains, and it brought up the millions of pounds of ammunition that mass production poured out of the factories. But without trucks, the forward railheads would have been constricting bottlenecks because horse transport, with its great demands for forage, would have limited what could be brought forward. Trucks could bring supplies to distribution points in operational zones, from which horse-drawn transport could finally take over distribution. By the end of World War I in 1918, military *mechanization* had

proven its usefulness; this term had been defined as the application of the internal combustion engine to land warfare in the transportation of men, weapons and supplies to and on the battlefield. By 1918, the German army had a large motorized park, including 25,000 cargo trucks, 12,000 cars, 3,200 ambulances, and 5,400 motorcycles.

## The vehicles of the Reichswehr (1919–1935)

The *Reichswehr* (Defense Forces) was the name of the German standing army during the period of the Weimar Republic and the opening years of the Nazi Third Reich (1919–1935). According to the Treaty of Versailles of 1919, the German army was restricted to a force of 100,000 professional men, of whom only 4,000 were to be officers, and which was divided into seven infantry and three cavalry divisions. Aircrafts, tanks, submarines, heavy weapons and fortifications were prohibited. Nevertheless, in contravention of the treaty, the chief of staff of the Reichswehr, General Hans von

*Geländewagen Horch 8 (1926). The 6 x 4 cross-country military car Horch 8 from 1926 weighed 2,680 kg. Length was 4.7 m, and maximum speed was 70 km/h. Fuel consumption was 26 liters/100 km (on road) and 33 liters/100 km (cross-country). Maximum range was 340 km (on road) and 270 km (cross-country). The Reichswehr Horch 8 could transport eight troops, including the driver.*

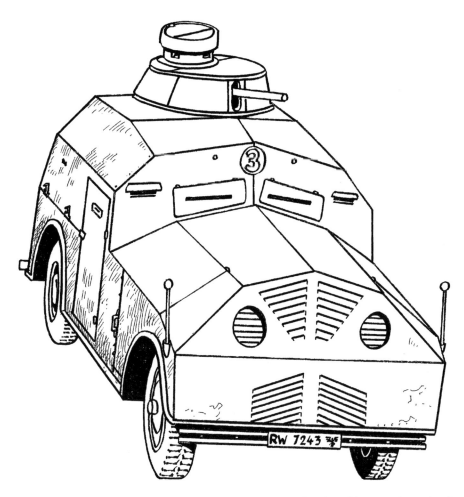

*Early German Panzerwagen c. 1930. This armored car was developed in 1930 from the chassis of the Adler Standard 6. Lightly armored with thin aluminum plates and fitted with a dummy turret armed with a mock gun, it was only an "Attrape," a dummy that would have been useless in combat conditions but provided a good training vehicle. The crew included four men: a commanding officer, a gun operator (who was idle), a radio operator and a driver.*

Seeckt (1866–1936), began rebuilding the army and extended armament production abroad. Von Seeckt represented the intellectual side of the German Reichswehr. In his role as commander in chief, he exercised an important role in changing the funda-

mental culture of the German forces. The long-term result was an army that valued rigorous, thorough training based on experience and one that had fully learned the lessons of World War I in a fashion that the rest of the European military authorities did

*OPPOSITE, TOP: Krupp-Daimler Panzerwagen SdKfz 3 M1574. The Reichswehr Krupp-Daimler heavy armored truck was designed in the late 1920s on the chassis of a Daimler DZVR and was used in the 1930s. Some 105 units were produced and issued to motor transport battalions of the Reichswehr. Some were equipped with radio sets and a frame antenna and were also used as command cars. It was an unarmed Mannschaftstransportwagen (armored personnel carrier) with a crew of two and 12 passengers. The vehicle had poor cross-country performance, even with four-wheel drive, because of its solid rubber tires; it weighed 10,600 kg, had a maximum speed of 20 km/h, and had a consumption of 90 liters/100 km. In 1935 the existing vehicles were relegated to tactical training duties.*

*OPPOSITE, BOTTOM: Light car Adler Kübelsitzwagen 1927*

*Dummy tank on NSU Dixi car 1931*

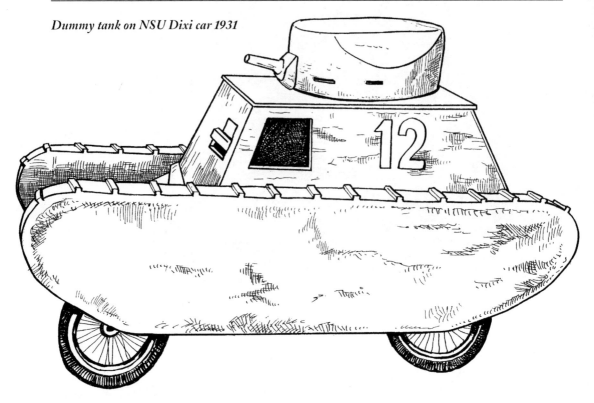

not. After 1920, von Seeckt could not avoid the army being involved in politics, as many officers and men had right-wing sympathies. Von Seeckt himself spent much of his tenure—between 1920 and 1926—as Reichswehr commander plotting but failing to understand political issues resulting from the German defeat of 1918. One of the greatest weaknesses of the Weimar Republic was its reliance on the army, which placed it at the mercy of the Right and deprived it of support from the Left. Throughout the twenties, the army, by its opposition to the Left and its ambiguous sympathy toward the Right, dangerously hampered the republic in its freedom of action. The small Reichswehr became a coveted body, a state within the state. Its senior officers had influence on foreign affairs and played a significant role in internal political issues, notably by supporting the *Freikorps* (militarized militia) in the period 1919–1921 and later Hitler's Nazi movement between 1930 and 1933. Political indiscretions in 1926 lost von Seeckt the

job, but he entered politics as a member of the Reichstag from 1930 to 1932, and in 1934 and 1935, he headed a mission to help Chiang Kai Shek reorganize the Chinese army.

If he was a poor would-be politician, von Seeckt had, however, the ability to take the long view. He was willing to abandon an immediate objective in order to obtain a greater goal. Technically speaking, he was the true father of Hitler's German army that went to war in 1939. He encouraged brilliant and modern-minded officers to update doctrine, and he introduced the latest organizations and methods, which led to the creation of the modern German air force, tank force and airborne troops. Right after World War I, he wanted to evade the restrictions of the Versaille Treaty without openly violating it, and he succeeded. He was instrumental in formulating a secret agreement of Russo-German military collaboration in 1921. Germany would help train the young Red Army and build up the Russian arms industry. In return, the agreement provided Germany with a place to train its officers and test new weapons beyond the watchful eyes of the Allied disarmament commission. Germany's secret activities for the circumvention of the military clauses of the Versaille Treaty were not confined to Bolshevik Russia. By using anonymous companies and foreign subsidiaries, the Krupp firm, for example, was able to carry out experimental weapons design and testing outside Germany in neutral countries such as Spain, Sweden, the Netherlands and Finland. From 1924 to 1927 the emphasis was placed on planning and designing prototypes. After 1927, with the departure of the Allied Control Commission, the budget of the army increased rapidly, German rearmament began and factories were adapted for the mass production of the prototypes designed abroad. At the same time, some of the cavalry units were used as a cover to develop transport and motorization, and secret orders were issued for the design of military vehicles. Several types of *Kübelwagen* (small personnel carriers) were produced, such as the Mercedes-Benz "Stuttgart" 260, the Adler Favorit, and the Hanomag 4/20. In 1926, the Horch Company produced the *Geländewagen Horch 8*, a cross-country personnel carrier with twin rear-bogie. Similar cross-country vehicles were designed, for example, the *Geländewagen Mercedes-Benz Typ G 1* from 1927 and the *Geländewagen Selve Typ M* from 1926. In 1930, the Reichswehr had 406 cars and 1,176 trucks, some lightly armored.

The German army also made use of so-called *Attrappen* (dummies). As early as 1925, push-along tricycles with canvas structures were used for the purpose of tank training. Attrappen training cars were fitted with dummy tracks on the sides, wooden armor and an imitation turret on top armed with a fake gun. Training vehicles included, for example, the Hanomag 10 from 1927, the Adler Standard 6 from 1930 and the Opel P4 from 1935.

## Hitler's rearmament

Rearmament was the key to Hitler's economic success. While rearmament was secretly taking place, Hitler pursued a foreign policy designed to throw other world powers into confusion about his ultimate aim: European domination by war. In 1934, Germany was still militarily weak and surrounded by hostile, suspicious and powerful neighbors: France and Poland. The short-term aims were the repudiation of the Treaty of Versailles and rearming without provoking a war. In 1935, Hitler took his boldest step by rearming Germany in defiance of the restrictions imposed under the Treaty of Versailles. Conscription was reintroduced with a view to increase the German army to 500,000 men, five times the figure allowed under the treaty. The name of *Reichswehr* was changed to *Wehrmacht* (Armed Forces), including the *Heer* (ground force), the *Kriegsmarine* (navy) and the newly constituted *Luftwaffe* (air force). Germany withdrew from cooperation with Russia and launched her own vehicle-building program. Hitler saw Russia as a threat and an eventual target, though Western nations could not be ignored.

A truck of 1916 was a clumsy machine put together by hand and not designed for large-scale manufacture. By 1936, thanks to Henry Ford and those who imitated or improved on him, gasoline vehicles could be turned out of vast factories in which they flowed together on conveyor lines, by the hundred thousands. Quantitative and qualitative improvement were spectacular. In the inter-war period, many improvements were done regarding development of road networks. The vital role of transport by truck had already been recognized by many military experts—particularly the British captain B.H. Liddell Hart who greeted the six-wheel truck as a landmark in military transport evolution. Technical progress enabled production of more powerful engines, larger payload capacity, better suspension and transmission, and stronger chassis and framework. Between the wars, mechanization stood at the forefront of the military debate, and the famous Heinz Guderian (1888–1954) borrowed heavily from British and French theory and practice to develop German armor and his audacious tactics of Blitzkrieg. After the seizure of power by the Nazis, the German army innovated and developed a doctrine emphasizing flexibility, initiatives at all levels, exploitation, leadership from the front and mechanization. Owing to two solid assets—a coherent strategical doctrine and technical knowledge of British and French experiments in the late 1920s and 1930s—they developed a sound framework that resulted in the gradual creation of a powerful armored force, composed of tanks (developed by Guderian) and motor vehicles (developed by Major-General Oswald Lutz).

New vehicles were ordered by Lutz, and the German War Department evolved a subsidy scheme and placed orders for military vehicles to manufacturers such as Krupp, MAN, Horch, Henschel, Büssing-NAG and Mercedes. Specifications were advanced but expensive and even luxurious, including permanent four-wheel drive, limited-slip differentials, independent suspension on all wheels, auxiliary low gears for country capability, and two spare wheels mounted on stub axles amidships where they acted to prevent the vehicle bellying on rough ground. The purely military vehicles were of quite elaborate design and this reflected the Nazi thinking that was behind the national rearmament program. What other army would produce beautifully designed tourer-type cars with independent suspension and other refinements just to transport four soldiers comfortably with their kit and equipment? What army would spend a small fortune on every one of thousands of highly sophisticated semi-track artillery tractors providing comfortable theater-type seating for every member of the crew of a dozen or so? This was prepa-

ration for war but somehow was interconnected with Göbbels's propaganda machine. The photographs, many in full color, of this equipment in such magazines as *Signal*, *Wehrmacht* and *Motor Schau* looked superb and must have impressed millions. These ideal specifications encouraged splendid vehicles but proved too expensive for quantity production, and gradually many civilian cars and trucks of all types were brought into military service, resulting in a great variety of models. Before 1938, there were about 113 different types of transport trucks, 52 models of cars and 150 different types of motorcycles, causing many complications.

## The Schell program

It was not very long, however, before the German military authorities decided that these fantastic and costly developments had to come to a halt. In 1938, a drastic scheme—the *Schellplan*—was named after Oberst (Colonel) Adolf von Schell—who was *Generalbevollmächtigter für das Kraftfahrwesen* (Director of Mechanization). Ironically, the Schell program was thought to have been originated after senior German officers read detailed reports of the American Quartermaster Corps's original standardization of the period 1930–1934. The Schell program was intended to reduce the chaotic situation.

German military vehicle production was reorganized, each manufacturer being limited to a few designs, and many models were discontinued. The program reduced the number of trucks from 113 to 30, cars from 52 to 19, and motorcycles from 150 to 30. Several so-called *Einheit* (standardized) types were axed for light, medium and heavy cars. The development of some special-purpose, over-elaborate and costly vehicles was abandoned or curtailed, and—as far as possible—designs that had both military and commercial applications were adopted. The army was persuaded to be content with a minimum number of reliable basic types that would meet most, if not all, transport requirements. The various models formed a universal transport fleet and were produced by a number of different firms in Germany and later Austria. In some cases, a vehicle that had proved to be of good quality was produced by more than one company, a typical example being the successful *Opel Blitz 3-ton* truck that was manufactured by both Opel and Daimler-Benz. The mass-produced *Volkswagen Kübelwagen* was another example of a universal, simple and reliable car that superseded much more expensive machinery. The system set up by Colonel Adolf von Schell worked reasonably well, although the Germans still managed to devise dozens of different versions of one basic truck with a universal house-type body.

In 1939 when the major nations went to war again, they were equipped with reliable, numerous and adapted military vehicles, but in general, German automotive equipment consisted of adaptations of civilian types, and these in most cases did not reach the high standard of American or British military vehicles either in reliability or performance.

At the outbreak of World War II, the following were the main classifications for *Wehrmacht* motor vehicles:

• Motorcycles: light (up to 350 cc), medium (350–500 cc), heavy (over 500 cc)

• Cars: light (up to 1500 cc), medium (1500–3000 cc), heavy (over 3000 cc)

• Field cars: as cars but open military-type bodywork

• Standardized *Einheit* cars: light, medium, and heavy

• Ambulances: one basic type on chassis of heavy car or light truck

• Buses: light (up to 15 seats), medium (up to 30 seats), and heavy (over 30 seats)

• Trucks: light (up to 2 tons payload), medium (2 to 4 tons), and heavy (over 4 tons)

• Cross-country trucks: light (up to 2 tons payload), medium (2 to 4 tons), and heavy (over 4 tons)

• Wheeled tractors: light (up to 25 bhp), medium (up to 40 bhp)

• Tracked tractors: light (up to 25 bhp), medium (up to 40 bhp), and heavy (over 40 bhp)

• Semi-tracked artillery prime movers: light (up to 3-ton towed load), medium (5 to 8 tons), and heavy (12 to 18 tons)

• Armored cars: light (with four wheels) and heavy (with six or eight wheels)

• Armored infantry half-track carriers and combat derivates: light (SdKfz 250 series) and medium (SdKfz 251 series)

• Armored fighting vehicles: tanks and self-propelled artillery

## German transport during the war

From 1936 to 1939, conscription had brought into being an army far bigger than anything that German industry could equip with motor vehicles. Those senior officers who wanted a small professional army on wheels knew it was out of the question. Apart from a tiny elite (armored divisions and, later, Waffen SS units), German World War II forces were mass armies of conscripted foot infantrymen with horse transport. It would remain so right through the war. In 1939 an average infantry division had about 5,000 horses and about 900 motor vehicles, and this required over 50 tons of hay and oats per day and about 20 tons of motor fuel. Although captured and civilian vehicles were used, there was not the slightest chance for Germany to have a modern, fully motorized army. Industrial production was simply pitifully inadequate.

On the whole, German military vehicles were less "modern" than those used by the Allies during World War II. Indeed, a large proportion of the Wehrmacht vehicles were pre-war types simply because they were of pre-war design and manufacture. The many ever-changing front lines, the vast occupied territories, and the immensely long supply routes into Russia called for large numbers of vehicles of various sorts. Moreover, not every type of vehicle was suitable for every type of combat area. The problems of making the same basic car or truck work satisfactorily under winter conditions on the Eastern front and almost the exact opposite in North Africa were enormous. Once the British and Canadian war industries had gotten into top gear in 1941, and much more so when by 1942 the gigantic U.S. automotive industry began to go all-out on producing war materials in huge quantity, there was no hope left for Hitler's Third Reich. The German industry was totally incapable of supplying enough materials to enable the army to retain the territorial gains it had made during the swift and

successful *Blitzkrieg* campaigns of 1939–1941. One of the reasons why Nazi Germany failed to knock Russia out of the war was the difficulty of maintaining supplies over long ranges across roads that broke up in wet weather.

Clearly but inexplicably, Hitler had expected the war to be of short duration. Together with the failure of the attack against the Soviet Union and the entry of the United States into the war, the mass bombings by the RAF and U.S. Air Force demonstrated to the Germans that the time of victorious *Blitzkrieg* was over. When the turning point came in 1943, the German forces changed from the offensive to the defensive with little or no choice but to employ whatever automotive equipment they could lay their hands on whether suitable or makeshift. The general results were chaotic. Added problems, of course, were those of material shortages and interruption in production as a result of sabotage and air bombings. Germany was then forced to

*Wrecked vehicle*

fight the industrial total war that Hitler had long sought to avoid. Reluctantly, the Third Reich began to mobilize for this new type of war, economically, militarily and psychologically.

Albert Speer (Minister of Armament and Ammunition) took complete control over the whole war economy with Hitler's backing and established a central planning board and a system of "organized improvisation" to mobilize the German economy for total war. In fact, Speer's efforts were desperate, short-term measures and expedients that undermined the structure of the German economy and accelerated its eventual collapse. Through the better management of this board, together with drastic rationalization, the massive closing down of small firms and the redistribution of skilled labor, factories producing war materials worked at high pressure. The war industry was dispersed for large-scale prefabrication, and components for war machines were produced in many different parts of the country and were brought together only when ready for assembly. In the short term, Speer was able to maintain, and in some cases increase, the output of essential weapons and ammunition. In 1944 Germany produced more armament than in 1940. Yet the so-called Speer miracle—which was able to answer the Allied bombing offensive with a considerable increase of war production in 1943–1944—was not realizable without the ruthless exploitation of human and material resources from occupied Europe. German workers, including women, and foreign workers, including prisoners of war, forced laborers and concentration camp inmates, were driven to the point of exhaustion by Speer's expedients.

## Foreign vehicles

Minister Albert Speer decided to engage as many foreign plants as possible, not only for the production of certain vehicles for which these factories were set up at the time of occupation, but also for additional output of the *Schell Plan* and other types of vehicles. The employment of captured material was a favored practice in the German army, and during World War II, captured military vehicles (and other equipment including artillery, tanks, weapons, uniforms and equipment) were collected, sorted, repaired and issued for further use by the three branches of the Wehrmacht: Heer, Luftwaffe and Kriegsmarine. Civilian cars, vans and trucks were also commandeered, but they were flimsy by military standards, with only two-wheel drive, a far cry from the all-wheel drive that was the army's preferred equipment.

France's motor vehicle industry and vehicles abandoned by the British after Dunkirk, as well as others taken from the other defeated West European nations, alleviated the German army's desperate shortages in the motorized infantry and motorized supply units. Germany's stockpiled fuel oil, deeply drained by the early campaigns, was replenished with enough to keep the war machine going for another two years. Captured vehicles and equipment played a non-negligible role in the World War II German armies. For example, in April 1941, the Germans were able to equip the 20th Armored Division and the 14th, 18th, 25th, and 36th Motorized Infantry Divisions with captured French vehicles. The rescue of the men of the British Expeditionary Force from the beaches of Dunkirk in 1940 is a legendary event in British history. The BEF was fully mechanized, unlike other armies that still used large numbers of horses. At Dunkirk a huge amount of equipment, weapons and vehicles was left behind. Some of these were destroyed in action or sabotaged or wrecked on purpose, but a considerable amount was still operating and was to see service with the German army. Of about one million vehicles operating on the Russian front, one in five was a captured French or British machine. Captured vehicles were used with nothing more than a new coat of paint, but some of them were fitted with local modifications (e.g., Notek night-drive lights, a new cab), and in a few cases more complicated conversions were carried out.

As a result of this predatory policy, a large number of foreign vehicles were used in the German armies, and their quantities justified the translating, printing and distribution of so-called *D-Vorschrifte* (manuals) for use by German personnel. Captured vehicles were indicated by a letter placed between brackets as follows: (e) *englisch* (English), (r) *russisch* (Russian), (t) *tschechisch* (Czech), (i) *italienisch* (Italian), (a) *amerikanisch* (American), (h) *holländisch* (Dutch), and (f) *französisch* (French).

The eventual result was an enormous variety of types, creating another chaotic situation that the Schell program had tried to reduce and control. This was, however, unavoidable as the military operations of World War II were so widely dispersed and of such enormous overall size that vehicle production had priority over development of new tactical types and standardization. Using a wide variety of foreign vehicles was a mixed blessing, as the huge variety of them made the situation inextricable. Hundreds of different models of vehicle, either manufactured or plundered from all over Europe, created unsolvable problems of maintenance and required the stocking of millions of different types of spare parts, a situation that was almost impossible to administer. Captured vehicles were used for a variety of tasks, and with the harsh conditions encountered in very different fronts (e.g., Russian front or North African campaign) and a chronic lack of spare parts, their numbers dwindled. However, some were still around as late as 1945, the final year of World War II.

The foreign companies who worked— more or less against their will—with the Germans made huge profits. Right after the war, there was a climate of revenge, and retaliations did not spare the top businessmen. Several high-placed automotive tycoons were tried, fined, fired or imprisoned for high treason and economic collaboration with the enemy (e.g., in France, Louis Renault and Marius Berliet). In January 1945, the Renault private automobile company, tainted by its collaboration with the Nazis, was nationalized without compensation.

The bloodless annexation of Austria and Czechoslovakia as early as 1938 and 1939 had given the Germans a huge production capacity. Austria and Czechoslovakia had very advanced motor industries and were turning out some of the best cars, trucks and tanks in the world when they fell intact into German hands. For Nazi Germany, the acquisition of a quantity of good quality military equipment and modern factories proved important. Vast numbers of trucks served in the Wehrmacht and remained in production for supply to Germany. The defeat and occupation of all industrial European nations after 1940 enabled the Germans to capture, confiscate or produce many civilian and military vehicles, notably in the Netherlands, Belgium, and France (Citroën, Peugeot, Panhard, Berliet, Latil, etc.). Other vehicles were taken over from or used by the Axis allies (Hungary, Italy, Romania).

Russian vehicles were also used by the Germans. Until the early 1930s, the Soviet Union had no automotive industry of great importance, and the country relied to a large extent on imports from Britain, Germany, Italy and the United States. The Second World War started for Russia when the Germans invaded the country on June 22, 1941. From that year, the Soviet Union received considerable quantities of war materials and vehicles under lend-lease from the United States, Canada and Great Britain. After the German smashing victory of summer 1941, large numbers of Russian-made and foreign Anglo-Saxon-imported vehicles were seized and pressed into *Wehrmacht* service.

Like Germany, Italy had begun building up its war machine long before the start of World War II. In fact, Italy was at war as early as 1935 in Ethiopia. After the collapse of Mussolini's fascist regime in 1943, the northern part of Italy (where most industry was concentrated) was occupied by the Germans, and the *Wehrmacht* got possession of large numbers of Italian military vehicles that were soon pressed into service. As a result of occupation, the Italian automotive industry was engaged principally in production of trucks and artillery tractors, which officially entered service with the *Wehrmacht*. By far the largest supplier of automotive equipment was the Fiat concern, which included several subsidiaries such as OM (Officine Meccaniche from Brescia), SpA (Ligure Piemontese Automobili from Turin) and many other companies, including Alfa-Romeo from Milan, Bianchi from Milan, Isotta-Fraschini from Milan, Lancia from Turin and Ansaldo-Fossati from Genoa. This did not help Germany much. It is on record that Fiat did everything it could to produce as little as possible. From September 1943 until April 1945, the Germans tried to make full use of Italian production facilities, only to meet sabotage, strikes and other forms of passive resistance. Under Mussolini, incidentally, the Italian war production efforts had not been outstanding either. Possibly this may explain in part why Italy's World War II fighting forces were comparatively weak, especially the mobile and armored variety, although in many cases Italian designs were excellent.

## The German automotive industry

Hitler was not an economical theorist but a pragmatical tyrant, and unlike Marxism, the ideology of Nazism had no underlying economic component. Nazism was fundamentally racist and *völkisch* in its conception—which was to make secure, preserve and enlarge the *Volksgemeinschaft* (racial German community). Economic factors were always subordinate, and Hitler aimed to create an autarkic system allowing Germany self-sufficiency. He also intended conquest and expansion in the East (*Lebensraum*, "vital space"), by force if need be. So, from the very beginning of the Nazi regime in 1933, the economy had been subjected to the preparation of war, while allowing a reasonable level of consumer affluence. In 1936, Hitler had restored what looked like prosperity, created a disciplined workforce, and reasoned that recovery from the traumatic depression of the early 1930s had been sufficient; he ordered then the launch of large-scale rearmament and the construction of a siege economy based on the policy of autarky. Although there were large investments in public equipment, the fastest expanding sector became the armament industry. So large were the plans for rearmament that neither the armed forces nor the economic administration thought them remotely feasible.

There was, however, no single, consistent economic program or master plan but a series of strategies followed by a succession of leaders trying to meet Hitler's will: Hjalmar Schacht in the period 1933–1934, Hermann Göring's Four Years Plan from 1936 to 1939, and finally the wartime economy directed by Albert Speer from 1942 to 1945. On the whole, the Nazi economical concept was nothing less than a deliberate unhinging of the German economy with the intention of recovering the financial losses by exploiting other national economies of Europe within the confines of German-dominated empire conquered by force. Hitler geared the German economy to war and conquest that would be necessary in order to achieve the *Lebensraum*, which would be its long-term economic salvation. The militarization of the economy forced a much higher level of state management and eroded the independence of private business. Against this background, the major German motor transport manufacturers were ordered to produce military vehicles. These are listed here below, including the main foreign plants in annexed or occupied territories.

Key: *Werke* means "manufacture." AG means *Aktiengesellschaft* (incorporated or joint-stock company). The French *Société Anonyme* (S.A.) and the German *Gesellschaft mit beschränkter Haftpflicht* (GmbH) mean "limited-liability company."

• Adler-Werk (formally Heinrich Kleyer AG), Frankfurt am Main

• Audi-Auto-Union AG Werke, Zwickau

• Austro-Daimler, Steyr-Daimler-Puch AG, Vienna (Austria)

• Auto-Union AG, Chemnitz and Siegmar-Schönau

• BMW, Bayerische Motoren Werke AG, Munich, Eisenau and Spandau

• Borgward, Hansa-Loyd-Goliath Werke AG (later Carl F.W. Borgward GmbH), Bremen

• Büssing-Neue Automobil Gesellschaft (Büssing-NAG), vereinnigte Nutzkw. AG, Braunschweig, Leipzig and Berlin-Oberschöneweide

• Citroën, Société Anonyme, Paris (France)

• Daimler-Benz (see Mercedes-Benz)

• Demag AG, Wetter/Ruhr

• DKW, Auto-Union AG Werke, Zschopau

• Famo, Fahrzeug und Motorwerke GmbH, Breslau

• Ford-Werke AG, Cologne

• Fross-Büssing KG, Vienna (Austria)

• Gräf und Stift Automobilfabriks AG, Vienna-Döbling (Austria)

• Hanomag, Hannoversche Maschinebau AG, Hannover-Linden

• Hansa-Loyd-Goliath (see Borgward)

• Henschel und Sohn GmbH, Kassel and Berlin

• Horch Werke, Zwickau

• Kaelble Motorenfabrik, Backnang

• Klöckner-Humboldt-Deutz AG, Cologne and Ulm am Donau

• Krauss-Maffei AG, Munich-Allach

• Krupp AG, Essen

• Laffly Etablissement, Asnières (France)

• Lanz Heinrich AG, Mannheim

• Latil (controlled by Daimler-Benz), Suresnes (France)

• Magirus AG, Ulm

• MAN, Maschinenfbrik Augsburg-Nurnberg AG. Augsburg, Nuremberg and Gustavsburg

• Matford SA Ford, Asnières (France)

• Maybach Motorenbau GmbH, Friedrichshaven

• Mercedes-Benz AG, Stuttgart

• NSU AG, Neckarsulm

• OAF, Osterreichische Automobil-Fabrik AG, Vienna (Austria)

• OM SpA, Milan (Italy)

• Opel, Adam Opel AG, Rüsselsheim am Main and Brandenburg

• Peugeot Société Anonyme, Sochaux (France)

• Phänomen-Werke Gustav Hiller AG, Zittau

• Porsche, Dr. Ing.h.c. Ferdinand Porsche KG, Stuttgart-Zuffenhausen

• Praga, Böhmische-Märische Maschinenfabrik AG, Prague (Czechoslovakia)

• Renault, Usines, Billancourt (near Paris, France)

• Saurer, Osterreichische Saurerwerke, Vienna (Austria)

- Skoda-Werke, Pilzen & AG (formally Skoda-Werke), Prague (Czechoslovakia)

- Somua-Werke, Saint-Ouen (France)

- Steyr-Daimler-Puch AG, Oberdonau and Vienna (Austria)

- Stoewer-Werke AG, Stettin-Neutorney

- Tatra, Ringhoffer-Werke, Prague (Czechoslovakia)

- Tempo, Vidal und Sohn-Werke GmbH, Hamburg

- Trippel Werke GmbH, Molsheim (Alsace, France)

- Unic, Société Anonyme Automobile, Puteaux (near Paris, France)

- Volkswagen (DAF/KdF) GmbH, Wolfsburg

- Wanderer, Auto-Union AG-Werke, Siegmar

- Zündapp-Werke GmbH, Nuremberg

## Various roles

Most German military vehicles were designed in order to be able to tow a supply- or an ammunition-trailer or a field gun; when towing a trailer, a hinged warning triangle was erected on the driver's cab roof. All classes of truck (light, medium and heavy, as well as heavy cars) sometimes included twin rear bogie versions of the same vehicles. An advantage of the 6 × 4 layout was its relative simplicity, the drive being confined to the rear bogie and the long chassis that was more suitable for the mounting of specialist bodies, but the disadvantage was the number of wheels and tires required. German military vehicles could be converted to various purposes, and the same chassis could be fitted with a different superstructure such as cargo, personnel carrier or bus, fuel tanker, field kitchen, ambulance, signal or radio truck,

engineering workshop and others, notably firefighting equipment, loudspeakers and amplifier for a propaganda role. Many vehicles were equipped with a winch or a crane to be used in a maintenance or recovery role. Some were actually used as combat platforms, for example, fitted with a searchlight, a field gun, an anti-aircraft gun, an anti-tank gun, or a rocket-launching system. Many German army vehicles were diesel-engined and even had gas generators, taking into account Germany's shortage of petroleum, which had to be imported. The gasoline shortage became a grave problem as the war proceeded due to blockade, bombing and loss of captured oil fields.

Trucks were also used as murder machines by SS *Einsatzgruppen* (task groups) charged with murdering all "enemies of the Reich," including members of the Polish intelligentsia, Soviet functionaries, "less valuable Asiatics," Gypsies and more particularly Jews. In the period 1939–1941, victims were starved, hung or shot by SS firing squads, but there were also experimentations of mass murder by means of gas trucks. From the sick brain of a Nazi engineer, SS-Untersturmführer Dr. Becker, were born the monstrous machines known as *Sonderwagen* (in short *S-Wagen*, "special trucks"). The S-trucks' true purpose could not be seen from the outside; they looked like ordinary closed vehicles but they were built so that when the engine was started, the exhaust gas was led inside the airtight body of the vehicle, bringing death to the occupants. The victims were loaded into the trucks, which were driven to the place of burial used for mass execution, generally a huge trench already half-filled with numerous corpses. The time of the journey was calculated to ensure their death, from ten to twenty minutes. The trucks, varying in size, could each take from fifteen to twenty-five persons who were told when climbing into them that they were to be transported elsewhere. Once the doors were closed, the inside of the body, rigorously sealed, became a gas chamber on wheels. The S-trucks were developed by SS-Obersturmbannführer Rauff and his adjutant, Zwabel, both belonging to the motor transport group of the *Reichssicherheitshauptamt* (RSHA—the SS Central Security Department of the Reich established in 1939). The trucks were modified by the Austrian firm Saurer and entered service in late 1942. They operated for several months in Russia, Poland and Czechoslovakia. The existence of these mass-murder groups was top-secret, and the SS Einsatzkommando personnel were bound to absolute secrecy regarding the activities of their units and the functioning of their vehicles. Contrary to what the Nazis had expected, however, the bringing into service of the S-trucks did not solve the problem of mass murder. Victims soon began to realize what happened as soon as they climbed into these death cars, resulting in "annoying" incidents. Although deceiving stratagems were used, the scheme did not work very well. Drivers and operators were submitted to heavy pressure when driving: behind them, bumped about at the hazard of the ruts, twenty-five men, women and children were dying of asphyxiation in the carefully upholstered iron prison. The murderers complained of violent headaches; they maintained that they, too, absorbed a large quantity of the gas when they opened the doors of the trucks on arrival. They also complained of the dirtiness and horror of the job, as they had to bring out bodies entwined together and sullied. The poisoning by carbon monoxide gas did not always take place as foreseen, and instead of dead persons, the murderers on arrival had to unload convulsing near-dead bodies. Moreover, the gas vans failed to dispose of sufficient numbers: the Nazis did not want only hundreds or thousands of people killed—their ambition was the extermination of millions. The S-trucks scheme was rapidly abandoned, and soon, the Nazis embarked upon a comprehensive *Endlösung* (Final Solution) of the "Jewish Question."

Then they created permanent extermination camps (e.g., Belzec, Lublin, Sobibor, Treblinka, Chelmo and Auschwitz), and the genocide was industrially organized. The whole process from collecting the victims by round-up, transporting them by train as cattle, murdering them and then disposing of their bodies became an industrial exercise, a matter of logistics applied on bureaucratic lines. The extermination camps were equipped with specially designed gas chambers (displaying the appearance of a large shower-room), into which hundreds of victims would be taken as if for a shower. Once inside and once the doors were locked, they would be liquidated by Zyklon-B poison gas; the bodies were subsequently taken out by non-German personnel and burnt in large incinerators.

## Nomenclature

German nomenclature was not always consistent, and sometimes there were several official designations for the same vehicle.

German military vehicles—if intended for any specific role—were given a *Kfz* number used as a prefix to ordnance designation. *Kfz* was the abbreviation for *Kraftfahrzeug* (motor vehicle). The Kfz ordnance number was attributed by the *Heereswaffenamt* (the Army Ordnance Office, often referred to as *Waffenamt*). The section of this department specifically responsible for mechanized vehicles was the *Waffen Prüfamt 6* (*Wa Pruf 6*, Weapon Test Section 6). Requirements for new designs were passed either to automotive, engineering or armament firms. Designs accepted and approved were ordered into production through the Reich Armament Ministry. There was an advisory body consisting of service chiefs and leaders of industrials firms involved in vehicle production.

Hitler took a great personal interest in vehicle and tank design. His maniacal devotion to minutiae led him to interfere in the procurement programs of all three armed services, but most particularly with the *Heer*, the ground army. The Führer often intervened in the deliberations or sent orders or suggestions. To be fair, some of his ideas were useful or even ahead of his advisers, but, on the whole, Hitler's general ideas were limited. His technical knowledge was broad but his military interests were narrowly restricted to the traditional weapons and limited by his own experience of World War I trench warfare. He had little feeling for innovations and new developments such as, for example, radar, the atom bomb, jet fighters and rockets. Hitler's interference sometimes delayed or obscured other important matters and often antagonized the staff.

The *Kfz* number indicated the vehicle's role, regardless of the make of its chassis. If the whole vehicle was of a special design, evolved by the army itself (including the most important foreign designs taken over, particularly French and Czech), it was given an *SdKfz* ordnance number (*Sonderkraftfahrzeug* or *SdKfz* for short, meaning "special purpose motor vehicle"). The allocation of *Kfz* and *SdKfz* numbers helped to distinguish vehicles in the ordnance vocabulary; it was used for labeling all working drawings and spare parts lists peculiar to that type of vehicle. The *Kfz* and *SdKfz* numbers followed a pattern, not entirely consistent, and the following list gives the main categories:

Kfz 1–10: light passenger cars

Kfz 11–20: medium passenger cars

Kfz 21–30: heavy passenger cars

Kfz 31: ambulances

Kfz 32–40: light *or* heavy trucks

Kfz 41–50: medium trucks

Kfz 51–60: medium and heavy trucks

Kfz 61–70: light and medium vehicles suitable for off-road operation

Kfz 71–80: heavy vehicles suitable for off-road operation

Kfz 81–90: light vehicles suitable for off-road operation *or* heavy passenger cars

Kfz 301 to Kfz 384: special vehicles for the Luftwaffe

SdKfz 1–100: special unarmored vehicles

SdKfz 101, 121, 141, 161, 171, 181 and 182: battle tanks from mark I to VI

SdKfz 130 to 140: captured Czech tanks and various Czech self-propelled mountings

SdKfz 221 and 231: special armored cars

SdKfz 250 to 253: armored personnel carrier half-tracks and their variants

SdKfz 260 to 299: various tracked and wheeled vehicles

SdKfz 301 upwards: special demolition vehicles

The ratio of wheel/powered wheel was usually indicated. The designation 4 x 2 meant a vehicle had four wheels of which two were powered; 4 x 4 was four wheel drive; 6 x 4 six wheels, four powered; 6 x 6 six wheels, all powered.

## Standard equipment

Cars, trucks, half-tracks (armored or not) and armored cars were fitted with a certain number of standard equipment.

A truck driver's cab was very often fitted with a *Rückspiegel* (driving mirror) and external turn signal indicating change of direction.

On top of a truck driver's cab there was sometimes a hinged warning triangle that was erected when the vehicle was towing a trailer.

The cab could be hard or soft canvas-topped. One of the results of material shortage by the ending phase of World War II was the substitution of the steel truck cab

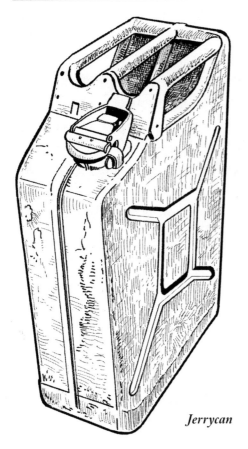

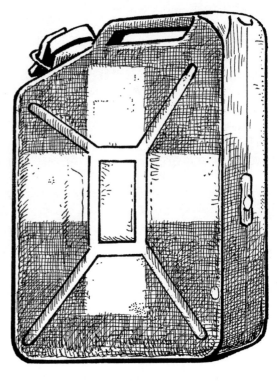

*Jerrycan*

*Jerrycan containing drinking water
(indicated by a white cross)*

by a standardized universal *Ersatz* or *Einheit* type. This cabin, called *Wehrmacht-Einheitsfahrerhaus* (army standardized driver's cabin) was made of pressed cardboard panels on timber framing and was used on the majority of new vehicles produced in 1944–1945. Due to the continuing shortage of raw materials in Germany after the war, the standardized *Einheit* driver's cab remained in production until 1947.

In many cases the windscreen could be folded down. Side vents were often fitted to the hood for improved engine cooling.

Hoods were made of simple pressed steel and often of squared-off shape. As they were often rather large, there were blind spots ahead of the vehicle, areas that could not be seen by the driver. To help the driver, vehicles were usually fitted with width indicator bars, these being a pair of small rods carrying balls at their ends and placed on both front wings.

Chassis were often fitted with a towing eye, haulage work hooks, sometimes a front-mounted winch, strong bumpers, guard bars protecting the radiator, headlamp guards, etc.

The bodywork—when suited for cargo—could be *Pritsche* (open), with *Seitenwände* (cart rails), or tilted with a *Wagenschutzdecke* (coarse canvas cover) that could be painted in camouflage patterns. The body work could also be arranged for *Kastenaufbau* (closed for special technical use) or *Krankenwagen* (ambulance).

Removable side canvas screens were often placed instead of doors.

The worst enemy of German armored forces in Russia was the weather. In summer there was dust, which not only choked the crews but also overcame air filters, thus causing a significant reduction of engine life. In autumn the heavy rain reduced

*Knüppelteppich
(log carpet)*

the countryside to a quagmire and stifled mobility. In winter temperatures could drop down to -30 degrees F, freezing and cracking crankcases and radiators, immovably fixing vehicles in suddenly frozen mud—frequently causing hundreds of vehicles to be abandoned to the enemy. For driving in snow, front and rear wheels could be fitted with snow-guards or skates known as *Schlittenkufen*. Some vehicles could be fitted at the front with a *Schneepflug* (snowplow). All German vehicles could be fitted with *Gleitschutzketten* (ice chains) attached on tires for driving on frozen ground. To help their vehicles drive in muddy or loose ground, the troops on the field devised the so-called *Knüppelteppich* (log carpet); this improvisation was made of logs or thick wooden sticks held together by iron wires, creating a corduroy path. The "carpet"—when not in use—could be rolled up and stored wherever a place was available, for example, on the bumper, over the hood, or on a rack placed on the wing of the vehicle.

Standard items included spare wheels,

spare parts, tools (shovel, pick or axe), towing cable, a camouflage net, canvas tarp cover, first aid locker, and fire extinguisher. There were also various stowing boxes and bins for individual weapons and ammunitions for the crew, supply and maintenance accessories, and personal effects (including helmets, gas masks, leather map cases, food, water, spare cloths, blankets, bags, etc.).

The Germans designed a very good fuel can, called *Einheits-Benzinekanister* (standardized gas can) or *Wehrmachtkanister* (army can) with a capacity of 20 liters (122 cu. in.). This was rectangular in shape with rounded corners, made of metal, robust, non-leaking, easy to carry and convenient to stack. The can was designed and manufactured by the Ambi-Budd company from Berlin-Johannisthal. Copied by all World War II combatants, the German container was universally known as a "jerrycan," from "Jerry," the nickname given to the Germans. In the German army, jerrycans were often intended to contain fuel (e.g., gasoline, diesel gas oil), but occasion-

*Tarnscheinwerfer (black-out front light). This was the front part of the Kfz-Nachtmarschgerät (vehicle night driving light)*

ally they were filled with drinkable water for men; in that case, a large white cross was painted on the side of the can to avoid accidents.

All items, jerrycans, tools and equipment were positioned using common sense and well on hand for immediate use by the crew. The inside of the vehicle became quickly cramped up, so accessories were attached in racks and clamps on the vehicle's hull sides and mudguards.

One characteristic item common to most vehicles officially taken into the German army was the *Tarnscheinwerfer* ("cat-eye" black-out lamp); this was a canvas cover used to dim headlights and so avoiding vehicles being spotted and strafed by aircraft. Another light dimmer was the *Kfz-Nachtmarschgerät* (night drive device). This device—introduced in 1939—was widely

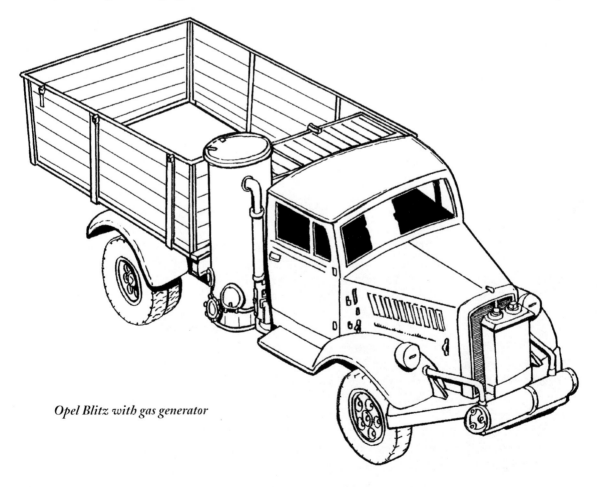

*Opel Blitz with gas generator*

*The standardized "Einheits" cab. Made of pressed cardboard panels on a wooden frame, the cheap Wehrmacht-Einheitsfahrerhaus (driver's cab) is shown here fitted to a late version of the Opel Blitz truck. Note the Kfz-Nachtmarschgerät (night driving device) fitted on the left front fender.*

used during the war for vehicles, half-tracks and tanks, especially after 1943 when the Germans had to move their motorized forces at night for black-out security reason. The *Kfz-Nachtmarschgerät* was developed by the army in cooperation with the firm Nova-Technik GmbH. This equipment consisted of three parts. The detachable *Tarnscheinwerfer* (black-out front lamp) had the shape of a flattened *Wehrmacht* helmet, enabling illumination ahead of the vehicle without being seen from the sky; this was placed on the left front wing or in an equivalent position. The *Abstandsrücklicht* (distance stop unit) was placed at the rear of the vehicle; it had two pairs of two square openings in a row that could be blanked off by a hinged lid, by which means the distance from the vehicle could be determined during convoy driving at night. If the four squares appeared

to the following driver as one light area, he was too far behind; if they looked like two lights, the distance was correct (35–25 m). Front and rear lights could be intensified, dimmed, and put on and off by a cylindrical-shaped *Stufenschalter* (regulating switch) placed in the driver's cab.

Toward the end of the war, when the Allied air force dominated the skies, many German vehicles had a so-called *Luftraumbeobachter* (air-observation post) popularly named *Lucki-Lucki* by the troops; this was a metal seat mounted on the right-hand front wing for an observer whose duty was to warn against aircraft. When possible, main roads were lined with drive-in dugouts at regular intervals into which the whole vehicle could be driven in case of air attacks.

The overriding worry for the Germans

*6.5-ton Tatra T 81 H truck equipped with gas generator*

as 1942 began was the looming threat of fuel shortage as their armies used up tons of oil in ever more mobile battles at the end of insufferably long lines of communication. By that time the decreasing availability of gasoline and diesel oil favored the appearance of the so-called *Gaserzeuger für Kohle* (gas generator). In this system, charcoal or green wood was burned in a twenty-gallon metal boiler strapped either to the hood or to the roof of the vehicle; the combustion products were then fed directly into the carburetor. The conversion from gasoline power to gas generator could be done rather quickly, and soon the sight of trucks, cars or buses with the unwieldy metal tanks puffing along the streets and roads was a familiar one. These conversions showed what efforts the Germans had to go to in the face of an ever growing fuel shortage as World War II progressed, as their front lines were pushed back from the oil fields and as Allied bombing took an ever heavier toll of their fuel reserves.

## Markings

In the heat of battle—during World War II but unfortunately this is still true today—there was always a chance of friends harming friends as the range of artillery and airplanes increased while mechanized and armored vehicles were of similar configuration. On land the *Identification Friend or Foe* (IFF) depended upon painted symbols or pennants, but mostly there was an optimistic dependence upon recognition training. Furthermore, the massive expansion of military forces and the huge increase in motor vehicles and military road convoys made some means of identifying military units essential for policing purposes. All German vehicles were therefore marked out with the national cross, with divisional insignia and with tactical symbols. The subject of markings for World War II German vehicles is in some ways complicated by the fact that there were so many variations and so many exceptions to the rules. Although official ruling dictated how markings were to be applied, a great amount of license seems to have been allowed, and the interpretation of the rules became somewhat lax as the war progressed. In fact, the subject of German vehicle marking is a quicksand with exceptions and anomalies to disprove every rule.

## NATIONAL IDENTIFICATION MARKS

The German *Balkenkreuz* (national marking) was a cross of Greek type with four arms of equal length, straight and parallel sides. In the period 1938–1940 the cross was white and later was black with contrasting white limbs to let the cross stand out against the background color. There were two main variants: thin and thick. The national cross—similar to the airplanes of the Luftwaffe—was painted on the vehicle's rear side, on doors or on the front plate, but its position was often governed by jerrycan stowage racks, spare wheels, exhaust pipes, tools and other pieces of equipment. The national marking was not frequent on "soft-skin" vehicles such as cars, trucks, and ambulances, but it was always displayed on front line combat vehicles such as reconnaissance armored cars, half-tracks and tanks. At the beginning of the war, and as long as

*National marking (Balkenkreuz). (1) white cross (beginning of World War II), (2) white outline, (3) thin black cross with white outline, (4) thick black cross with white outline.*

the Germans had air superiority (that is, roughly speaking, until 1943), a national flag (a black Nazi swastika in a white disc on a red background) was often displayed on the hood of vehicles; Nazi flags were also displayed for propaganda purposes. Flags and national crosses were omnipresent on captured vehicles in an attempt to identify them against mistaken air attacks from friendly artillery and airplanes.

## DIVISIONAL INSIGNIA

The divisional insignia was applied by stencil and often painted white or yellow on the front mudguards and repeated at the back. Divisional insignia of motorized units were numerous and varied; they ranged from the simple to the complex. They represented an animal, a geometric pattern or a stylized symbol using simple signs and straight lines to be easily applied, remembered and recognized. For example, the emblem of the 6th armored division was two *X*s or a battle-axe blade, that of the 13th armored division a cross within a circle, that of the 3rd armored division the standing

*Afrika Korps Emblem*

bear of Berlin, that of the 24th armored cavalry division a horseman within a circle, that of the armored regiment *Grossdeutschland* a German helmet, that of the *Afrika Korps* a swastika on a palm tree, and that of the

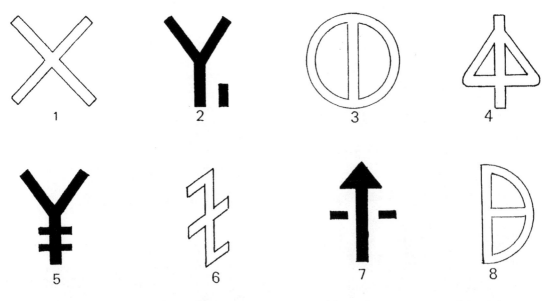

*Examples of divisional insignia. (1) 5th Panzer Division, (2) 8th Panzer Division, (3) 11th Panzer Division, (4) 15th Panzer Division, (5) 17th Panzer Division, (6) 19th Panzer Division, (7) 20th Panzer Division, (8) 21st Panzer Division.*

Panzer-Regiment IV a warrior with sword and shield.

During important campaigns such as operation *Barbarossa* (the invasion of Russia in June 1941), vehicles could be marked with a letter or a symbol indicating which Army Group they belonged to. For example, a *G* on the mudguard showed Guderian's *Panzergruppe* (Armored Group); a *K* indicated von Kleists's.

## TACTICAL MARKINGS

The *taktische Zeichen* (tactical markings) found their way on signposts, maps and battle orders. Their purpose was twofold: to enable military police to identify a vehicle to report it or to direct it to its proper destination, and to identify knocked-out vehicles brought in for light repairs. Vehicles sent back for major over-

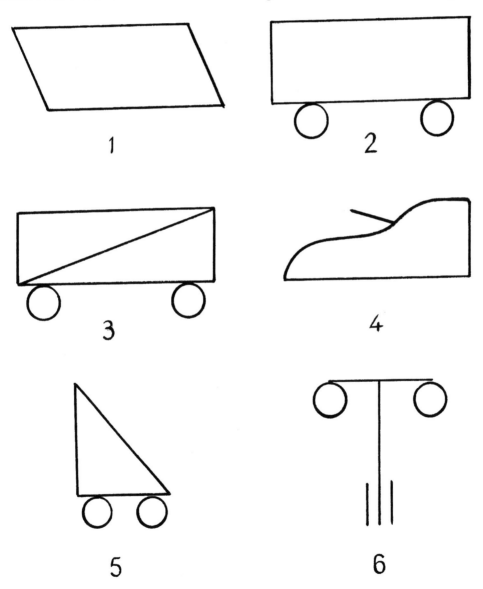

*Examples of tactical markings. (1) Armor and armor support unit, (2) Motorized infantry in trucks, (3) Motorized reconnaissance units, (4) Armored car reconnaissance units, (5) Self-propelled anti-tank gun, (6) Towed artillery.*

haul or rebuilding were re-issued to any unit as required.

On vehicles tactical markings were not always applied. When this was the case, they were generally painted in white or yellow with recommended sizes and line thicknesses. They too were applied on the front mudguards, repeated at the back and designed to be instantly recognizable. As so often happens, a simple idea was soon made complex by numerous additions to the obvious basic symbol, the result being complex and cumbersome. Soon tactical markings formed a complicated system of geometric signs, digits, combinations of letters and numbers and stylized symbols in many variations denoting rank of the user and hierarchy in command, depicting function, load transported, weapon used, specialties, degree of motorization and so on. No explicit names were used for security reasons. Officially the signs were standard throughout, but in November 1942 the symbols for certain units were often simply omitted, slightly simplified, and in some cases changed. The overall picture was further confused by the fact that units often removed or modified the tactical markings on their vehicles in an effort to confuse spies and the resistance movements.

## REGISTRATION NUMBER

Each vehicle carried a standard rear and front *Nummerschild* (number plate) indicating individual registration figures and prefixed RW for *Reichswehr* (the German Army in accordance with the Treaty of Versailles until early 1935). After 1935 the indications were prefixed by:

- WH (*Wehrmacht Heer*) for the ground forces,

- WL (*Wehrmacht Luftwaffe*) for the air force,

- WM (*Wehrmacht Marine*) for the navy,

- POL (*Polizei*) for the militarized police forces,

- SS (in runic letters) for the *Schutzstaffel* (SS) and *Waffen SS* (armed SS),

- OT for the nationalized militarized building company *Organisation Todt*,

- RP (*Reichspost*) for the National Mail Service,

- DR (*Deutsche Reichsbahn*) for the German National Railway Company.

## VEHICLE STATISTICS

Further information was also displayed on the driver's door or in an equivalent position including the vital statistics of each vehicle. The information usually appeared on a panel surrounded with a broken line, but sometimes the broken line was omitted and only the information was shown. These consisted of four items: the abbreviated Kfz number (vehicle ordnance nomenclature), *Leergewicht* (empty weight in metric tons), *Nutzlast* (payload) and *Verlade Klasse* (load-class for railway shipping). For example, the statistics of a Ford medium truck looked like this:

Kfz. M. Lkw. (V3000S/III)

Leergew: 2.85 to.

Nutzlast: 3.-to.

Ve. Kl.: la

## OTHER MARKINGS

The tire pressure was often indicated in atmospheric units with small figures on the mudguards.

Sometimes at the back of some transport vehicles the indications *Abstand 30 m* or *Abstand 50 m* could be carried, indicating the distance (30 or 50 m) that was to be observed between each vehicle of the column. The statutory speed limit could sometimes be marked in km/h (kilometers per hour). Non-official names could be given by the crew to a vehicle—usually in small let-

*Vehicle statistics displayed on the door of a Mercedes-Benz model 170 VK (Kfz 2)*

ters as this habit was not encouraged by the military authorities. The names were various and linked to the private life (e.g., the name of girlfriend, wife or children), to the army life (e.g., the name of a fallen comrade), or patriotically inspired (e.g., illustrious heroes, historical characters, etc.), but this practice was officially frowned upon. By 1945 some military cars and trucks could carry slogans intended to boost morale.

*Markings on a Mercedes-Benz 170 V. (1) Front registration number plate, (2) G showing that the vehicle belonged to Guderian's Army Group during the invasion of Russia in 1941, (3) Tactical marking, (4) Divisional marking, (5) Tire pressure in atmospheric units, (6) Weight data shipping panel, (7) Rear registration number plate.*

Others carried warnings painted large on the sides of their bodywork such as *Auch das Mundwerk verdunkelt!* (Blackout, also for the mouth!) or *Feind Hört mit!* (The enemy is listening!). The latter warning was also displayed on radio equipment.

In operation and action in combat zones, all markings could be swept away, concealed with mud, or adopted in a sober form for the purpose of camouflage.

## Camouflage

In all combat zones it was—and still is—vital for escorts to secure from ambush both the road ahead and the ground dominating it. In mountainous sites the picket-ing of the heights and the guarding of defiles and other significant points were standard practice. Transport convoys, in close order or well spaced, needed to maintain formation to facilitate command and control. Air power, however, called for greater dispersion and cover from detection, it made night driving necessary, and it required anti-aircraft artillery moving along with the columns. Air power also made camouflage a vital measure. The purpose of camouflage was to reduce or erase the effects resulting from the "three S's": shape, shadow and shine.

The subject of World War II German vehicle camouflage is—just like markings—a complicated matter as there were numerous variations and exceptions to the official

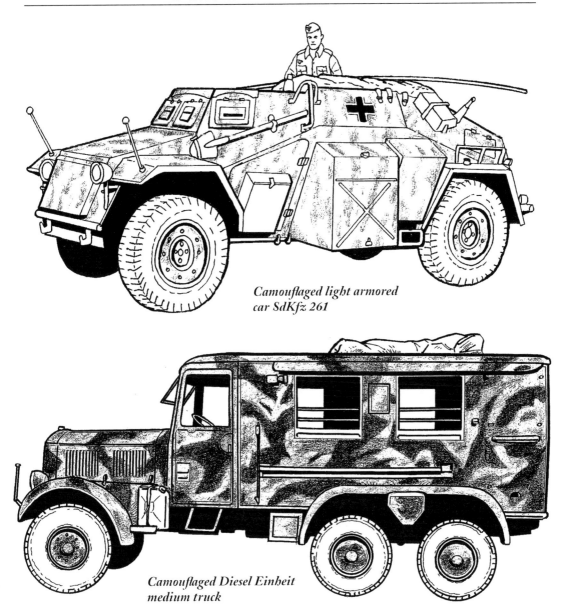

*Camouflaged light armored car SdKfz 261*

*Camouflaged Diesel Einheit medium truck*

rules. Originally, most German vehicles (including half-tracks, tanks and self-propelled guns) were painted in a dark blue/grey color known to modelers as *Panzer Grey*. Pictorial evidence suggests that by 1940 there was an additional shade of dark grey with a distinct green tinge, known as *Slate Grey*.

Alongside their standard equipment, the Germans used many specially adapted vehicles for operations over the varying terrain from Northern Africa to Russia, for which different forms of camouflage were devised to blend in with the terrains and the seasons, from sunny green spring and hot summer to the bitterly cold winter with heavy snowfalls, ice and blizzards. Depending on operation conditions, tanks, self-propelled guns, cars, trucks, trailers, bikes, armored reconnaissance cars and half-tracks were camouflaged. They were painted in sand yellow in northern Africa or combined various tans of dark yellow, green and brown patterns in Europe in spring and autumn,

*Camouflaged Mercedes-Benz 170 Kfz 1*

for example. All vehicles, tanks and other armor were brushed in white or covered with white sheets during winter operations, notably on the Russian front and in mountains.

Orders concerning camouflage colors and patterns were issued periodically but whether they were obeyed, or in fact could be obeyed by lack of means, is open to dispute. No doubt paint was in short supply, and random camouflage patterns due to individual efforts and local improvisations were evident. In June 1943, it was announced that dark yellow would gradually be adopted for the whole of the German vehicles in service. Subsequently all vehicles were repainted and additional colors (brownish-red, green, brown and any colors that happened to be available) were sprayed over the basic yellow in various mottled patterns, irregular patches or wavy lines (verti-

cal or diagonal) to take into account local conditions, break up the vehicle's outline and take away the harsh, bright effect of the yellow. The paint, of varied quality and viscosity, was sprayed, brushed or spattered with a broom by the crews themselves. When Allied aircraft began to dominate the skies from 1943 onward, vehicles and tanks were camouflaged with fresh cut tree branches, brushwood and foliage held by wires and nets intended to break up the outline of the vehicle and to blend in with the local surroundings. This did not help much, and the transport and redeployment of German troops were severely hindered by Allied ground-attack aircraft. In an attempt to minimize the losses, the German divisions advanced in widely separated, heavily camouflaged march columns with vehicles and half-tracks armed with Flak guns inter-

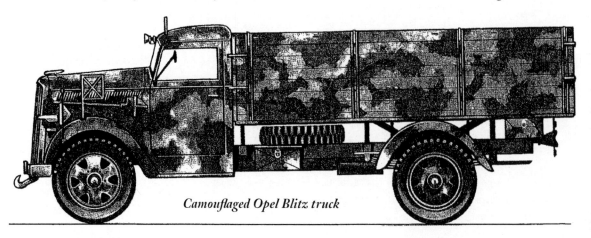

*Camouflaged Opel Blitz truck*

spersed with supply trucks and tanks. Very often these columns were spotted and attacked by Allied *Jabos* (fighter bombers, e.g., De Havilland Mosquito, Hawker Tempest, Hawker Typhoon, North American Mustang, Lockheed P-38 Lightning or Republic P-47 Thunderbolt). When observers spotted low-flying Allied airplanes, the vehicles screeched to a halt, and the crews leaped into the ditches that ran along the sides of the roads, while a few foolhardy gunners would continue to man and fire machine guns and Flak guns. The aircraft attacked again and again until the column was a smoking and charred wreck. The German soldiers at the front were left entirely at the mercy of Allied tactical air power, which combined low flying, strafing fighter-bomber attacks in direct support of land operations, strategic carpet bombings from a high altitude, and intense preliminary artillery fire plans before any offensive. Those who were not killed, wounded or driven insane by devastating infernos of exploding rockets, bombs and shells were driven to despair by the incredible force that was unleashed on them. Only a relatively small number of units retained their cohesion. So great was the threat from the air that transport by land was only possible at night and by cloudy or misty weather.

By 1944–1945, on all fronts, there were vehicles with all types of colors, camouflage patterns and many styles of markings, and it is impossible to be dogmatic about what was and was not standard.

Italian military vehicles in their homeland were painted a shade of greyish green. For use overseas, vehicles were painted in desert-sand yellow, and various camouflage patterns of green and brown were used additionally.

*Driver. The man wears the standard German army Feldgrau (grey/green) field service uniform. Headgear is the peakless Feldmütze (forage cap).*

## Transport troops

Every German division included in its organic components logistical services. The divisional transport troops were called *Fahrtruppen* or *Nachschubtruppen* and placed under the command of an officer called the *Divisionsnachschubführer*, in short *Dinafu*. The size of the *Nachschubdienst* (transport service) was of course in accordance with the degree of motorization of the division. The supply system of the German army was simple and flexible. Its main objective in combat was to replace all supplies used during one day. Rules and regulations were not mandatory. Much discretion remained with the supply *Dinafu* officers, who were encouraged to move supplies as far forward as possible without reloading, to salvage all usable material, and to limit expenditure of supplies as much as possible.

Drivers and mechanics, privates, NCOs and officers were officially combatants wearing the normal Wehrmacht fieldgrey uniform including various headgear (steel helmet and caps), tunic, greatcoat, trousers, and marching boots. They were also issued various boiler suits, work dresses and overalls. Ammunition pouches, gasmasks, breadbags, bayonets, drinking bottles and other personal infantry items were standard issue. The men were equipped with small arms such as pistols, carbines, submachine guns, grenades and machine guns. As the war went on, the communication lines in the occupied territories were often unsafe due to ambushes and sabotages—particularly in Russia and in the Balkans. Transport columns were then

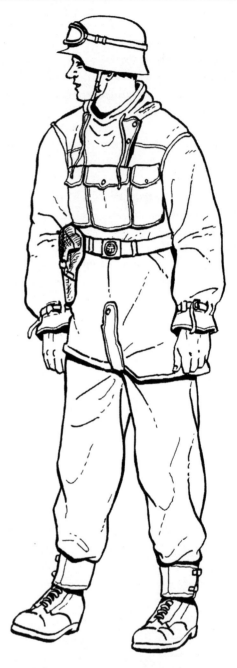

*Driver in winter suit. The driver wears the standard pull-over, reversible, windproof anorak. Worn on the Russian front, this had three frontal pockets, a draw string waist, sleeves with elastic wrist, attached draw string hood, and a fastened tail strap between the legs. The anorak was field-grey, and was worn over the field service uniform for extra warmth. The man is armed with a pistol attached to his belt.*

*Driver's award*

*Army goggles (left) and Luftwaffe goggles (right). The use of sun-glasses and Windschutzbrillen (protective goggles) was widespread for drivers, motorcyclists, and gunners operating in the open air. Two main sorts were issued: the army goggles were round or ovals with plain glass or sometimes a deep brown tint lenses. Very popular and widely used by ground troops were the Luftwaffe goggles designed for air crews. Manufactured by the Leitz company, these had interchangeable curved lenses in plain glass or brown tinted glass for use in bright sunshine or snow. Both goggle types were fixed on a grey leather mask and held by an elastic and adjustable strap.*

accompanied by armed escorts and, increasingly, drivers and mechanics had to make use of their weapons to defend themselves.

German—and also foreign volunteering—transport troopers who distinguished themselves while driving in difficult conditions in certain eastern, northern and African theaters of war for a given number of operational days (between 90 and 185 days) might be awarded the *Kraftfahrbewährungsabzeichen* (motor transport driver's award). This medal was instituted on October 23, 1942. It was issued in three grades: gold, silver and bronze. The metal award represented a steering wheel surrounded by oak leaves, and it was worn on the left lower sleeve or on the breast. It could be forfeited for neglect of vehicle, drunkenness while driving, exceeding the speed limit or causing an accident.

Transport/supply troops had a standard that was displayed at parades, ceremonies, commemorations and other solemn events. The flag, designed by master painter Paul Casberg with Hitler's approval, consisted of a fringed piece of silk cloth (75 cm in length and 51 cm in height) with a swallow-tailed cut-out section running on the horizontal axis of the central field. The cloth was nailed on an oak staff (2.85 m in total length) painted black and polished; the finial included a socketed point decorated with an aluminum eagle and swastika from which hung two streamers with plaque and tassel. Its left field was light blue with a large black iron cross and a superimposed embroidered garland of silver oak leaves containing a stylized Wehrmacht black eagle clutching a black swastika; in each of the four corners of the standard there was a small swastika

*Transport troops' standard*

standing on its point. The right side of the flag was the same in mirror image. Other units had standards identical in size, design and quality; only the *Waffenfarbe* (color-of-arms) differed. That was gold-yellow for cavalry, white for motorized infantry, lemon-yellow for signal units, black for motorized engineers, and pink for armored troops.

## Repair

At the end of 1942, the *Fahrtruppen* were separated into two services: the drivers and the motor maintenance troops (mechanics), the latter including workshop companies (*Werkstattkompanien*) and mobile repair shops (*Kraftwagenwerkstätte*), as the fundamental principle was that repair and maintenance should be done as close as possible to the front line. If the damages inflicted were too extensive for the facilities of the mobile workshops, vehicles were gathered to a collecting point and sent back to a *Kraftfahrpark* (Army motor transport park). There were several such parks in each army corps area, controlled by the *Heimatkraftfahrbezirk*. (Home Motor Maintenance District Headquarters). In Berlin, for instance, there were three parks, each with the capacity of holding 1,000 vehicles and repairing 30 daily. Most parks, however, had a daily repair average of probably fewer than 10 vehicles. A typical motor transport park included a reception point, where vehicles defects were inspected, and a number of specialized workshops with storage of spare parts where vehicles were repaired, scrapped or cannibalized. At the end of the chain, there was a final inspection point where they were controlled and repainted, after which they were dispatched back to units for further use.

Supply of spare parts and tires was procured from the *Zentralersatzteillager* (ZEL, Central Spare Parts Depot) and the *Reifenlager* (Tire Depot).

Associated with equipment depots were the army depots attached to motor transport manufacturers; the main function of these was to facilitate transfer of vehicles from factories to equipment depots and repair centers. This organization showed great recuperative powers, but its importance was, however, greatly diminished, particularly after 1943, owing to the dispersion of stores among the smaller supply centers, and the increasing Allied air bombardments.

The supply of fuel and lubricant was organized by the Ministry of Economic Affairs through its central Petroleum Office. In spite of captured and controlled oil fields and synthetic fuel production, the fuel supply was to remain a constant problem for Germany. Because of the critical condition of German fuel supply, the collection and

*Mechanic. The depicted man wears a duty overall.*

distribution of fuel were always sources of problems. Throughout the war, and more particularly in the closing phase of World War II, the Germans expected in many cases to keep their tanks and vehicles operating by the seizure of enemy fuel dumps.

## Transport regulations

According to the German army regulations, there were several sorts of convoy.

A *Kraftwagen Kolonne* (Kw-K in short) was a motorized convoy composed of trucks and cars.

A *Troß* was a convoy transporting *fechtende Truppe* (fighting troops).

A *Gepäcktroß* carried the soldiers' equipment, often including rolling field kitchens, field bakeries and coffee kettle, placed on trailers.

A *Thermoskolonne* was a convoy of refrigerator trucks transporting meat and other perishable products.

A *Gefechtstroß* was a transport of ammunition.

A *Verpflegungstroß* was a convoy evacuating casualties in ambulances.

A *Kw-Kolon für Betriebstoff* or a *Kesselwagenkolonne* (in short *Kewa*) was a motorized convoy composed of tanker-trucks transporting fuel, lubricant, gas and oil.

But very often the transported supply of a motorized combat unit was mixed, in accordance with its needs. For example, a Flak Kompanie of twelve half-tracks armed with anti-aircraft guns was supported—at least officially—by a *Troß* including four trucks (or half-tracks) carrying ammunition, two trucks carrying fuel, one field kitchen, one truck with equipment, one medical truck, seven staff cars, one radio/signal car, and five motorbicycles.

Convoys were also classified in accordance with their transport capacity.

A *klein Kw-Nachschubkolonne* (small convoy) could transport an average of 30 t of supply;

A *groß Kw-Nachschubkolonne* (large convoy) could carry about 60 t of supply.

For special tasks and larger tonnage of about 120 metric tons, there was a special service, known as *Großtransportraum* (GTR, large transport) including three special transport units, the regiments 602, 605 and 616 equipped with heavy trucks.

Finally, and they were the most numerous, *Bespannte Fahrkolonnen* were horse- or oxen-drawn cart units composed of an average of 40 carts transporting between 17 and 30 t of supply. According to German regulations, well-cared for and trained horses could cover 12 to 15 miles per day and under favorable conditions up to 20 miles, with a day of rest following. If oxen were used, the rate of movement was slower.

In mountainous terrain, *Tragtierkolonnen* (pack trains) with mules were employed carrying up to 5 tons of supply, but their capacity and speed were obviously dependent on the trails and grade.

Regulations were issued for the troop movements. The average speeds of division marches were as follows.

An infantry division had to march 3 miles per hour by day or by night; but depending on weather and road conditions this could be as little as 10 miles or 16 miles a day;

A motorized division should drive 16 mph by day and 10 mph by night;

An armored division should drive 12 mph by day and 7 mph by night;

A motorized division could maintain an average daily march of between 90 and 150 miles and an armored division from 60 to 90 miles a day.

The road space between units varied from 5,700 m (6,234 yd.) to 1,420 m (1,553 yd.). Including the intervals between the individual units, the average length of an infantry division was about 30 miles (at 3 miles per hour), that of a motorized division 80 miles (at a speed of 16 mph) and that of an armored division was 70 miles (at 12 mph).

On long distances, vehicles were transported by inland boats or more frequently by rail (on flat cars). *Infanteriezüge* were standard infantry troop trains. *Kraftfahrzeuge-Züge* were trains for motor vehicles. *Sonderzüge* were special trains, intended for tanks and half-tracks. *Sonderpanzerzüge* were special trains for tanks. For transport by rail, vehicles were divided into several *Verlade Klasse* (Verl.Kl., weight classes) according to their weight and length.

| Class | Weight | Length |
|---|---|---|
| I | up to 17.5 t | from 7.21 m to 11.14 m |
| Ia | up to 12.5 t | from 6 m to 7.20 m |
| Ib | up to 10 t | from 5 m to 6 m |
| II | up to 7.5t | from 3.54 m to 5 m |
| III | up to 5 t | from 2.51 m to 5.53 m |
| IV | up to 4 t | up to 2.50 m |
| A | between 17.5 t and 26.5 t | up to 9.28 m |
| S | no limit | more than 11.14 m |

For obvious and practical purposes, the flat cars of the German *Reichsbahn* (National Railroad Company) were divided into capacity categories. A type *R-Wagen*, for example, could transport two class-II vehicles.

## Military police

Military policemen were organic in every German division.

The *Feldgendarmerie des Heeres* (military police of the ground force) was intended to maintain order and security among the fighting units, to regulate circulation and organize road traffic including signalization. The *Feldgendarmerie* would help to mark roads, work out schedules, and flag on convoys. They were also responsible for control duties in ports and airfields, administrative control of aliens, patrol duties, collecting and evacuating prisoners of war, rounding up of deserters, marshalling refugees, etc. A branch of the military policemen—called *Wachtruppen*—was concerned with the guarding of headquarters and senior officers in the field. The army policemen were generally recruited from the ranks of the *Ordnungpolizei* (Orpo), the major uniformed order police force of the

Third Reich composed of *Schutzpolizei* (security police), *Gemeindepolizei* (town police) and *Gendarmerie* (rural police). Military policemen formed self-contained detachments under the command of army divisions. They were organized into battalions of three companies, each of three pla-

*Policeman of the Feldgendarmerie. The status of the policeman was indicated by the traffic wand, the gorget, the orange badge and the cuff title both worn on the left sleeve.*

toons, generally transported in trucks or busses and mounted on motorbicycles for quick movement.

Their *Waffenfarbe* (color of service) was orange. The military field policemen wore the normal army uniform and, on duty, often the standard *Schutzmantel*, a double breasted waterproof rubberized greatcoat.

On the upper left arm there was the national emblem composed of eagle and swastika set against an oval wreath of oak leaves; for officers this was silver grey and for other ranks it was orange with a black swastika. Occasionally on the cuff of the left sleeve German military policemen had a brown cuff-title with a grey edging inscribed with the word "Feldgendarmerie" in silver gothic lettering. On duty, their most characteristic feature was the *Ringkragen* (gorget), a metal plate in the form of a half moon positioned just below the collar on the breast and held by a chain; the gorget was lettered "Feldgendarmerie" and decorated with embossed buttons and an eagle/swastika emblem; letters, buttons and emblem were finished with luminous paint so that they were easily visible in the dark.

In all armies of the world, army policemen were (and still are) rather unpopular (e.g., American "snowdrops" and British "red caps"). German soldiers called their MPs "head-hunters"; because of the gorget they were also pejoratively nicknamed *Kettenhunden* (chained dogs). Military policemen were armed with the army standard small arms: pistols and submachine guns.

The Nazi state was a bloody dictatorship dominated by police forces. These were not bodies of men whose task was to

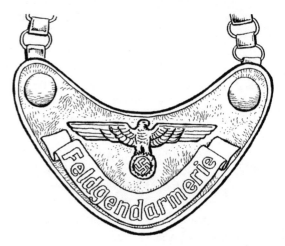

*Feldgendarme. The military policeman wears the greatcoat.*

*Ringkragen. The gorget was worn around the neck in service.*

preserve constitutional law and public order but units (controlled by Himmler's SS) intended to impose National Socialism by force, to repress and destroy all real and supposed enemies of the regime. There were many other services linked with the German transport system, and there was a large overlap of duties among the different German police services.

The other branches of the Wehrmacht had their own police: *Luftwaffe Feldgendarmerie* for the air force and *Marine Feldgendarmerie* for the navy.

The *Waffen SS Feldgendarmerie* was the police counterpart of the military police for the armed branch of the SS.

The *Geheime Feldpolizei* (GFP, Secret Field Police) was a special investigative

branch of the military police. Formed in July 1939, its functions were many: counter-sabotage, counter-propaganda, detection of treasonable and defeatist activities, investigations for martial courts, personal escort of high-ranking military VIPs, interrogation of captured enemy soldiers and many others.

The *Heeresstreifendienst* (Army Patrol Service) was tasked with maintaining order and discipline in garrison areas.

The *Bahnhofswache* (Station Watch) and the *Zugwache* (Train Watch) were responsible for policing stations and trains by checking travel papers, identity documents, hunting for deserters, escorting trains in unsafe areas, and assisting in the security and smooth flow of rail traffic.

The *Feldjägerkorps* (Corps of Field Police), created in 1943, operated behind the front line. Their functions were, among others, to preserve order and discipline, check identity papers, control traffic, arrange removal of destruction, prevent panic, collect stragglers and deserters, assemble rapid-acting units in the case of enemy parachute landing and many others.

## National Socialist Motorized Corps (NSKK)

The *Nationalsozialistischen Kraftfahrer Korps (NSKK*, National Socialist Motorized Corps) was founded in 1930. It regrouped mechanics, drivers and vehicles to transport Nazi party formations and leaders. It included wealthy car-owners who sympathized with the Nazis and put themselves at the party disposal in their free time. The Nazis gave great attention to modern means of transport. Hitler was keen on cars and

*Officer of the Geheime Feldpolizei (1940). The depicted officer wears the standard army officer's field grey uniform. The tunic had a dark green collar, shoulder straps wearing the gilt mono-gram GPF, and a cuffband bearing the mention Geheime Feldpolizei on the lower left sleeve.*

*ABOVE, LEFT: NSKK Truppführer (Sergeant) 1939. RIGHT: NSKK tank instructor. The instructor wears the typical armored force uniform (see Part 5: Uniforms).*

planes, and being driven at top speeds was one of his greatest joys; he never drove himself, and even during the "Time of Struggle" (the period 1920–1933), he had a private chauffeur and owned several cars that he paid for with his own money coming from royalties of his book *Mein Kampf.*

The *Sturmabteilung* (SA, the Storm Troopers of the Nazi Party) had its own transport service, called *Motor Sturmabteilung* (MSA). After the bloody elimination of the SA leadership in June 1934, the MSA was disbanded and its members were transferred to the NSKK. From then on and until the end of the Nazi regime, the NSKK became an important official *Gliederung der NSDAP* (sub-organization of the Nazi Party) directly placed under Hitler's authority. The NSKK (counting 500,000 members in 1938) was militarily organized with the traditional Nazi ranks, rather similar to those of the SA, SS and Waffen SS. The organization was headed by a *Korpsführer* and divided in five geographic regions called *Obergruppen* (North, East, South, West and Middle, each headed by an *Obergruppenführer*). Each *Obergruppe* (division) was divided in four or five *Motorgruppen* (groups) headed by generals called *Gruppenführer* and *Brigadeführer*. Each *Motorgruppe* was composed of five to six *Motorstaffeln* (regiments) headed by colonels called *Standartenführer*,

*NSKK arm eagle cloth badge. The emblem of the NSKK displayed an eagle holding in its claws a swastika in a wreath of oak leaves surmounted by a scroll bearing the mention NSKK. It existed in cloth form for wear on uniforms (on the upper left sleeve) and in metal form at the front of headgear.*

*Oberstaffelführer* and *Staffelführer*. Every *Motorstaffel* included six *Motorstürme* (battalions) headed by captains called *Hauptsturmführer*, *Obersturmführer* and *Sturmführer*. Each *Motorsturm* was divided into transport *Truppen* (companies), *Scharen* (platoons) and *Rotten* (squads) headed by lieutenants, sergeants and corporals called *Haupttruppführer*, *Obertruppführer*, *Truppführer*, *Oberscharführer*, *Scharführer* and *Rottenführer*. A driver/private was called *Sturmmann* or *Obersturmmann* (driver first class).

The members of the NSKK were volunteers recruited among the Nazi party, senior ranks from the Hitler Youth and men exempted from military service for medical reasons. The members of the NSKK not only drove and maintained vehicles but they also gave mechanic and driving lessons to candidate truck and tank drivers in *Fahrschulen* (driving schools). Closely connected to the Nazi party, they were often politically active, participated in party rallies and ceremonies, and dispensed Nazi ideology lectures; they channeled the enthusiasm of all automobile-minded Germans by organizing car and bicycle races, visits to factories and manufactures for propaganda aims, etc. The politically-involved NSKK thus allowed Hitler to have a grip on the Wehrmacht: all transport and army logistics were controlled by the Nazi organization placing the regular national armed forces in a totally dependent position.

During the war, the NSKK became a major asset to Hitler's regime both in Germany and in the occupied territories, and its members often assisted the military police with enforcing traffic regulations and public order. After 1941, as many German nationals were drafted into the army, the NSKK also recruited pro-Nazi Frenchmen, Belgian, Dutch and other volunteers from occupied nations. As the war progressed and more fighting troops were needed, large numbers of NSKK members were drafted to form army combat groups, Waffen SS units and Volkssturm battalions.

# 2

# Cars and Motorcycles

## Light cars

Light cars had an engine capacity under 1500 cc and included several types, many of which were *(o) models* that were commercially available. The seating capacity was maximum four men including the driver. Often the chassis were made specifically for the fitting of military bodywork and thus converted to open-top, light cross-country vehicles. When intended to transport troops they were popularly known

*Civilian French Peugeot 202*

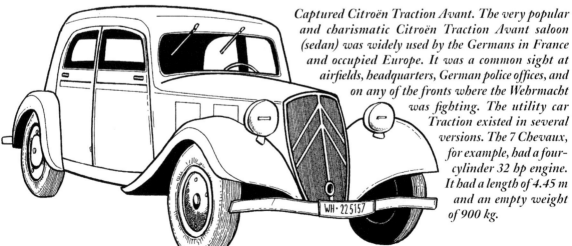

*Captured Citroën Traction Avant. The very popular and charismatic Citroën Traction Avant saloon (sedan) was widely used by the Germans in France and occupied Europe. It was a common sight at airfields, headquarters, German police offices, and on any of the fronts where the Wehrmacht was fighting. The utility car Traction existed in several versions. The 7 Chevaux, for example, had a four-cylinder 32 hp engine. It had a length of 4.45 m and an empty weight of 900 kg.*

as *Kfz 1 Kübelsitzer*, *Kübelwagen* or just *Kübel* (bucket). Of course, many foreign-made light cars were pressed into German service after the victorious period of 1940–1941. For example, captured French civilian cars included the Peugeot 202 and the famous Citroën "traction avant."

m, height was 1.65 m and weight was 970 kg. Maximum speed was 90 km/h, fuel consumption was 38 liters/100 km, and range was 380 km. Produced by the Ringhoffer-Tatra company from Czechoslovakia, some 6,000 Tatra 57 K were built for the German forces between 1936 and 1943.

## TATRA 57 K

The light car *Tatra 57* K had an air-cooled, 4-cylinder, 23 bhp, 1.3-liter B4L engine. Length was 3.98 m, width was 1.55

## HANOMAG REKORD KFZ 1

The light car Hanomag Rekord from 1934 had a four-cylinder engine, and it was a Wehrmacht Kfz 1 Kübelwagen that could

*Light car Tatra 57 K*

*Light car Hanomag Rekord Kfz 1*

accommodate four soldiers including the driver. It was built in the period 1934–1938.

## Opel P4 Kfz 1

The light car *Opel P4 Kfz 1* had a 4-cylinder, 23 bhp engine. Length was 4.11 m, width was 1.58 m, height was 1.8 m and weight was 930 kg. Maximum speed was 85 km/h, fuel consumption was 10 liters/100 km, and range was 250 km. It was basically a three/four seater with removable canvas side doors. This vehicle was also used with a light truck body and also as the basis for a dummy tank for training purposes with dummy tracks and fake armor.

## BMW type 315

The BMW 315 was a four-seater Kübelwagen Kfz 1. Built by the Bayerische Motoren Werke München (BMW, Bavarian Engine Works Munich), it had a six-cylinder, 1.5-liter engine. Its weight was about 1,000 kg, length was 4.1 m, width was 1.5 m, and height was 1.6 m. It had removable canvas side doors. Based on a civilian model, it was built in the period 1934–1936 and saw service during the first years of World War II.

*Light car Opel P4*

*Light car BMW type 315*

*Utility car Wanderer
W23S Kfz 11 (1938)*

## WANDERER 23 S KFZ 11

The *Wanderer W23 S* was a utility car introduced in 1938. It was one of the many tourer cars used by the German army. It was based on the commercial civilian *Wanderer model W23S*. The Wanderer 23 S was given a military type body, a six-cylinder 60 hp engine, detachable doors, and a large stowage box at the rear. Later-type bodies (1937–1939) featured removable steel doors but civilian-type front and rear wings. It was used as a staff and utility car with almost any kind of military unit. Weight was 1,650 kg, maximum speed was 90 km/h, fuel consumption was 17 liters/100 km, and range was 410 km.

## MERCEDES-BENZ TYPE 170

The light car *Mercedes-Benz 170*, designed in 1934–1935, was used for light staff duty and troop transport. The engine was the water-cooled, 1,700 cubic centimeter MB type 136; this was a side-valve, gasoline engine with an L-shaped cylinder head, with the camshaft and valve gear on the

*Light car Kfz 2/40 Mercedes-Benz 170*

*Light car Mercedes-Benz 170 Kfz 1*

right side. The engine developed about 38 brake horsepower. The fuel tank, located in the engine compartment, contained 11.5 gallons. Maximum speed was 60 km/h, fuel consumption was 13 liters/100 km, and range was 380 km. The *Mercedes-Benz 170* was a commercial car modified for military service. It was basically more a civilian car than a military vehicle. It could transport four passengers including the driver. Some 19,179 were built between 1934 and 1942 in several versions including four-wheel drive. It was also issued to Nazi party associations and agencies.

When used as a light repair car, the type 170 was known as Kfz 2/40, with re-

movable doors and a large tool locker at the back. The same car could also be fitted with a wireless radio, and that variant was known as *Kleinfunkwagen* (small radio car).

## STANDARDIZED LIGHT CAR BMW TYPE 325 KFZ 3

The *leichte Einheits-Personenkraftwagen Kfz 3* (le.Einh.Pkw) was designed and manufactured by *Bayerische Motoren Werke München* (BMW, Bavarian Engine Works Munich) but also produced by the Hanomag and Stoewer companies. Weight was 2,200 kg, maximum speed was 75 km/h,

*Standardized light car BMW type 325 (1.E.Pkw light utility car BMW Kfz 3)*

fuel consumption was 17 liters/100 km on road (25 liters/100 km cross-country), and range was 350 km on road and 240 km cross-country. It was a light cross-country car with a standard chassis designed for several military bodyworks including open tourer for four crew, small repair car (with only two seats and a large locker at the rear), small cargo carrier, machine gun carrier, and even as the basis for a dummy tank for training purposes. Popularly known as *Kübelsitzer*, *Kübelwagen* or *Kübel* (bucket), about 3,225 units were built in the period 1937–1940. Introduced in the late 1930s, it was intended to replace the multitude of models of the early mid-1930s. But it was the mass-produced *Kübelwagen Volkswagen 82* which was successful in achieving at least part of this ideal.

## KdF Volkswagen "Beetle"

An early aspect of the Nazi regime was the attempt to make the automobile a reality for as many Germans as possible. Car ownership in the 1930s in Germany was the prerogative of the rich; one in fifty Germans owned an automobile compared with one in five Americans. To this end, the world famous *Volkswagen* "Beetle" (the People's Car, originally called *KdF Wagen*) was designed by professor Ferdinand Porsche (1875–1951) in 1936. An extensive system was set up by the Nazi agency DAF (German Labor Front) to allow nearly anyone to purchase and own one for 997 Mark. The DAF had a successful and popular sub-organization known as the *NS-Gemeinschaft Kraft durch Freude* (National Socialist Organization Strength through Joy), in short *Kraft durch Freude* (KdF). All members of the *Deutsche Arbeitsfront* were automatically members of the *Kraft durch Freude* organization. Created in November 1933, *Kraft durch Freude* was essentially designed for the purpose of providing organized leisure for the German work force including cruises, skiing trips, tennis lessons, retreats, day trips, excursions, hikes, tours, concerts and musicals, theater, cabaret, opera and operetta performances,

*KdF Volkswagen "Beetle." The famous Käfer (Beetle) is shown here in service of the Deutsche Reichsbahn (DR, German National Railroad Company).*

art exhibits, and other cultural and historical displays and events, all of which were supposedly designed to aid the "average" German enjoy their free time more. It was hoped that this would help in creating a healthier, more educated, flexible, disciplined and productive workforce. For the KdF/DAF project of the *Volkswagen*, the cheap popular civilian car, a huge production complex was developed at Wolfsburg near Hanover. For marketing the car, Robert Ley (head of the DAF/Kdf) devised a scheme by which the customer paid 5 Reichsmark weekly and received a stamp to paste in a saving book. When the sum of 997 RM was saved, the purchaser became eligible to receive his KdF-Volkswagen. Some 336,668 Germans started buying their vehicles on the installment plan, paying some 280 million Mark ($112 million) but the buyers were destined to disappointment. In the end, as with many other Nazi "social" measures, the KdF-car scheme turned out to be a large-scale swindle. By September 1939, war broke out and the KdF-Wagen project was postponed. The existing Volkswagen were allocated to party officials and state agencies.

Ferdinand Porsche's design was a brilliant, tiny, beetle-shaped vehicle with a 23 bhp, four-cylinder, air-cooled engine placed in the rear. From 1936 to 1945 several types and versions were manufactured with slightly different performances, including four-wheel drive (known as VW Limousine Typ 82 E), and a "tropical" version—known as VW Limousine Typ 87—produced for the Africa Korps in North Africa. The rather common 1939 version had the following features: Weight was 650 kg, length was 3.75 m, width was 1.55 m and height 1.6 m; speed was 83 km/h, fuel consumption was 9 liters/100 km, and range was 440 km.

In 1946, a new, denazified Volkswagen company was constituted that honored the old saving stamps, and at last the world-popular VW began cruising the civilian roads. The last Volkswagen "Beetle" was produced in July 2003.

### VOLKSWAGEN K1
### TYP 82 KÜBELWAGEN

The KdF People's Car automotive facilities at Wolfsburg were transformed and militarized when World War II broke out.

*Kfz 1 Kübelwagen Volkswagen 82 (with canvas top)*

Hitler ordered Porsche to modify the VW Beetle as an all purpose military vehicle known as the *VW 82 Kübelwagen*. The mass-produced *KdF Volkswagen K1 Typ 82 Kübelwagen* was intended to replace the multitude of models of the early and mid-1930s. As seen above, the *Kübelwagen 82* (meaning "bucket-car") was the military version of the 1936 sedan Volkswagen "beetle" with a redesigned roofless look and rear-axle reduction gear to improve traction and increase the ground clearance to the army's requirements. The *VW Kübelwagen type 82* was designed by engineer Dr. Ferdinand Porsche. In December 1939, the military version was tested and favorably received, being easy to handle and having good cross-country performance. It became the most widely used and best-known Wehrmacht vehicle, plying the roads of all World War II fronts, and one of the passenger cars to remain in production for the German army. It was a light passenger car—to a certain extent comparable to the legendary U.S. jeep. It was, however, inferior in every way except in the comfort of its seating accommodation. The chassis consisted of a central, welded-steel tube bifurcating at the rear to support the engine and transmission. The steel floor on both sides of the central member provided the means of supporting the body. The box-like open structure was made of flat steel panels for ease of production and assembly. The *Kübelwagen* was powered by a four-cylinder, overhead valve, air-cooled, 1131 cc gasoline engine (25 bhp at 3000 rpm) that was situated at the rear. The gasoline tank was below the instrument panel in front of the right seat. There were four forward speeds and one reverse. The maximum speed in high gear was about 50 mph. The vehicle weighed 725 kg and employed a torsion bar suspension system. For use in the North African special desert, smooth tires were fitted to cope with the soft terrain. The German "jeep" could be armed with a single MG 34 machine gun and could accommodate a crew of four. Throughout the war, production continued, and between 1940 and 1945, a total of 51,334 were manufactured. The popular vehicle could perform a number of functions including staff car, light reconnaissance vehicle, ambulance, ammunition carrier, assault engineer carrier, and maintenance/repair car. The *Kfz 1* was the basic, light car

*Kdf/VW 82 Kübelwagen*

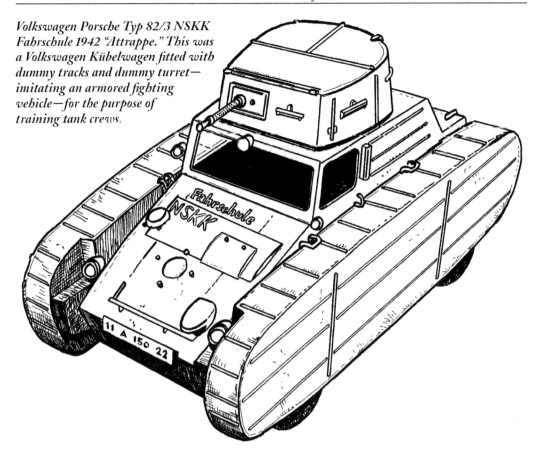

*Volkswagen Porsche Typ 82/3 NSKK Fahrschule 1942 "Attrappe." This was a Volkswagen Kübelwagen fitted with dummy tracks and dummy turret— imitating an armored fighting vehicle—for the purpose of training tank crews.*

design. The variant *Kfz 2* was a radio and communications car. The *Kfz 2/40* was a maintenance and repair car. The *Kfz 3* was a light surveying car. There was an experimental four-wheel drive version. The *type 82/3 Panzerkampfwagen-Attrappe* was a Volkswagen Kübelwagen with dummy tracks and dummy turret—imitating an armored fighting vehicle—for the purpose of training tank crews. An amphibious version was produced, known as the *Kfz.1/20 k2 Schwimmwagen* (floating car). An experimental version equipped with tracks on the rear wheels for use in snow was known as the *VW Typ 155 Schneeraupe Ausf. IV.*

## Medium cars

Medium cars had an engine capacity between 1500 and 3000 cc, but the 3000 cc limit was not always adhered to for foreign-made medium cars. Their story is much the same as the light cars. From the late 1920s until the mid-1930s, first the *Reichswehr* and later the *Wehrmacht* purchased civilian type car chassis and fitted them with either closed or open military bodywork. The seating capacity was maximum five men including the driver. Confiscated and captured vehicles of roughly the required specifications were also employed, including Austrian, Czechoslovakian, Italian and French military types.

### MEDIUM CAR KFZ 12 ADLER (3GD)

The *mittlere Kübel-Personenwagen* (medium car) *Kfz 12 Adler (3 Gd)* was a special *Wehrmacht* model introduced in 1938. It was derived from the civilian *Adler Diplomat*. It could accommodate four or five passengers including the driver and was fitted with a towing hook for light artillery pieces or light trailers. It had a 6-cylinder, 60 bhp engine. Length was 4.8 m, width was 1.8 m, and gross weight was 2,210 kg. Maximum speed was 80 km/h, fuel consumption on road was 17 liters/100 km, and maximum range on road was 410 km. Production stopped in 1943.

The chassis of the Adler (Gd) Kfz 12 was used to constitute a *leichter Panzerspäh-wagen Kfz 13* (light armored car).

## HORCH 830

The medium car *Kfz 15 Horch 830* was a personnel carrier for four or five soldiers including the driver. Designed in 1933, it was a reliable car that stayed in service in the German army until 1943. It had a V8 70 bhp engine. Length was 4.8 m, and weight was 1,820 kg. Maximum speed was 110 km/h, fuel consumption on road was 18 liters/100 km, and maximum range on road

*Medium car Kfz 15 Horch 830, shown here as troop transport for a crew of four*

*Medium car Kfz 12 Adler (3 Gd)*

was 350 km. The Horch 830 could carry a load of 380 kg.

It was also used as a signaling service and radio car and in this role was known as the Horch 830 Kfz 17.

## HORCH 830 KFZ 17

The *Horch Kfz 17* was the standard German army *Kleinfunkwagen* (light radio car) used in the mid-1930s. In production from 1933 to 1935, it consisted of a standard *Horch 830* touring car chassis with a wooden van-body housing signaling equipment, extra batteries, locker at the rear, cable reel holders and other equipment. The closed body could be used as a telephone exchange and in similar roles. It was also used as a staff car in open tourer form with a squared-off locker at the back. It was also built by Opel. Later productions were dispensed with stub axle-mounted support/spare wheels. Maximum speed was 110 km/h, fuel consumption was 18 liters/100 km, and range was 350 km.

## STANDARDIZED MEDIUM CAR AU/HORCH (KFZ 15)

The widely used 4 x 4 standardized universal medium type (known as *mittlere Einheits-Personenkraftwagen*, in short *m.E. Pkw*) was intended to replace earlier designs such as the Mercedes 260 Stuttgart, Mercedes 200, Wanderer W23 S, Adler 3Gd and Horch 830R. Designed in 1937, it was built by the Horch company, the Auto-Union AG company and the Adam Opel AG company and was known as Horch/Wanderer 901 Typ Efm. The engine, fitted at the front, might be either of two types: a Horch V-8 type 901, water-cooled, 3.5-liter, gasoline engine developing 82 bhp at 3,600 revolutions per minute, or an Opel straight-six, water-cooled, 3.6-liter gasoline engine developing 68 horsepower at 2,800 revolutions per minute. The car had two gasoline tanks. The main one holding 18.7 gallons was suspended in the center of the chassis frame, and the reserve holding 10.8 gallons was at the rear. The wheels were all driven and sprung independently by two coil springs. The spare wheels were carried on each side of the chassis on stub axles to prevent bellying when traveling over rough ground. The car was 4.7 m in length, 1.85 m in width, 2 m in height, and weighed about 2,500 kg empty. Its payload was about 600 kg. Maximum speed was 90 km/h on road and 40 km/h cross-country, fuel consumption was 18 liters/100 km, and range was 400 km on road and 300 km cross-country. It could be used as staff car (open or closed), command car, radio car, troop carrier (four or five crew) or supply carrier, the various bodies being manufactured by

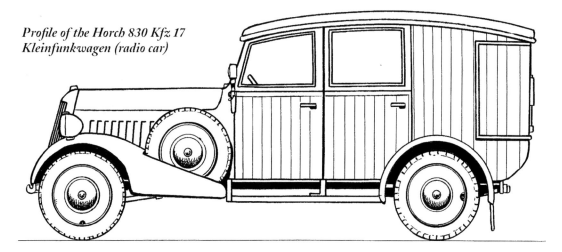

*Profile of the Horch 830 Kfz 17 Kleinfunkwagen (radio car)*

*Standardized medium car AU/Horch Kfz 15. The m.E.Pkw is shown here as a cargo carrier.*

*Auto-Union/Opel/Horch m.E.Pkw. The standardized medium car Kfz 15 is depicted here as a personnel carrier.*

Ambi-Bud from Berlin-Johannisthal and Gaubschat from Berlin-Neuköln. About 30,000 standardized medium cars were built, some 14,902 produced by Horch, 12,298 by Wanderer and the rest by Opel. Widely used in the German forces on all fronts and all through the war, the popular *m. E.Pkw* was generally called *Horch* by the troops, regardless of the manufacturer.

## MEDIUM CAR STEYR 250

The medium *Kübelsitzer Steyr 250* was Austrian-built. It had a 4-cylinder engine. Weight was 1,650 kg, maximum speed was 75 km/h, fuel consumption was 11 liters/ 100 km, and range was 400 km. It could be arranged as a troop carrier for four soldiers, including the driver, or as a light cargo

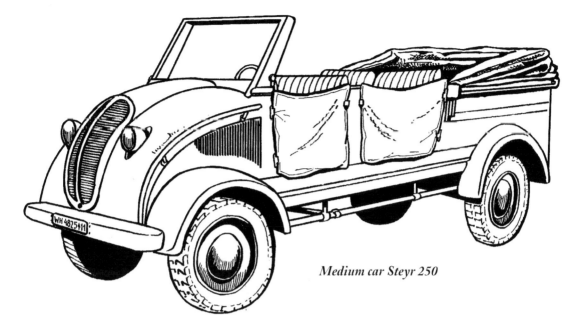

*Medium car Steyr 250*

carrier. About 1,200 were produced for the German army between 1938 and 1940.

## Heavy cars

Heavy cars had an engine capacity of 3000 cc and over. Some of them were especially built for military use and originally intended to replace various vehicles built previously on light truck chassis of the *Schell program* of 1938. Some had air-cooled engines, which had obvious advantages for use in North Africa and Russia. There were also six-wheel (twin rear-bogie) heavy cars for special purposes, such as light trucks, ambulances, *Kommandeurwagens* (command cars) or propaganda reporter's cars. All through the war, confiscated civilian chassis (mainly American makes) with simple, open, six-seater rear bodies with back entrance were used as raid cars and personnel carriers.

*Heavy 4 x 2 command car Kfz 21 (Skoda Superb Type 952 Kabrio)*

## SKODA 952

The heavy command car *Kfz 21* was basically a civilian *Skoda Superb Type-952 Kabrio*. It had a V8 engine. Its length was 4.8 m, width was 1.9 m and weight was 3,080 kg. It was a luxurious four-door coach-built convertible *Kommandeurwagen* (command car) used by high officers in the field, including Heinz Guderian and Erwin Rommel.

## HEAVY CAR SKODA 903

The 6x4 *Convertible Skoda 903* had a 3-liter, 6-cylinder, 80 bhp engine, the same as the civilian *Skoda Superb 300*. It was produced in limited numbers in the late 1930s for the Czech army and issued as staff car for high ranking German officers in the period 1941–1943. The staff car *Skoda 903* could accommodate six passengers (including the driver).

*Heavy car Skoda 903 staff car*

*Heavy car Mercedes-Benz 320. The car shown is in service of the Kriegsmarine (navy).*

Similar designs of luxurious heavy car/ light trucks with twin rear-bogie were the 6x4 Steyr 640, the Tatra T93, the 6x4 Convertible Krupp L2H143 and the *Mercedes-Benz G4.*

## MERCEDES-BENZ TYPE 320

The heavy *Mercedes-Benz 320* had a 6-cylinder, 78 bhp engine. It was one of the various types of Mercedes-Benz civilian cars that were used by German senior officers. There was also a *Kübelwagen* variant with military body for troop transport with a capacity of five soldiers. Some 1,764 specimens were built in the period 1937–1941.

## AUTO-UNION/HORCH 108

The *Auto Union/Horch 4x4 108* (known as the *schwerer geländegängiger Einheits-Personenkraftwagen* or s.gl.E.Pkw.) was produced in two main variants: the rear engined type for armored cars and the Type II for soft skinned vehicles with open and closed bodywork. Early production had a 3.5-liter engine and some had 4-wheel drive capabil-

ities. A 3.6-liter, V8 side valve, liquid-cooled gasoline engine was fitted to models produced by Ford of Cologne. This was their own model engine, which could provide 81 bhp at 3600 rpm. It was also equipped with a dry clutch plate, 5F1R gearbox with lockable differentials at rear and in the gearbox. Front wheel drive was also an option on this vehicle and was supplied direct from the gearbox differential. It had independent suspension with coil springs and was equipped with 12-volt electrics and had a 120-liter fuel capacity.

## STANDARDIZED HORCH/FORD KFZ 70

This vehicle, also known as the *schwerer Einheits Personenkraftwagen* (heavy standardized car), was introduced in 1938, and it was intended to replace the numerous types of utility vehicles previously in service. It was built by the Horch company from Zwickau and the German Ford company from Cologne. It had a Horch V8 90 bhp engine (or a Ford V8 78 bhp engine) and four-wheel drive, and early models had

*Mercedes-Benz 320 with military body*

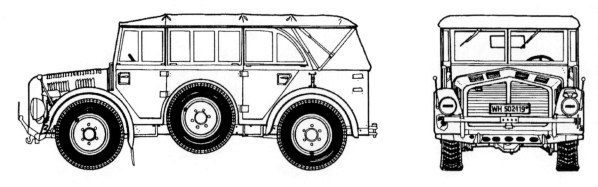

*Profile and front-view of standardized Horch Kfz 69/70*

*Standardized light truck Horch Kfz 69*

steering rear wheels, but this expensive luxury was soon discontinued. It had detachable doors, and the free revolving spare wheels—carried on each side—provided extra support if the vehicle bottomed traveling cross-country. Length was 4.8 m, width was 2 m, and height was about 2 m depending on the bodywork. The heavy car/light truck *Kfz 70 Horch* was intended as a personnel carrier for six soldiers (including the driver), and it was used as staff car, personnel carrier or light artillery tractor, often with a tourer canvas folding top. It could also be fitted with a closed bodywork and converted to ambulance or command or radio car. Some models were employed as *Selbstfahrlafette* (mobile artillery or self-propelled gun) carrying a Flak gun upon an open platform. On the whole, the standardized Horch/Ford was a very sturdy, reliable and popular model, but its only drawback was its weight, which (unloaded) was approximately 3,150 kg. Widely used in the first phase of World War II, this vehicle was replaced after 1942 by several other types, notably the Steyr 1500A and the Mercedes L 1500. In all, a total of about 10,000 standardized heavy cars were produced and used in the German forces.

## STEYR 1500A

The heavy command car *Kfz 21 Steyr 1500A/01* had a V8 85 bhp engine, which allowed a maximum speed of 100 km/h. It was 5 m long, 1.8 m wide, 2.1 m high and

*Standardized Horch/Ford with 2 cm Flak gun. The 2 cm anti-aircraft gun was fitted with a shield to protect the gunners, and the side rails around the open platform were covered by light wire mesh and opened sideways when the weapon was cleared for action. Ammunition and equipment were often carried in a two-wheeled trailer model Sd.Ah 51 towed by the light truck.*

*Heavy command car Kfz 21 Steyr 1500A/01*

weighed 2,500 kg. Maximum speed was 90 km/h on road and 40 km/h cross-country, fuel consumption was 24 liters/100 km on road and 36 liters/100 km cross-country, and range was 350 km. The version shown was a *Kommandeurwagen* (command car) for senior officers. Produced between 1941 and 1944, it could also be fitted with a cargo

*Profile of Steyr 1500 A troop carrier (Mannschaftswagen)*

*Heavy car Steyr type 1500A/01*

bodywork and in this role was known as light truck *Steyr 1500A/02* with a payload of 1,675 kg.

## MERCEDES-BENZ L 1500

The heavy car *Mercedes-Benz L 1500 Kfz 70* had a 6-cylinder, 60 bhp gasoline engine with a maximum speed of 84 km/h. Fuel consumption per 100 km was 19 liter on road and 30 liter cross-country. The vehicle was about 5 m long, 2 m wide and 2.22 m high. It was a typical *Schell Pro-*

*gramm* heavy car/light truck designed with various body types. The *L 1500 A (Allrad)* was a military four-wheel drive troop carrier. The *1500 S (Standard)* was mainly used as a cargo and fire-fighting vehicle.

## HEAVY STAFF CAR MERCEDES-BENZ G4

This impressive six-wheeler was produced in 1936 as a military troop transport. Very expensive, it was soon specifically used as staff car for senior officers in the German army and for Nazi party high officials. The powerful G4 could accommodate six passengers, including the driver, and became familiar because Hitler and Göring used one as a personal transport for both parade car and cross-country vehicle. Mechanically the G4 was based on the Mercedes 5-liter. It had a 100-hp Daimler-Benz 8-cylinder engine. Weight was 3,500 kg, length was 5.4 m, width was 1.89 m, height was 1.8 m, maximum speed was 65 km/h, and fuel consumption was 27 liters/100 km. Fifty-seven were built.

Another heavy staff car was the Großer Mercedes Typ 770 W 150 or Staatskarosse. It was a luxurious vehicle used by the top leadership of the Third Reich. Only a few were built, amongst which one bearing the police registration IA v 148697. Built in carly 1940, with the factory number 429334, it was handed over to the Adjudancy of the Führer at Hermann Göringstraße 16— the location of the car pool of the Reich Chancellery—in July 1940. It was used on many occasions by Hitler over the following years. At the end of April 1945, the

*Heavy car Mercedes-Benz L 1500 A Kfz 70. The vehicle is shown here as the Allrad Mannschafts-kraftwagen Kfz 70 (four-wheel drive troop transport).*

*Heavy staff car Mercedes-Benz G4*

Führer's bullet-proof car—left abandoned on a flat-bed railway wagon near Salzburg—was captured by soldiers of the 20th U.S. Armored Division. It was shipped to the United States and extensively used for U.S. Victory Bond drives. Purchased by various collectors of vintage cars, Hitler's Mercedes was finally offered to the Canadian War Museum of Ottawa where it has been on display since 1971.

## Amphibious vehicles

### VW SCHWIMMWAGEN

The most popular amphibious car was the light *Kfz1/20, K2 Volkswagen VW 166* known as the *Schwimmwagen* (literally "floating car"). The *Kfz1/20 Schwimmwagen*—designed after the Kübelwagen—was manufactured by Volkswagen. Mechanically similar to the VW Kübelwagen, this amphibious utility vehicle was employed by the German army on all fronts. It had a bath-

shaped, pressed steel body, and this gave it quite a comical appearance, yet it proved a reliable vehicle during the war. It was powered by an air-cooled, 4-cylinder, 1,131 cc gasoline engine. At 3,300 rpm its power output was 24.5 hp. When used on water, it employed a rear three-bladed propeller on a lifting rear arm that was used to power it along. It was steered in the normal way, its front wheels acting as a rudder. As the engine was mounted in the rear of the vehicle, the propeller was connected via a dog clutch to the crankshaft of the engine; however, this neutralized the gears and no backward movement was possible whilst in the water. When traveling overland, the propeller and shaft folded over the back of the vehicle. The bulkhead was obviously completely waterproof, with the rear axle housing protected by rubber bushes. Transmission was four forward gears and one reverse, with a top speed of 75 km/h on road and 12 km/h on water. Suspension was by means of torsion bars, the favored German method of suspension. It was sometimes

*Amphibious Volkswagen Schwimmwagen Typ 166*

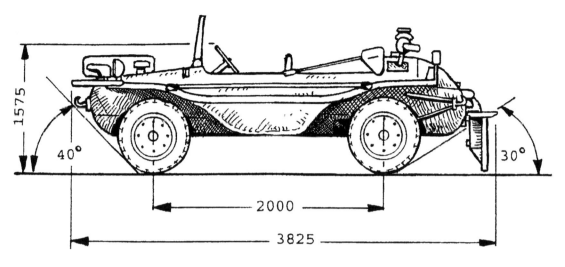

*Profile of the VW Schwimmwagen Typ 166 (measurements in millimeters)*

armed with a single MG 34 machine gun. A total of 14,267 Schwimmwagens were built, and production ceased in mid-1944.

### AMPHIBIOUS MEDIUM CAR
### TRIPPEL SG6/41

The amphibious Trippel SG6 was the successor of another amphibious car, the Trippel SG6/38, first made in 1935 with a 4-cylinder, 2-liter Adler engine. The SG6/41—and other amphibious vehicles— were designed as a private venture by a young engineer named Hans Trippel. Trippel had taken over the Bugatti works in Molsheim (Alsace, France) and produced his cars in the period 1941–1944. The Trippel firm did not enjoy official Nazi or army support, so production was limited. The Trippel amphibious car was not that common in the German army; total production was about 1,000 units, mainly privately pur-

*Amphibious medium car Trippel SG6/41*

chased and issued to the elite Waffen SS. The Schwimmwagen SG6/41 had an Opel 6-cylinder, 55 bhp engine, and variants included the Tatra V8 engine. The vehicles weighed 1,750 kg and had a length of 4.825 meters. It could accommodate four passengers including the driver and had a payload of about 1,000 kg.

In the period 1941–1942, Hans Trippel's company designed a small *Spähwagen* (armored reconnaissance car) fitted with a turret, named *Schildkröte* (tortoise). Based on the SG6 design, this was fitted with an air-cooled Tatra V8 engine and used faceted armor plates. Lacking support, work on the idea was ceased at the end of 1942. Only three prototypes were produced: the *Schildkröte I* was armed with one 7.92 mm MG 81 with armor 7 mm thick, the *Schildkröte II* was armed with one 2 cm MG 151 with 10 mm armor, and the *Schildkröte III* was armed with a 2 cm MG 151 with 10 mm armor. Two further prototype 4 x 4 amphibious armored vehicles, known as the Trippel E3, with a turret mounting a small gun were built. A similar but turretless munition transporter (Trippel E3-M) was also designed in 1944. These vehicles failed to attract the German military authorities' attention because they were not successful. Trials were therefore discontinued, and the projects were abandoned.

## SNOW CAR TATRA V 855

The Germans designed curious vehicles. Among those rarities there was an experimental design of a medium *Schnee-Automobil* (snow car) intended for the Wehrmacht for possible use on the Eastern front. This vehicle, the snow car *Tatra V 855*, was designed in 1942 and was derived from the Czech 1938 model 4x2 *Tatra 87*. The V 855 (V in model designation stood for *vojensky*, "military") snow car rested on four skis, the air-cooled engine was placed at the rear, and it was driven by a roller and an air propeller both placed at the rear. Steering was done by the front skis. The maximum speed was 80 km/h, and the experimental car could transport four passengers (including the driver). Only one prototype was ever built.

## Motorcycles

The 1914–1918 war gave a great impetus to the motorcycle, which was used for dispatch-carrying and even as machine gun carrier with a sidecar. After the war, motorbikes were used in the German army in the 1930s with many models in service. *Krad* (plural *Kräder*) was the official abbreviation of *Kraftrad* (motorcycle). After the 1938

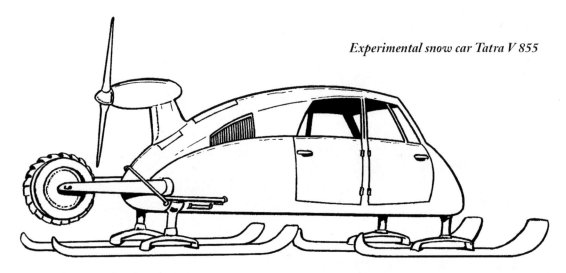

*Experimental snow car Tatra V 855*

Schell reorganization, the Germans used bikes in a relative large number, as motorcycles were regarded to be a comparatively cheap means of mass infantry motorization, a convenient substitute to military horses. All tank divisions had motorcycle infantry units. Two or three motorcycle companies and an HQ company formed a motorcycle battalion. An average infantry division on the Eastern front in the early stages of the war used 452 motorcycles, including those with a sidecar, made up as follows: 17 (HQ company), 45 (reconnaissance unit), 32 (signal battalion), 141 (infantry regiment), 40 (artillery regiment), 45 (anti-tank gun battalion), 44 (engineer battalion), and 88 (supply unit).

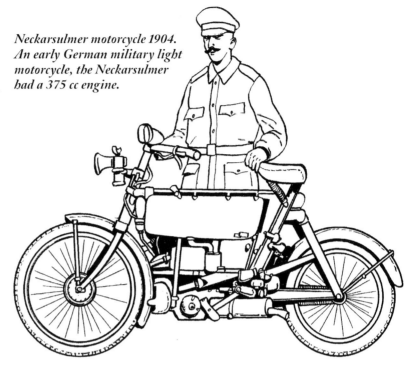

*Neckarsulmer motorcycle 1904. An early German military light motorcycle, the Neckarsulmer had a 375 cc engine.*

Each motorcycle could be fitted with a *Seitenwagen* or *Beiwagen für Krad* (sidecar). The sidecar was often of a standardized *Einheit* type. The *Beiwagen* could carry one man as well as panniers for stores, one spare wheel and one machine gun (on pintle mount) with ammunitions; some could even accommodate a light mortar. The soldiers rode to battle and dismounted to fight just as in earlier centuries the *dragoons* using horses.

Actually, motorbikes rapidly proved to be quite unsuited to modern warfare. Motorcycles offered no protection to the rider against wind, cold and rain—German motorbikes were not fitted with windshields, so a ride could be an uncomfortable and miserable experience. Motor-bike riders were vulnerable to small arms fire, grenades, mines and

*Zündapp KF 600 motorcycle*

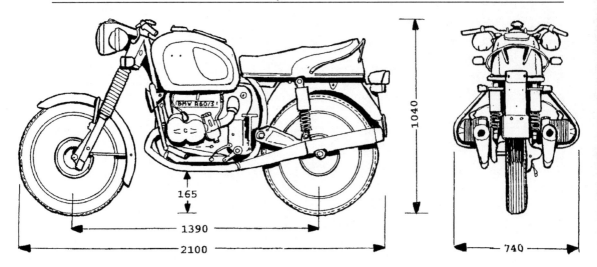

*Two-view of the German BMW R60/5. BMW stands for Bayerische Motor Werke, meaning "Bavarian Engine Works," located in Munich (measurements in millimeters).*

*BMW R75 with sidecar. The BMW's traditional 2-cylinder, flat 750 cc engine gave the 400 kg motorcycle with a sidecar a maximum speed of 90 km/h. The production of the heavy BMW R75 was begun in late 1940 and about 16,500 were produced up to the end of World War II. Its reliability was such that after the war, the Russian army used faithful copies of the BMW R/75, referred to as K-M72.*

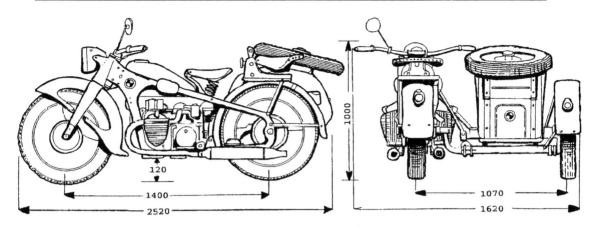

*Two-view of the BMW R12 with sidecar. Measurements are indicated in millimeters. The BMW R12 has a BMW 2-cylinder engine, a speed of 100 km/h, and 85 km/h with a sidecar.*

*Captured French Bernadet bike with sidecar. The sidecar is armed with a light machine gun FM 1924/29.*

to mantraps (such as deliberately spilled oil). On soft ground or on bad roads, motorcycles became useless. After the Polish campaign motorcycles, with or more often without sidecar, were relegated to the role of runners taking messages from headquarters to frontline troops and regrouped as *Kradschutzen* (motorcycle light reconnaissance battalions). Most early models of German military motorcycles proved unre-

*German motorbike rider. The depicted man wears the standardized M35 steel helmet with goggles, heavy waterproof gloves, and a rubberized, full length, water proof greatcoat—which could be gathered in and buttoned around the ankles for easy riding; there were two large pockets positioned in the front and to each side of the coat, each with a large buttoned pocket flap. At the waist belt, the man carries a leather pouch for messages and dispatches.*

liable after the invasion of Russia in summer 1941, and only the BMW R75 was rugged enough for liaison and reconnaissance purposes. The average infantry division in 1943 to 1944 came to use an increasing number of light *Kübelwagen* "bucket" personnel cars, which had excellent durability and various uses in place of motorcycles.

The German army originally grouped motorcycles into three classes:

• *leichte Kräder* (light bikes) under 350 cc,

• *mittlere Kräder* (middle bikes) 350–500 cc, and

• *schwere Kräder* (large bikes) over 500 cc.

The Germans mainly employed Zündapp, Triumph, Puch, NSU and BMW motorbikes with 125 cc, 500 cc and the powerful 750 cc engines driving both the rear wheel of the bike and the sidecar wheel to greatly improving the performance. About 35,000 motorbikes, *Zündapp KS 750, NSU 251 OSL* and *BMW R75*, were produced during the war. Captured motorcycles were also used in large numbers, of course, such as the Belgian FN M12, the French Gnome & Rhône AX2, the French Terrot 500 R and Bernadet. Italian captured motorcycles included, for example, the 1-cylinder *Guzzi Alce*, the heavy *Gilera Marte*, and the machine-gun carrier tricycle *Guzzi Trialce*.

Motorcyclists were issued goggles, large gloves, waterproof overshoes and leggings. They were often wearing the practical *Schutzmantel*, a double breasted, waterproof, rubberized, heavy duty greatcoat; this could be buttoned around the man's legs to allow easier and safer movement while riding the motorbike.

Worthy of mention is the *NSU Kettenkrad HK 100 SdKfz 2*. The *Kettenkrad* was unique in being a sort of cross between a motorcycle and a small half-track chassis. It was designed in 1940 by the *Waffenamt* (Ordnance Department) and produced by the NSU AG company from Neckarsulm,

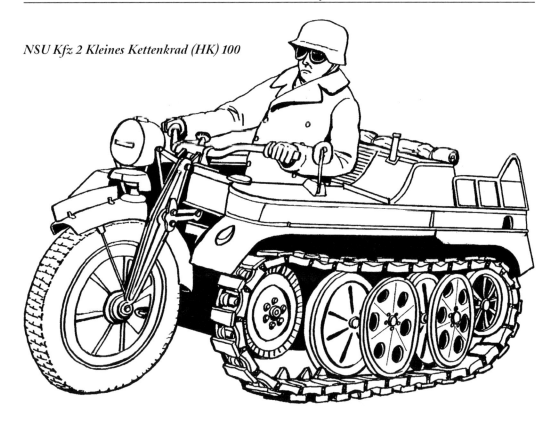

*NSU Kfz 2 Kleines Kettenkrad (HK) 100*

the well-known motorcycle firm. The vehicle was also manufactured by other companies, notably Stoewer from Stettin. The Kettenkrad went into service in 1941 and was originally intended for paratroopers to tow airborne light artillery (2.8 cm or 3.7 cm guns). It was moved by an Opel Olympia 1.5-liter, four-cylinder, 36 bhp gasoline car engine. Seats were provided for three men: the driver and two passengers at the rear. The bodywork was in pressed steel, but its weight (1,235 kg) and its dimensions (3 m—about 9 ft. 10 in. in length, 1 m in width and 1.20 m in height) were calculated in order to fit into a three-motor transport plane Junkers Ju 52, which was the standard carrier of the *Luftwaffe.* The Kettenkrad had a payload of 325 kg, and it could tow a load of 450 kg. The track system was that of a half-track with large double and overlapping rubber-tired bogie wheels suspended by torsion bars, running almost four-quarters of the length of the vehicle, giving increased traction and excellent

cross-country performance. Fuel consumption was 16 liters/100 km on road and 22 liters/100 km cross-country. The fuel tank had a capacity of 42 liters, thus allowing a range on road of 260 km and of 190 km cross-country. Its maximum speed was rather impressive: 70 km/h on good roads.

The *NSU Kettenkrad HK 100* was first used in the landings at Crete in 1941. After Hitler's rejection of the airborne concept in 1942, the paratrooper force became almost exclusively infantry units, and so the *Kettenkrad's* original role became redundant. The machine was then deployed as a supply vehicle in difficult terrain by paratroopers, and several vehicles found their way into army hands. It was employed with success in North Africa in 1941–1942 and proved an extremely versatile machine, being able to tow light guns or a matching trailer that could accommodate ammunition and supplies. It could also help tow bogged or wrecked light vehicles. A variant, known as the *Kettenkrad SdKfz 2/2,* was a telephone

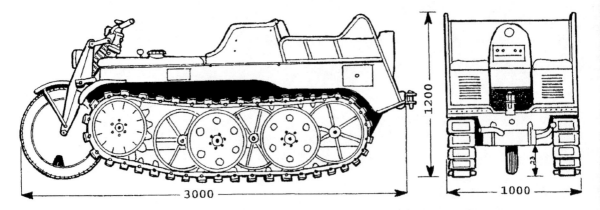

*Profile and back view of NSU Kettenkrad Kfz 2 (all measurements in millimeters)*

cable layer with a reel carried in a cradle over the central engine compartment. By the end of the war, some 8,345 *Kettenkräder* were produced and used on all fronts as cross-country utilities, and several of them were captured and used by the Allies during the Battle of Normandy in July 1944. By the end of the war, NSU designed a more powerful version with a 2-liter engine and the capability of carrying five soldiers, but this project came much too late and never reached the front troops.

*Soldier on bicycle*

## Bicycles

In the 1930s many European armies raised bicycle troops. This would seem curious, odd and ridiculously old-fashioned today, but the importance of the bicycle as military troop transportation must not be underestimated. Western Europe offered a dense network of relatively good metalled roads. Under favorable conditions, bicyclists could cover long distances; with regular breaks, on flat land, dry weather and good road, an average speed of 20 km/h may be easily sustained. A troop on bicycle could approach a fighting zone quietly for a surprise attack—much quieter than a horse-mounted cavalry unit or a column of vehicles anyway. It could be instantly deployed for combat without the services of horseholders. Bicycles are cheap devices, and they require none of the specialist care and supply of horses (food, water, veterinary care, etc.) or of motorized vehicles (fuel, maintenance, etc.). It should be noted that bicycles were extensively used as transport by the Vietnamese forces in the Indochina/Vietnam wars from 1946 to 1975. Disadvantages were, however, numerous. These included the muscular strain imposed on the rider and the limited load that each bicyclist could carry with him—though heavy weapons and cumbersome equipment could be transported in accompanying motorcycles with sidecars or engine-driven cars and trucks. Other drawbacks were similar to those of the motorbike: the absence of protection (as much from weather conditions as from enemy fire) and the fact that such a troop was totally road-bound. Nonetheless, the German Wehrmacht made wide use of the cheap *Fahrrad* (bicycle) as a means of transportation all through World War II. In the cavalry, for example, one squadron per regiment was formed of men mounted on bicycles. Wehrmacht bicyclists generally used the standardized German-made M1939 Patria WKC bicycle, but many foreign cycles were captured and used.

# 3

# Trucks and Tractors

## Light trucks

The majority of German light trucks were basically commercial types with payload capacities of up to 2 tons, but the line between heavy car and light truck was not always clearly drawn. Even though the *Schell Plan* of 1938 curtailed the multitude of them, there were many models in use during World War II, and to list them all would be prohibitive. There were mainly two categories: the *S-Wirtschaftstyp* (commercial road S model) and the *A-Wehrmachtstyp* (military cross-country A model). Here again, there were many captured or confiscated foreign types pressed into German service. There were also six-wheel light trucks, generally known as *Protzkraftwagen*, that were more particularly employed to tow light field artillery and anti-tank guns.

### BÜSSING-NAG G 31

The light 6 x 4 truck *Büssing-Nag G31 (Kfz 61)* was a typical example of a standard 1.5-tonner used by the German army in the mid-1930s, and some 2,300 were built between 1931 and 1935. Length was 5.63 m, height was 2.8 m and weight was 3,990 kg. Speed was 60 km/h, and fuel consumption was 27 liters/100 km on road and 35 liters/100 km cross-country. Range was 450 km on road and 350 km cross-country. The G31 was also built by Daimler-Benz and Magirus. Numerous bodies could be fitted to the basic chassis such as cargo, troop carrier, ambulance, signal or engineer truck, and so forth.

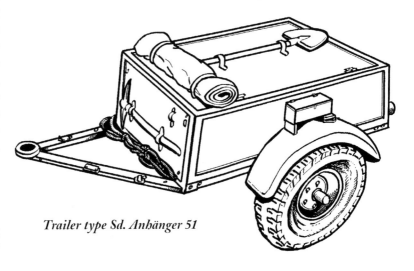

*Trailer type Sd. Anhänger 51*

*Light truck Büssing-NAG G31*

*Light truck Tatra T92*

### TATRA T92

The 6 x 4 light truck *Tatra T92* had a V8 70 bhp, air-cooled 4-liter engine. Length was 5.5 m, width was 2 m and weight was 3,580 kg. The truck had a payload of 2 tons. Speed was 70 km/h, and fuel consumption was 35 liters/100 km on road. Range was 370 km on road. It could also be fitted with other bodywork such as an ambulance. About 500 were produced between 1937 and 1940. There was a variant known as the Tatra T93 intended for the Romanian army.

## PRAGA RV

The *Praga RV* light cargo truck (6 x 4) was 5.69 m long, 2 m wide, 2.5 m high and weighed 3,810 kg. Speed was 70 km/h, fuel consumption was 35 liters/100 km on road, and range was 390 km on road. Payload was 2,000 kg. The truck could be fitted with a 3-ton winch at the rear. About 2,000 of

these trucks were built during the period 1935–1939, mainly for the Czech and Romanian armies. Later in the war they were used by the German forces.

## STEYR 40 D

The light truck *Steyr 10D*, designed in 1935, was the standard 6 x 4 vehicle of the

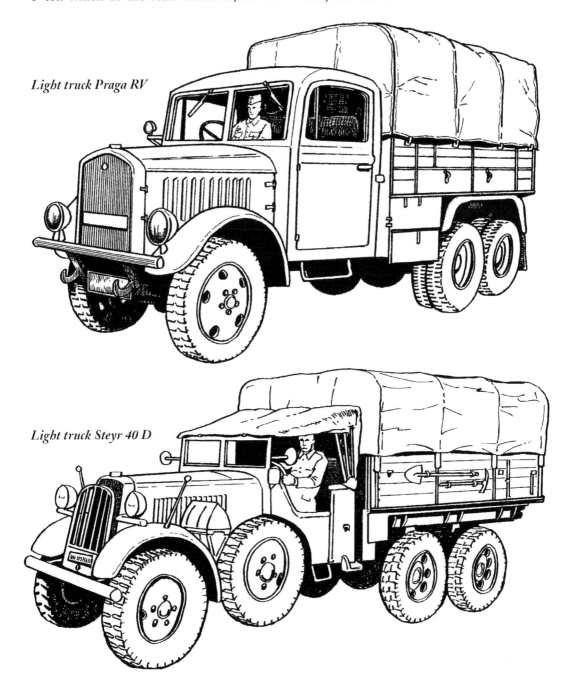

*Light truck Praga RV*

*Light truck Steyr 40 D*

*Light cross-country truck*
*Kfz 81 Krupp L2H143*

*Krupp L2H 143*
*Radio truck (Kfz 17)*

WH- 1288544212

Austrian army. It had a 45 bhp, six-cylinder gasoline engine giving a top speed of 70 km/h. It had spare wheels, which were carried on each side of the cabin. These were attached to the chassis frame and free to revolve, thus giving added traction when the truck was crossing rough ground. More than 700 of these lorries were impressed in the German army after the annexation of Austria in 1938.

## KRUPP L 2 H 143

The six-wheel *Krupp-Protze L2H143* was designed by Krupp and introduced in the late 1930s. It was intended to be used exclusively by the German army for several purposes. The low-profiled vehicle had a sloping hood, enabling excellent vision for the driver. It had a Krupp M 304 four-cylinder, 3308 cc air-cooled engine, hydraulic brakes, all-independent suspension and added free-revolving spare wheels on both sides for cross-country performance. Maximum speed was 70 km/h. Range was 450 km on surfaced road and 350 km cross-country. Fuel consumption per 100 km was 24 liters on road and 30 liters cross-country. The vehicle weighed 2,450 kg, its length was 5.1 m, width was 2 m and height was

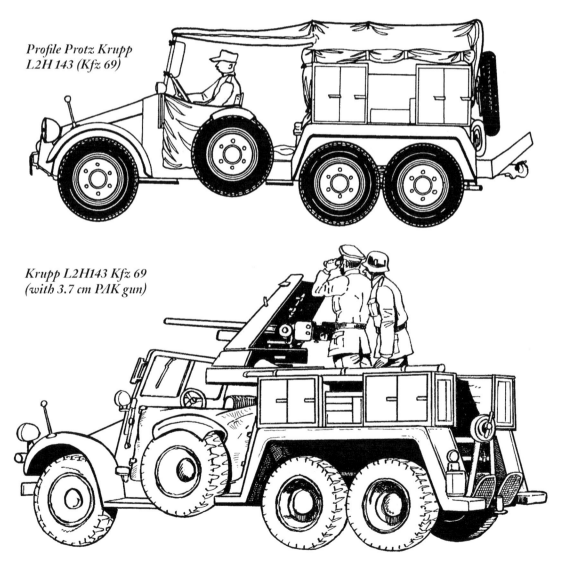

*Profile Protz Krupp L2H 143 (Kfz 69)*

*Krupp L2H143 Kfz 69 (with 3.7 cm PAK gun)*

about 2 m. It could carry a load of 1,150 kg. Probably due to the appearance of the sloping hood, it was popularly nicknamed by the troop *Krupp-Schnauzer* (Krupp snout). The *Krupp L2 H123* chassis was used for a variety of body types and conversions.

The most common version was the *Kfz 69 Protzkraftwagen* (tractor) towing a 3.7 cm anti-tank Pak 36 gun and carrying the team of gunners.

The *Fernsprechbetrieb Kraftwagen Kfz 19* (communication vehicle) was fitted with a closed body, telephone switchboard and related equipment.

The *Funkwagen Kfz 17* was a radio conversion with a closed body housing the radio equipment and fitted with an antenna frame on the roof.

The *Mannschaftskraftwagen Kfz 80* was a troop carrier with a capacity of ten soldiers, including the driver.

Two variants were also used by the Luftwaffe.

The *leichter Flakkraftwagen Kfz 81* was intended to tow a light, 2 cm Flak 30 anti-aircraft gun; occasionally, the gun was placed on a platform on the vehicle itself.

The *Scheinwerferkraftwagen Kfz 83* was intended to tow a 60 cm Flak searchlight, and the truck carried a generator to provide the energy required by the searchlight.

Finally, there was a conversion known as the *Standardenwagen* (standardized car); that was a 6 x 4 Krupp-Protze L 2 H 143 truck with sloping armored body intended to be used as a *Panzerspähwagen* (armored reconnaissance car).

## DIESEL EINHEIT

The light truck known as the Diesel Einheit was a standardized 6 x 6 diesel-engine vehicle in the 2.5 ton class. Designed and manufactured by Man, Henschel, Magirus and Büssing-NAG, it was a typical example of a standardized, fully cross-country military truck used by the German army in the period 1937–1940, many of which served until 1945. Numerous bodies could be fitted to the basic chassis, such as cargo, troop carrier, ambulance, signal or engineer truck, artillery observation role and many others. The vehicle was fitted with a standardized diesel engine type Baumuster Hwa 526 D, 80 bhp, giving a maximum speed of 70 km/h. Length was 5.84 m, height was 2.8 m, and weight was about 5,000 kg, but these dimensions could vary slightly according to basic type. Diesel fuel consumption per 100 km was 30 liters on road and 45 liters cross-country. Range was 360 km on road and 260 km cross-country.

*Einheit Diesel.*
*The vehicle is shown*
*here as the radio car*
*Kfz 61.*

## MORRIS PU

The British light truck *Morris Commercial PU* was designed and built by Morris (Nuffield) Motor Ltd. from Cowley Oxford. It had been issued to the British army since 1936 and used for a variety of bodies including staff car, utility, ambulance, general service and wireless vehicle. It was powered by a Morris OH 6-cylinder, 3.48-liter, 60 bhp engine. After the retreat of Dunkirk (France) in June 1940, the quasi-totality of British vehicles was abandoned and sabotaged. Many were repaired by the Germans and pressed into service in the Wehrmacht. The Morris Commercial PU was known in the German forces as the *Kfz 15 (b)*.

## GAZ-AΛ

The *Russian truck GAZ-AA* was designed and built by the Gorki Automobile

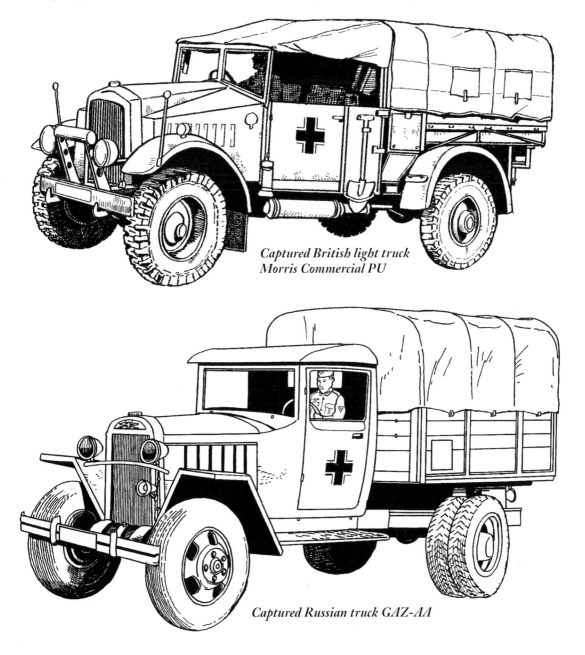

*Captured British light truck Morris Commercial PU*

*Captured Russian truck GAZ-AA*

Zavod company in 1932 with the technical assistance of the American company Ford. The GAZ-AA was actually a copy of the U.S. Ford Model AA 1.5-ton truck; hence its nickname *Russki-Ford*. Many thousands were produced and built until 1945, many of which were captured by the Germans in 1941. The vehicle had several conversions for special purpose variants including ambulance, breakdown truck, anti-aircraft gun carrier and rocket-firer. The GAZ-AA had a four-cylinder, 50 bhp side-valve engine. There was a six-wheel version, the *GAZ-AAA*, identical to the AA except for the twin rear bogie. The chassis of the six-wheel GAZ-AAA was often used as the basis for an armored reconnaissance car conversion known as the GAZ-BA 32.

## Medium trucks

Most German medium trucks were commercial types designed to transport cargo with a payload of about 3 tons. In early stages, many models were fitted with a stan-dard soft-top cab instead of the civilian all-steel type. In 1944, a standardized substitute was introduced for practically all types of trucks then in production. This cab, as already said, was known as the *Einheits-fahrerhaus*. It was made of wood and pressed cardboard, the object being to save steel, which by this time was in short supply. In addition the Germans (especially the NSKK, the National Socialist Drivers' Corps) used large quantities of confiscated civilian and captured military medium trucks, such as U.S. Chevrolet and Oldsmobile as well as French Citroën and Renault. Relatively large numbers were produced—some with twin rear bogie—and a wide variety of standard and special bodies was used, including house types for signals and other specialist roles. Before the outbreak of World War II, medium trucks were available to civilian users and for export (Spain, Hungary, Romania, Turkey, etc.), mainly in order to boost production and to reduce unit costs. They were also issued to government departments, including the *Deutsche Reichsbahn* (railway company) and the *Reichspost* (mail service).

*3-ton Ford medium truck*

## FORD V 3000

The 3-ton Ford medium 4 x 2 truck was built by the German branch of the Ford Motor Company established in Cologne. In 1935 this branch had become an independent firm named Ford-Werke AG. The company mainly produced 3 tonners, of which about 50,000 were built between 1941 and 1944. The engine was a 3.9-liter Ford V8, maximum speed was 85 km/h, and payload was 3,300 kg. Fuel consumption was 32 liters/100 km on road, 45 liters/100 km cross-country; range on road was 330 km and 230 km cross-country. The 3-ton Ford had several conversions including cargo carrier, ambulance and bus. The company also manufactured the same truck with track fitted to the rear bogie known as the *Ford Maultier* (about 15,000 produced).

## OPEL BLITZ

The 4 x 2 *Opel Blitz LKW 3.6–36S* 3-ton truck was the mainstay of German transport. Designed in 1938 by Opel (the German subsidiary then of General Motors), the *Blitz* was a very successful truck with a quite conventional layout. It had a 3,626 cc, six-cylinder Opel engine develop-

ing 75 bhp and a five-speed gearbox. Suspension was by conventional leaf springs. Length was 5.4 m, height was 1.94 m, and weight was about 1,525 kg. Maximum speed was 80 km/h, fuel consumption was 16.5 liters/100 km and range was 340 km. The Opel Blitz had a reasonable cross country performance and was designated *mittlerer geländegängiger Lastkraftwagen* (medium cross-country truck). By the end of the war, some 100,000 of them had been produced and engaged on all fronts; a total of 40,000 was scheduled for 1945 production alone. There were over 100 different types recorded. The most important versions were troop carrier, field kitchen, cargo truck, ambulance, radio truck, fuel tanker, mobile laboratory, fire brigade truck, mobile cipher office, cistern or workshop carrier and many others. There were a *3-ton Allradantrieb* (four wheel drive) version and a half-track variant designated as the *Opel-Maultier* (mule). Another version included an armored cab and a platform designed to house a light anti-aircraft gun; the vehicle was then transformed into a light *Selbstfahrlafette* (self-propelled gun) and called the *Opel Blitz 3t mit 2 cm Flak 38*; ammunitions for the gun were usually transported in a two-wheeled trailer towed by the truck. Early vehicles were fitted with pressed

*Opel Blitz 3-ton Type S*

*Opel Blitz 3-ton Type S (with Wagenschutzedecke, "canvas cover")*

*Opel Blitz tanker*

steel cab and hood, but later 1944 models had the cheap wooden *Einheits* (standardized) driver's cab, as well as gas-generator engine.

The *Opel Blitz* was the major German military truck of World War II, and its production was continued well past the end of the war, forming the mainstay of post-war German commercial civilian transport.

*Armored Opel Blitz with 2 cm Flak 38*

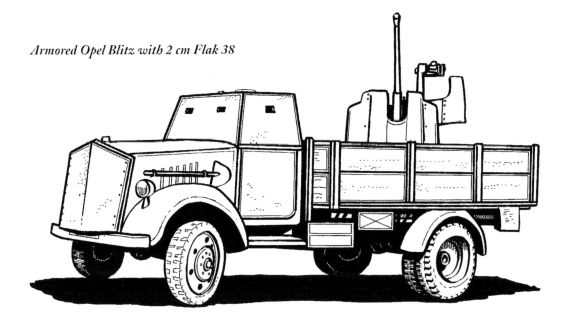

## HENSCHEL 33 G1

The *Henschel 33 G1 mittler gelän-degängiger Lastkraftwagen* (medium cross-country truck), designed in 1934, was one of the most long-lived models of the early 1930s period. It was a 6 × 4 transport with a 100 hp, six-cylinder diesel engine, a five-speed gearbox and airbrakes. Speed was 52 km/h, and diesel fuel consumption was 30 liters/100 km on road and 45 liters/100 km cross-country. Range was 380 km on road and 250 km cross-country. Length was 7 m, height was 2.5 m, and weight was about 6,450 kg. Also built by Magirus, the Henschel 33 G1 was widely used until 1945. There were several conversions possible, notably a radio variant known as the *Fernsprechbetriebkraftwagen Kfz 72*, a *Mannschaft-Entgiftungskraftwagen Kfz 92b* (gas decontamination vehicle for personnel), and a *Tankspritze Kfz 343* (fire truck) with pump

*Mittler Lastkraftwagen*
*Henschel 33 G1*

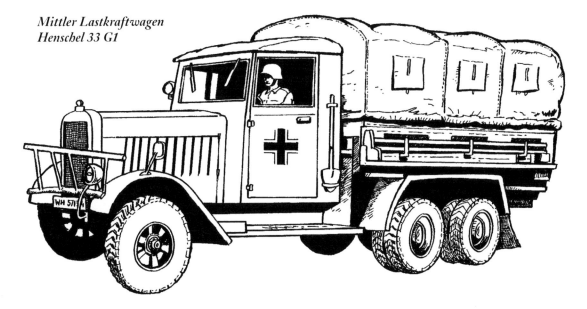

*Medium truck Klöckner-Deutz-Magirus A 3000*

and water tank containing 2,500 liters and a four-man crew. In all, some 3,600 of them were manufactured.

## KLÖCKNER-DEUTZ-MAGIRUS A 3000

The Klöckner-Deutz-Magirus 3000 was produced in two categories: the *S-Typ Wirtschaftstyp* (4 x 2 commercial model) and the *A-Typ Wehrmachtstyp* (4 x 4 military cross-country model). Produced in the period 1941–1944, the vehicle was fitted with a diesel engine type Deutz F 4 M 513, giving a speed of 75 km/h on road and 40 km/h cross-country. Length was 6.6 m, height was 2.5 m, and weight was about 6,450 kg, but these dimensions could vary slightly according to S or A type. Diesel oil consumption per 100 km was 20 liters on road

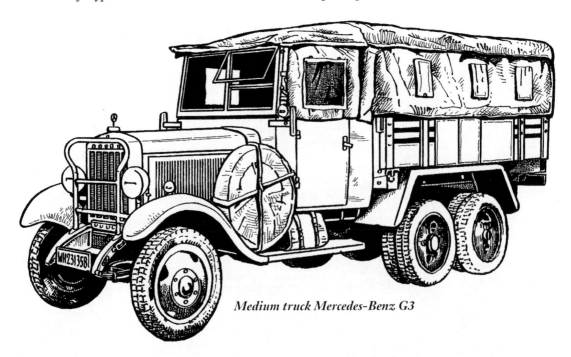

*Medium truck Mercedes-Benz G3*

and 30 liters cross-country. Range was 350 km on road and 230 km cross-country.

## MERCEDES-BENZ G3

The 6 x 4 medium cross-country truck *Mercedes-Benz Typ G3* was designed in 1928 and was produced until 1935, but many of them stayed in use with the German army until the end of the war. It had a 6-cylinder, 3,689 cc Daimler-Benz M09 gasoline engine, giving a maximum speed of 60 km/h. Fuel consumption per 100 km was 25 liters on road and 33 liters cross-country.

*Medium truck Mercedes-Benz Type G3a with field kitchen*

*Medium 3-ton truck Borgward B3000 A/D*

The type G3 was about 6 m long, 2.1 m wide and 2.65 m high. It was a versatile vehicle with a payload of 1,500 kg that existed in various bodies, configurations and chassis for specialized technical roles (observation, fire-fighting, ambulance, radio, command, weather station, etc.) designated SdKfz 61, 62, 63, 64 and 76. Some 2,000 were built. The chassis of the *Mercedes-Benz Typ G3* was also used to build the *Schwerer Panzerspähwagen SdKfz 231 (6-Rad)* (6-wheel heavy armored reconnaissance truck), issued in 1932. An improved version—known as type G3a—was designed in 1929 with increased payload of 1,800 kg and a speed of 65 km/h.

## BORGWARD B3000

The 3-ton medium truck B3000, built by the Borgward company between 1939 and 1944, existed in four versions. The

*3-ton medium Mercedes-Benz L3000A*

*L3000 Mercedes-Benz truck (with canvas cover)*

B3000 S/O was a 4 × 2 gasoline engine cargo carrier. The B3000 A/O was a 4 × 4 gasoline engine cross-country truck. The improved B3000 S/D was a 4 × 2 diesel engine truck. The improved B3000 A/D was a 4 × 4 cross-country diesel engine carrier. Data of the type B3000A/D were as follows: Length was 6.45 m, height was 2.3 m, weight was 6,610 kg, and payload was about 3,515 kg. Maximum speed was 70 km/h, diesel oil consumption per 100 km was 25 liters on road and 32 liters cross-country. Range was 480 km on road and 370 km cross-country.

## MERCEDES-BENZ L3000

The 3-ton medium truck B3000, built by the Mercedes-Benz company between 1939 and 1943, existed in three versions. The L3000 was a 4 × 2 diesel engine cargo carrier. The improved L3000 S was a 4 × 2 diesel engine truck. The improved L3000A was a 4 × 4 cross-country diesel engine carrier. Data of the four-wheel drive cross-country type L3000A were as follows: Length was 6.255 m, height was 2.35 m, weight was 4,020 kg, and payload was about

3,000 kg. Maximum speed was 70 km/h, diesel oil consumption per 100 km was 250 liters on road and 30 liters cross-country. Range was 450 km on road and 300 km cross-country. The L3000 could be fitted with various bodies, including cargo carrier, tanker, and radio vehicle.

## CITROËN U23

In 1939 the medium 2-ton *Citroën U 23* was widely used in the French army as troop and freight carrier, ambulance, radio car, and anti-aircraft weapon carrier (e.g., armed with a Hotchkiss 8 mm model 28 machine gun). The U 23 was also very popular in civilian use. Some 14,000 of these vehicles were produced as both military and civilians trucks. About 6,000 were pressed into German service after the French defeat of June 1940.

## CITROËN 23 R

The French 2-ton medium truck *Citroën 23 R* was designed to replace the 1.5-ton U23. The new truck had a 4-cylinder, 28 bhp engine. Length was 5.54 m, width

*French Citroën 1.5 t U 23*

*French medium truck Citroën 23R*

*Captured French Peugeot DMA 1.5 t LKW*

was 1.98 m, height was 2.7 m and gross weight was 2,200 kg. Over 5,000 of these 2-tonners were produced during World War II for the German army. They were mainly employed on the Eastern front.

## PEUGEOT 1.5 T DMA

Another French truck of the medium class used by the Germans was the *Peugeot 1.5 t DMA*.

*French medium truck Renault AHN*

*Italian medium truck 2.5 t Fiat/Spa T40*

## RENAULT AHN

The French-built 4 x 2 *Renault AHN* was a medium cargo carrier with a payload of 3,500 kg. It had a 6-cylinder, 75 bhp Renault engine. This truck had a maximum speed of 60 km/h, a weight of 3.5 t, a length of 6.4 m, a height of 2.6 m and a width of 2.4 m. It was produced between 1941 and 1944 by the French company Renault from Billancourt (a suburb of Paris) for the German army.

## FIAT T40

The Italian medium *2.5-ton Fiat/Spa T40* had a 6-cylinder, 108 bhp diesel engine.

*Italian medium truck Fiat/Spa Dovunque 35. The Dovunque served as the basis of constituting the armored truck Fiat Auto Blinda 611.*

Length was 5.31 m, width 2.18 m, height 2.78 m and weight (unloaded) was 5,650 kg. The Fiat T40 was basically a *Tipo TM40* tractor chassis and is shown here with the German standardized low-cost *Einheits* driver's cabin. This vehicle was produced from 1941 to 1948. Another Italian vehicle of this class was the medium truck Fiat/Spa Dovunque 35.

## Ambulances and buses

Mechanization and the use of motor ambulances, which had hastened evacuation of casualties in World War I, were put to even better use in World War II. Casualties unable to walk were carried from the bat-

tlefield by stretcher bearers, while those still capable of walking were directed to the *Verwundetennest* (Aid Station), located as close to the frontline as was practicable, where they received first emergency medical attention. The stretcher cases (severely wounded) were sent to a *Hauptverbandplatz* (Main Dressing Station), where the surgical unit performed amputations, applied dressings and splints, checked hemorrhages, gave blood transfusions, and administrated sedatives and preventive injections. After treatment, casualties were evacuated further rearward to a *Lazarette* (hospital) by train or by automobile ambulance.

All ambulances used by the German forces were designated *Kfz. 31 Krankenkraftwagen* (Krkw). They were also referred to as

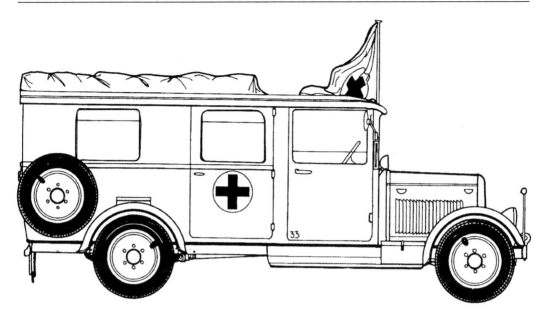

*Profile Kfz 31 Phänomen-Granit 25H ambulance*

*Sanitätskraftwagen* (*Sanka* or *Sankra* in short). Mobile operating theaters were known as *Operationswagen*. The chassis on which the ambulance body was built could originally be any heavy car, light truck or medium truck. By 1940 the standardized heavy car chassis with ambulance body was issued to the front troops, with a capacity of four stretchers or eight sitting patients. Shutter and mushroom type ventilators were often incorporated on the roof of the bodywork for extra ventilation. A common model was the Opel Blitz Typ S. Many captured ambulances were also taken into German service, varying from the British Austin K2 and Bedford ML and the French Peugeot 202U to the Soviet ZiS and GAZ-05–193. In case of emergency, military or civilian-type buses could be temporarily used or converted to ambulances for the conveyance of casualties. According to the international Geneva convention, ambulances were marked with a red cross on a white disc displayed on the sides, the back and sometimes on the roof of the vehicle for air recognition. There was often a waving white flag with a red cross attached on top of the driver's cabin.

## PHÄNOMEN-GRANIT 25H

The *Kfz 31 Phänomen-Granit 25H* was a common ambulance used by the German army. It could accommodate four stretchers or eight sitting patients. Length was 5.4 m, width was 2 m, height was 2.3 m, and weight was 2,400 kg. Maximum speed was 73 km/h. Fuel consumption was 16 liters/km, and range on road was 340 km. The vehicle could be fitted with either an all-metal closed cab or a canvas-top cab and folding windscreen.

## PHÄNOMEN GRANIT 1500A

The *Kfz 31* ambulance *Phänomen Granit 1500A* was the smallest standardized class under the *Schell Programme*. It was built on the chassis of a 1.5-ton heavy car, known as the *schwerer Personenkraftwagen Phänomen Granit 1500* (heavy personnel carrier). It had an air-cooled, four-cylinder diesel engine, a length of 5.5 m, a width of 1.98 m, a height of 2.08 m and a weight of approximately 3,750 kg. Maximum speed was 85 km/h. Fuel consumption was 17 liters/km, and range on road was 430 km.

*Ambulance 4 x 4 Kfz 31*
*Phänomen Granit 1500A*

*Ambulance (Krankenkraftwagen)*
*Mercedes-Benz L Kfz 31*

Late types were generally fitted with the low-cost *Einheits* driver's cab. A rather similar design was the Mercedes-Benz LE 1100 ambulance.

## STEYR 640

The Austrian-made 6 x 4 *Steyr 640 Krankenkraftwagen Kfz 31* was derived from the 1.5-ton medium cross-country truck,

*Steyr 640 ambulance*

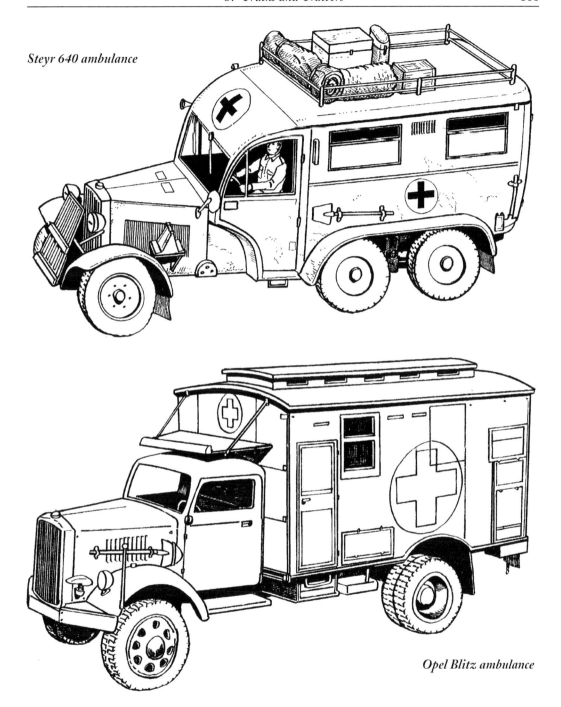

*Opel Blitz ambulance*

built in the period 1937–1941, of which 3,780 were produced. It had a six-cylinder, 2260 cc, 55 bhp engine; hydraulic brakes; and a maximum speed of 70 km/h. Fuel consumption was 22 liters/km on road and 28 liters cross-country. Range on road was 340 km and 260 km cross-country. Length

was 4.88 m, width was 1.8 m, height was 2.5 m and weight was 2,885 kg.

## OPEL BLITZ AMBULANCE

This common German ambulance was a version of the Opel Blitz S-Typ 3-ton

*Schwerer Einheits-PKW Horch/Ford
(ambulance version)*

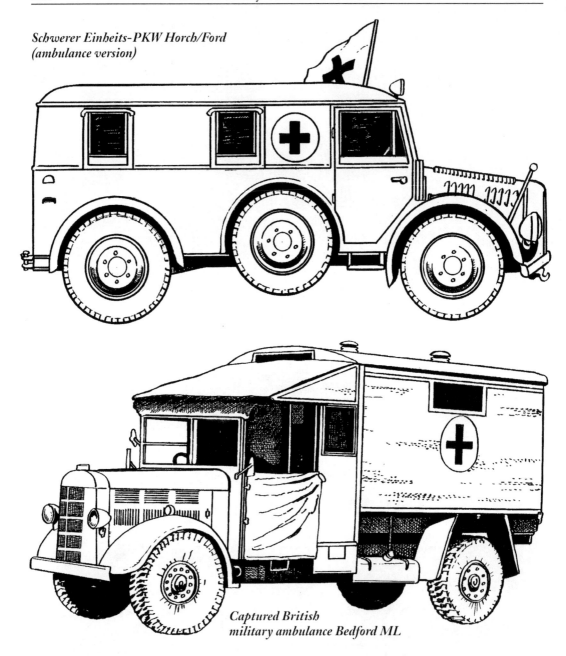

*Captured British
military ambulance Bedford ML*

truck. Its interior could be adapted for use as bus, command center or ambulance.

## STANDARDIZED AMBULANCE HORCH/FORD KFZ 31

This vehicle was the ambulance version of the *schwerer Einheits-Personenkraftwagen* (PKW heavy standardized car) built by Horch and Ford.

## BEDFORD ML

The British ambulance *Bedford ML* had a 6-cylinder, 72 bhp engine, and it could accommodate four stretchers or ten sitting patients. A certain number of these vehicles were captured and used by the Germans after the evacuation of Dunkirk in 1940.

*Captured Russian ambulance GAZ-05–193*

*Wehrmacht-Bus*

## RUSSIAN AMBULANCE
## GAZ-05–193

The ambulance GAZ-05–193 was based on the chassis of the 6-wheel GAZ-AAA, produced from 1936 to 1945. The vehicle had accommodation for nine casualties and a maximum speed of 65 km/h. It weighed 3,140 kg, and fuel consumption was 27 liters/100 km.

## WEHRMACHT OMNIBUS

The *mittlerer Personenkraftwagen*, also called the *Wehrmacht-Omnibus*, was a conversion of the popular *Opel Blitz* medium

truck. It had approximately the same performance as the medium Blitz but featured
a longer chassis (length was 7.2 m) fitted
with an enclosed omnibus-type body (built
by the Karosseriefabrik Gebruder Ludewig
from Essen) with 26 seats. It was thus a
medium bus, light buses having a capacity
of maximum 15 seats and heavy busses being
able to carry more than 30 passengers. The
seats were removable, and the vehicles could
be fitted with stretcher racks to accommodate about ten wounded and an emergency
medical team. As yet another alternative,
the bus could be arranged as a command

vehicle or map caravan for senior officers.
About 2,900 were produced between 1939
and 1944.

## MERCEDES-BENZ BUS
## TYP 02600

The light/medium bus Mercedes-Benz
02600 was a variant of the medium 2/3-ton
class Mercedes cargo truck. It had a 4-cylin-
der, 4.94 liter diesel engine using 17 liters
diesel oil per 100 km. Maximum speed was
60 km/h. The bus could also be used as an
ambulance or adapted to various roles such

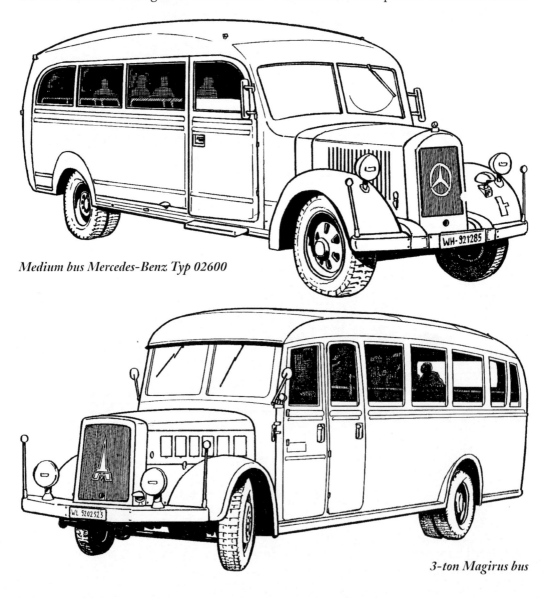

*Medium bus Mercedes-Benz Typ 02600*

*3-ton Magirus bus*

as command or radio vehicle. Other variants included a fire-fighting vehicle known as the Mercedes Lo 2750.

### THREE-TON MAGIRUS BUS

The Magirus firm from Ulm produced vehicles for the German army as early as the First World War. In 1935 the company was incorporated in the larger Klöckner-Humboldt-Deutz AG (KHD). The KHD company produced mainly diesel engines and tractors while Magirus remained specialized in trucks. For the German army, the Magirus firm produced the type M206 (1,150 units), the so-called Standardized Diesel truck (2,500 units), and the model 33 G1, designed by the Henschel company (3,800 units). The most produced Magirus truck was the 3-tonner (between 16,000 and 20,000 units built), including cargo trucks, personnel carriers, buses, and *Maultier* versions. The 3-ton Magirus, designed in the early 1930s, had a 6-cylinder, 70 bhp engine.

## Heavy trucks

Heavy trucks were designed to transport heavy cargo with a payload of over 4 tons, and this could be greatly increased by towing a trailer. They were basically commercial types or *S-Wirtschaftstyp* (commercial model) and "A" military cross-country versions of the 1938 *Schell Plan*. Many were replicas of German/Austrian types built under license abroad. Others were military captured or civilian confiscated models. There were German-made heavy trucks with twin rear bogie used in various roles (open, specialist bodies; transport of engineer and other heavy equipment including crane for lifting; recovery and loading roles). A few were designed as light tank transporters to the battle zone, thereby conserving the tracks and motors to the last minute before going into action. These vehicles could carry light armor such as the PzKpfw I and II. They had folding ramps that were wound up and down by hand winches. With much bigger and heavier tanks coming into service after 1943, however, the tank transporting trucks went out of use in that role. Medium and heavy tanks—including PzKpfw III, IV, Panther and Tiger—were so heavy that they could only be transported by rail.

### BÜSSING-NAG 4500

The heavy truck *Büssing-NAG 4500* existed in both standardized S "civilian" and

*Heavy truck Büssing-NAG (4.5-ton) 4500A*

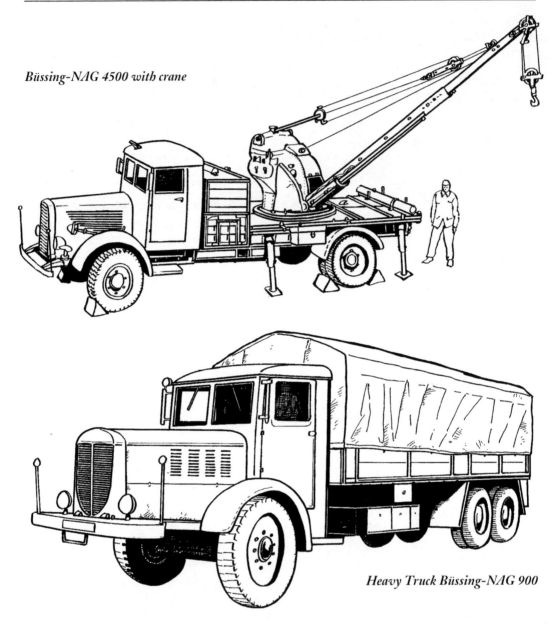

*Büssing-NAG 4500 with crane*

*Heavy Truck Büssing-NAG 900*

A cross-country military versions. The latter was representative of the series of the *schwerer geländegängiger Lastkraftwagen* (heavy cross-country trucks) in the 4- or and 5-ton class. Introduced in 1941, it had a six-cylinder, 105 bhp type LD diesel engine. Maximum speed was 65 km/h. Fuel consumption was 28 liters/100 km on road and 42 liters/100 km cross-country. Range was 390 km on road and 260 km cross-country. Payload was 4,500 kg (cross-country), length was 8.05 m and weight was 5,450 kg.

The vehicle was produced in the period 1942–1946. There was also a version fitted with a crane for a recovery/loading role; and this version could be converted for use on railroad tracks.

## BÜSSING-NAG 900

The heavy truck *Büssing-NAG 900* was introduced in 1937 for carrying cargo and light tanks (PzKfw I and II). It had a 6-cylinder, 150 bhp diesel engine. Length

*Heavy truck Mercedes-Benz L4500A
(with Einheits cab)*

was 10.4 m, width was 2.5 m, height was 2.6 m, and weight was 8,900 kg. A similar, heavy tank carrier was the *schwerer Lastkraftwagen Faun L900* with a payload of 8,800 kg.

## MERCEDES-BENZ L4500

The heavy truck *Mercedes-Benz L4500* was in the load class 3.5–5 tons. It appeared in 1938 under the *Schell Plan* specifications that made the *schwerer Lastkraftwagen* (heavy truck) class all look identical except for differing details such as cabs and hood. It existed in two versions: the standard "civilian" 4 x 2 L 4500S and the cross-country "military" 4 x 4 L 4500A.

The *L 4500A* had a 6-cylinder, 7,274 cc diesel engine giving a maximum speed of 66 km/h. Fuel consumption per 100 km was 28 liters on road and 42 liters cross-country. Range was 500 km on road and 330 km

cross-country. Length was 7.86 m, width was 2.35 m, height was 3.345 m, and weight was 5,715 kg. Late production had the low-cost *Einheit* driver's cab. There was a conversion for use on railway and a *Maultier* semi-track variant. A few Mercedes-Benz L4500A were converted to self-propelled, anti-aircraft guns with a *Kabinenpanzerung* (enclosed armored cab), armed with various weapons, usually a 2 cm-Flakvierling, or a 3.7 cm Flak 36 or 37 gun mount on a flat bed body. Ammunition was carried in a standardized *Anhänger* (trailer).

## MAN ML 4500

The heavy truck MAN ML4500 existed in two version: the standard 4 x 2 ML 4500 S and the cross-country 4 x 4 ML 4500 A.

The MAN ML 4500 A had a 6-cylinder, 110 bhp MAN D 1040 G diesel engine.

*Armored Mercedes-Benz*
*L4500 A with 3.7 cm*
*Flak 36*

WH-778554215

*Heavy truck MAN ML4500S*

*Heavy truck 4 x 2 Saurer BT 4500*

Maximum speed was 63 km/h. Fuel consumption was 28 liters/100 km on road and 42 liters/100 km cross-country. Range was 460 km on road and 300 km cross-country. Payload was 4,350 kg (cross-country), length was 7.5 m and weight was 5,550 kg. The vehicle was produced in the period 1940–1946.

## SAURER BT 4500

The 4 x 2 heavy truck Saurer BT 4500 had a 6-cylinder, 120 bhp Saurer type T diesel engine. Maximum speed was 66 km/h. Fuel consumption was 25 liters/100 km on road. Range was 500 km. Payload was 4,500 kg, length was 8.2 m and weight

*Heavy truck Tatra 6500/111*

was 5.930 kg. The vehicle was produced in the period 1941–1945.

## TATRA 6500

The Czech 6 x 6 heavy truck *Tatra 6500/111* was rated as 6–5 tons. This *schwerer Lastkraftwagen*, built in the period 1942–1944, was about 8.55 m in length and had a V12 diesel, air-cooled engine. Maximum speed was 75 km/h, and diesel fuel consumption was 35 liters/100 km on road. Range was 450 km on road. Late produc-

tion had the low-cost *Einheit* driver's cab. It remained in production in Czechoslovakia for many years after the war.

## MERCEDES-BENZ L6500

The heavy 4 x 2 *Mercedes-Benz Typ L 6500* had a payload of nearly 6,000 kg, and this could be increased by towing a trailer. Built between 1938 and 1940, it had a 6-cylinder, 12,528 cc diesel engine, giving a maximum speed of 60 km/h. The vehicle was 9.45 m in length, 2.5 m in width and

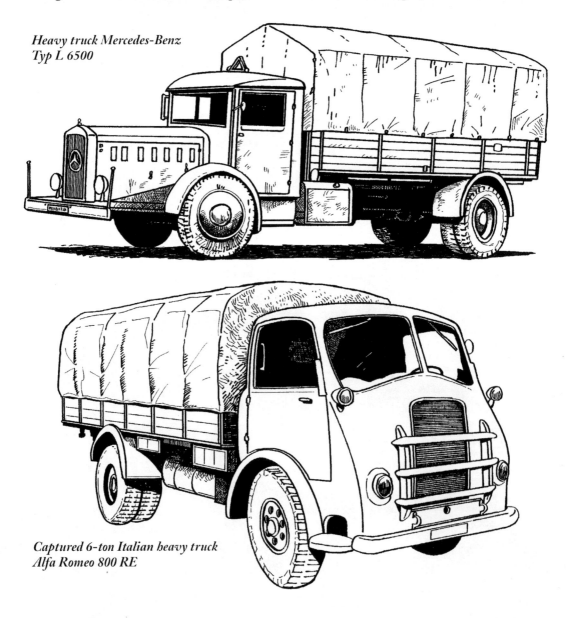

*Heavy truck Mercedes-Benz Typ L 6500*

*Captured 6-ton Italian heavy truck Alfa Romeo 800 RE*

2.42 m in height. Fuel consumption was 36 liters per 100 km, and range was 430 km.

## ALFA ROMEO 800 RE

The Italian heavy 6-ton truck *Alfa Romeo 800 RE* had a 6-cylinder, 108 bhp diesel engine. Length was 6.8 m, width 2.35 m, height 2.85 m and gross weight was 5,500 kg. The *Autocarro Unificato Pesante* (heavy standardized truck)—as it was designated—was produced between 1940 and 1944. Some had full doors rather than half doors. Some Alfa Romeo 800RE were also converted as German *Maultier*, with the rear bogie replaced with tracks. Similar in appearance and capacity was the Italian truck Tipo 430.

# Maultier

German trucks proved to be totally unequal to the demands made of them during the Russian campaign in the winter of 1941–1942. The *Maultier* (mule) was designed to overcome the severe conditions of the East

that defeated even four-wheel drive. The design reportedly originated from a field improvisation by engineers of the 2nd Waffen SS Division Das Reich in the winter of 1941–1942 when a 3-ton Ford V3000 truck was converted into a semi-track by replacing the rear wheels with modified British Carden-Loyd track bogies for improved off-road performance. The drive shaft was reduced in length and the axle was moved forward to line up with the sprocket wheels. The existing brake drums were retained for steering at the rear. The idea was sound and applied to other "Mule" vehicles. The track bogies, replacing the rear wheels, were often discarded light tank track bogies from Panzer I and II, which were being phased out at that time. The term *Maultier* is often associated with the German medium truck *Opel S Blitz*, which was the most produced, but other vehicles were converted as well. As the war proceeded, some *Maultier* trucks were armored and armed with various weapon systems, for example, rocket launchers, searchlights, anti-aircraft guns, and so forth. In this combat role, they could resemble

*Opel S Maultier*

half-tracks. *Maultier* should, however, not be confused with proper half-tracks. Although the *Maultier* design was successful and the cross-country performance was greatly improved, the conversions were slow, with a high fuel consumption and thus a poor range, particularly in off-road conditions. After all, the Maultier series were low-cost makeshift substitutes, merely commercial "civilian S" or "military A" trucks on which tracks were placed instead of rear wheels, while half-tracks were elaborate *Sonderkraftfahrzeuge* (SdKfz, special military vehicles) especially intended for cross-country hauling and combat roles. Altogether well over 5,400 two-ton *Maultier* trucks of various models were produced and saw service until it was decided to replace them with a new, standardized semi-track vehicle known as the *schwerer Wehrmacht Schlepper* (sWS).

Interestingly, the British and Australians also produced some similar semi-tracks, including the 3-ton Bedford GS (QL modified), the AEC Matador, the 3-ton Chevrolet, the 3-ton GS Ford 218T, and the 3-ton International K6, for example.

## OPEL BLITZ MAULTIER

The two-ton *Opel Blitz Maultier* was produced at Opel's Brandenburg-Havel plant. The vehicle had a 3–6-liter, 6-cylinder, 3626 cc Opel engine; it was six meters long and weighed 3,930 kg. Top speed was only 38 km/h. Fuel consumption was 50 liters per 100 km on road and 100 liters per 100 km cross-country. It had a range of 160 km on road and 80 km cross-country. The Opel Blitz Maultier had usually an open cargo body. There was an experimental version with improved cross-country capacity whereby the rear axle remained in the original position with sprockets replacing the rear wheels that drove the tracks and bogies placed on a pivoting subframe. Some 300 *Opel Blitz Maultier* were fitted with an armored body and transformed into half-tracks; known as *SdKfz 4/1*, they were used as weapon systems mounting the 10-barrel rocket launcher *15 cm Panzerwerfer 42 (Sf)*.

## MERCEDES-BENZ L4500R MAULTIER

The *Mercedes-Benz L4500R Maultier* was a 4.5-ton *Mercedes-Benz L4500* fitted with a light tank Panzer II track bogie. The vehicle had a 6-cylinder, 112 bhp diesel engine with a top speed of 36 km/h. Length was 7.9 m, width was 2.36 m and height was 3.2 m. Fuel consumption was 70 liters per 100 km on road and 140 liters per 100 km

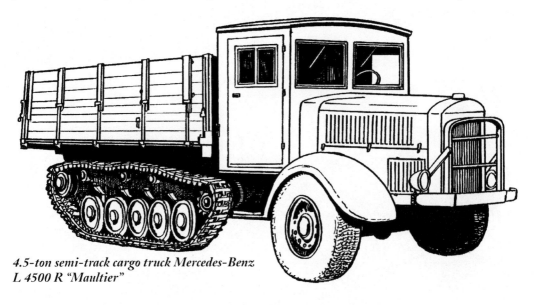

*4.5-ton semi-track cargo truck Mercedes-Benz L 4500 R "Maultier"*

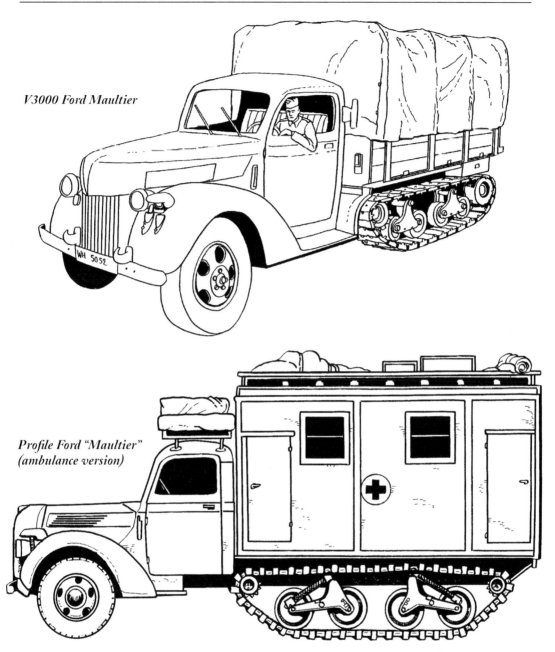

*V3000 Ford Maultier*

*Profile Ford "Maultier"*
*(ambulance version)*

off-road. It had a payload of 4,500 kg and a range of 200 km on road and 100 km cross-country. It was produced in 1943–1944, and many models were fitted with the cheap standardized wooden *Einheit* driver's cab.

## FORD MAULTIER

The *Ford Maultier* was a modification of the standard 3-ton *Ford model V 3000*

truck; it was supplied by the Ford factories in Cologne (Germany), Amsterdam (the Netherlands) and Asnières (France). Maximum speed was 40 km/h on good roads. The vehicle was 6.325 m long, 2.245 m wide and 2.1 m tall. Fuel consumption was 60 liters per 100 km on road and 120 liters per 100 km cross-country. It had a range of 170 km on road and 80 km cross-country. The Ford Maultier had a payload of about

*Büssing-NAG sWS (schwerer Wehrmacht Schlepper) (cargo half-track) 1943*

2,000 kg. The vehicle could also be fitted with a radio configuration or an ambulance body.

## SCHWERER WEHRMACHT SCHLEPPER (SWS HEAVY ARMY TRACTOR)

In May 1942, Hitler decreed that a new series of standardized vehicles be built to replace the *Maultier* and the existing light

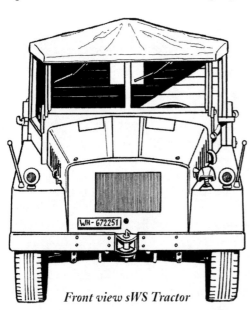

*Front view sWS Tractor*

3-ton *SdKfz 11* and medium 5-ton *SdKfz 6* half-tracks. The new vehicle, known as the *schwerer Wehrmacht Schlepper* (sWS, heavy army tractor) was entrusted to Büssing-NAG, and prototypes were ready by early 1943. The vehicle was well-designed and very powerful. Actually it was more a proper half-track than an improvised *Maultier*. It weighed 9,500 kg; had a Maybach HL 42 TRKMS 100 bhp gasoline engine, a maximum speed of 27 km/h, and a payload of 4,000 kg; and could tow a load of 8,000 kg. Fuel consumption was 80 liters/100 km on road and 180 liters/100 km off-road. Range was 300 km on road and 150 km cross-country. The sWS had generally a crew of two placed in an open cabin that could be protected by a canvas top. Orders were placed for over 7,000 *schwerer Wehrmacht Schlepper*, but the new vehicle never fulfilled Hitler's intention of replacement. No more than 150 sWS were manufactured in 1943, and fewer than a thousand were completed and had reached the troops on the front by the end of the war. The existing sWS served mainly in the role of cargo carrier. A few of them were fitted with armored cab and hood and were used as self-propelled anti-tank

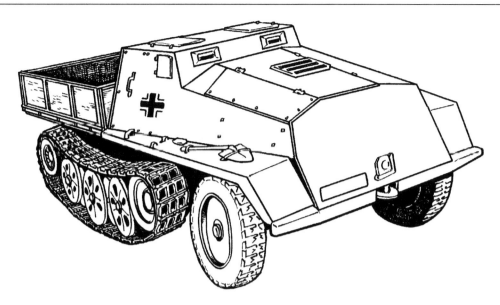

*Armored Büssing-NAG sWS. This conversion could serve as mount for a 3.7 cm Flak 43 anti-aircraft gun, or as carrier for a 10 barrel-rocket launcher 15 cm Panzerwerfer 42.*

guns, or anti-aircraft gun carriers or *Panzerwerfer* armed with rockets.

A slightly modified version continued in production at the Tatra works in Czechoslovakia after the war. Fitted with a V12, 180 bph, air-cooled Tatra 111 engine, they served in the Czech army until 1953.

## Trucks for use on railway

The Germans also made several designs for *schienengängig* conversions for use on railway. Some trucks had their tires removed and fitted with flanged steel wheels adapted for use on railway, and the chassis

*Heavy truck Henschel 6J2 for use on railway*

*Tractor MSZ 10
Krauss-Maffei*

was equipped with railroad buffing plates at both front and rear. The vehicle became a self-contained locomotive that could haul trailers along the track. It could also be used as a switcher at railheads or marshalling yards. The railway conversions included notably the heavy truck 4 x 2 *Henschel 6J2* (possibly with a trailer), the *Mercedes-Benz L4500A* cargo carrier, and several other heavy trucks.

## Wheeled tractors

Wheeled tractors or prime movers were used by the Germans for a large variety of roles such as towing of heavy artillery pieces, heavy trailers, refueller trailers on airfields, low-loader trailers, rocket equipment, etc. Some could be used as recovery vehicles and were fitted with a crane or a winch. Many were fitted with gas-producers or compressed gas, due to fuel-oil shortage. Heavy wheeled tractors were reminiscent of German and Austrian artillery steam tractors of World War I.

### KRAUSS-MAFFEI MSZ 10

The wheeled tractor MSZ 10 was based on a commercial model designed in 1926 by the Krauss-Maffei company. The tractor—intended to tow a cargo trailer—had a 4-cylinder Daimler-Benz diesel engine. Its length was 3.8 m and width was 1.7 m.

### SKODA 175

The *Skoda 175 Ostradschlepper* (east-wheeled tractor) was designed in 1942 by engineer Dr. Ferdinand Porsche (the brilliant creator of the Volkswagen). The vehicle was intended as an artillery tractor for use on the Eastern front. It was powered by a 80 bhp, four-cylinder, in-line, air-cooled diesel engine and had large solid metal wheels, 4 feet 10 inches in diameter. It was thought that oversized wheels were the answer to the severe mud and snow problem encountered in Russia. In fact the "big foot" *Ostradschlepper* offered no great advance over conventional wheeled tractors and were less easy to handle. The vehicle was four-wheel drive with locking differential. It had five

*Heavy wheeled tractor
4 x 4 Skoda 175 "Ost"*

*Italian heavy artillery
tractor Breda 40*

gears forward and one reverse. Average speed on road was 6 miles per hour. Weight unloaded was 9 tons. Useful load was 4.5 tons, trailed load was 5.6 tons and winch capacity was 5.6 tons. Two hundred Skoda 175 Ost were produced during the war by the Czech firm Skoda from Pilsen.

## BREDA 40

The *Trattore Pesante Campale 4 x 4 Breda 40* could tow 5-ton loads. Introduced in 1940, it was also produced with open-type bodywork, and some had solid tires. The Breda 40 reflected the characteristics

*Tractor Fiat TM 4*

*Italian light tractor Fiat-Spa TL 37*

of the Italian artillery tractors, including a powerful engine, four large oversized wheels (usually with single or dual solid rubber tires), and the four-wheel steering system that, in conjunction with their short length, made very short turns possible. This was generally desirable as the Italian artillery was often engaged in mountainous battle zones.

## FIAT TM 40

The *Trattore Medio Fiat/Spa TM 40* was an Italian medium artillery wheeled tractor of compact dimensions (length was just about 15 ft) for short turns. The vehicle was powered by a 6-cylinder, 50 hp diesel engine and weighed 5,500 kg. The open-topped body held seats for the gun crew, and there was a locker for ammunition stowage at the back. Some were fitted with solid wheels. Some TM 40 were fitted with a truck body for use as a supply carrier and, despite their comparatively low payload capacity, were of great value as *Autocarretta da Montagna* (mountain cargo trucks). The German designation of the TM 40 as tractor was *Radschlepper 110 PS Spa (i) TM 40*.

## FIAT-SPA TL 37

The short *trattore leggero 37* produced by Fiat-Spa was intended as a cross-country light artillery tractor. It had a 4-cylinder, 4053 cc, 57 bhp Spa engine. Length was 4.25 m, weight was 3,300 kg and payload was 800 kg. It had optional oversize tires and could also be fitted with a cargo truck body.

## LATIL TAR-H

The Latil vehicles had been among the earliest trucks in service with the French army. Since 1916 Latil tractors were used with the French artillery, and in the 1930s, the company produced new models such as the *Latil TAR 5* and the *Latil TAR-H*. Characterized by its squared-off hood, steel-framed body, enclosed cabin, and rather good performances the *Latil TAR-H* entered service in 1935 and was the standard French heavy artillery tractor until the outbreak of World War II. Many of them were pressed into German service after the fall of France in 1940.

## LAFFLY V15 R

The French artillery tractor Laffly V15 R was another captured vehicle used by the German army. After the capitulation of June 1940, some sixty such tractors were captured and another 900 built during the war. Another Laffly tractor was the very advanced six-wheel drive G35 T from 1935

*Captured French Tracteur
Latil TAR-H 1936*

*Captured French tractor*
*Laffly V15 R*

with articulating independent rear bogie suspension. A typical Laffly feature was two small, non-driven wheels placed at the front for improved cross-country performance.

## Full-track tractors

Full-track tractors were employed in a way similar to the wheeled prime movers, but they were specifically designed for use on the Eastern front; during the latter part of World War II, they were also used in the West. Full-track tractors were slow, but in the conditions of snow, slush and mud prevailing in Russia for a good part of the year, they were at an advantage as roads were often impassable to wheeled transport—as the Germans found to their cost in the successive winter campaigns on the Eastern front. Some full-track tractors were converted tanks, for example, the *Munitionsfahrzeug auf Fahrgestell PzKpw 38 (t)*. This was a munition and artillery tractor based on a Czech design in which the turret and weapons were removed for additional room.

Numbers of captured artillery full-track tractors were also used by the Wehrmacht, amongst them the Soviet STZ Komsomolets, Stalinet 65 (r) and Stalin 607 (r).

### Steyr RSO

The *Raupenschlepper-Ost Steyr RSO/1 SdKfz 232* (tracked tractor "East") was specially designed in 1943 to face the difficult terrain in Russia. The RSO was built by both the Steyr and Klöckner-Deutz-Magirus companies. It was a very efficient prime mover and was in service from 1944; it was a fully tracked supply truck with a payload of 1,700 kg, or an artillery tractor that could pull loads up to 3,000 kg. The vehicle had a Steyr 1500A V8, 3517 cc, 70 bhp gasoline engine. Length was 4.425 m, and weight was 3,800 kg. Maximum speed was about 15 km/h. The gasoline consumption for the Steyr version was 60 liters/100 km on road and 120 liters/100 km cross-country, with a range of 300 km on road and 150 km off-road. The RSO had generally a crew of two. It was steered by two

*Steyr Raupenschlepper-Ost (RSO)*

*Steyr RSO (Raupenschlepper Ost) with 7.5 cm Pak 40*

upright levers with right-angled handlebars and was quite difficult to drive until experience was gained. It had tank-like torsion bar suspension and steel tracks. The tracks were usually adapted to snow with a width of 600 mm, and for normal conditions conventional 340 mm tracks were fitted. About 2,500 of these vehicles were built.

There was also a conversion with removed driver's cab for a self-propelled

*KHD-Magirus RSO/03*

*Panzerjäger* (anti-tank combat vehicle) using the chassis of the Steyr RSO and mounting a 7.5 cm Pak 40 anti-tank gun. Eighty-three *RSO Panzerjäger* were produced in 1944, illustrating a desperate policy of creating combat vehicles from existing tractors.

The latest edition of the *Raupenschlepper* (known as *RSO-03*) was produced by KHD-Magirus in 1944; it was fitted with a 4-cylinder Deutz diesel engine and a simplified bodywork including a squared-off open cab and canvas top. This model was continued in production for a while after World War II as the *Waldschlepper RS 1500* (forest tractor).

## Sachsenberg LWS

The full-tracked tractor *Sachsenberg LWS* (for *Land-Wasser-Schlepper*, or amphibious tractor) was an amphibious tractor-cum-tug ordered in 1935 by the Engineer

Branch of the *Heereswaffenamt* (Army Ordnance Office). It was designed by the Alkett and Sachsenberg companies and manufactured by the firm Rheinmetall-Borsig from Düsseldorf. The LWS was a large and strange machine, halfway between a vehicle and a boat powered by a tank gasoline engine (type 300 PS V12, 300 bhp Maybach). In appearance the LWS was a motor tug built on tracks with a clean pronounced bow and a boat-like compartment with portholes for the crew of three and extra room for twenty passengers; on top of the cabin was a funnel-like air intake for the engine. Length was 8.6 m, width was 3.16 m, height was 3.13 m and weight was 13,000 kg. The engine was mounted amidship and was fitted with an inertia-type starter driven by a handle from the rear and clutched in by the driver through a control lever. The LWS had twin propellers, a rudder on slipstream of each, and a bollard winch at the rear. Speed on land was 35 km/h and 12.5

*Profile amphibious tractor Sachsenberg LWS*

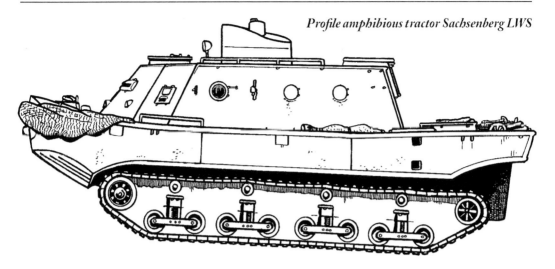

km/h in water. The tractor would be able to tow behind it a floating trailer capable of accommodating vehicles or other cargo weighing up to 18,000 kg. The Sachsenberg LWS could be discharged from a landing craft, and some were armored against small arms. It could be used as tractor on land and tug in (sheltered) water with pontoon bridging equipment.

The cumbersome Sachsenberg LWS was tried for the preparation of Operation *Seelöwe* (Sea Lion, the invasion of Great Britain in 1940). The LWS program was for a while carried out with urgency but never fully materialized. About 20 units were built in 1939 and tested in 1940; they proved more suited for calm inland waters than for the tempestuous English Channel. By 1941, when the Germans invaded Russia, the conquest of Britain was postponed and the LWS project was dropped. Whether the existing machines were ever engaged in war operation is not known, but it seems that toward the end of World War II, some of them were employed as ferries with buoyant decks slung between two tugs.

## STZ-5–2TB

The Russian full-track artillery tractor STZ-5–2TB was originally an agricultural tractor. In military use, it was a cab-over-engine prime mover and load carrier. It was powered by a six-cylinder diesel engine, and the suspension was copied from the American Holt type. A similar design was the *Stalinietz S2*. The Germans used captured vehicles of this type under the designation of Artillerie Schlepper CT3–601 (r).

## STZ KOMSOMOLETS

The Russian full-track light tractor *STZ Komsomolets* was designed as personnel and ammunition carrier and as artillery tractor for towing the M 1937 45 mm anti-tank gun. The vehicle was 3.45 m in length and weighed 4,200 kg. It could carry a crew of 8 soldiers, consisting of driver and machine-gunner in the lightly armored front compartment (fitted with three vision ports, a ball-mounted machine gun and two escape hatches); above the engine at the rear of the tractor there was a curious and somewhat uncomfortable arrangement for three artillerymen on each side, back to back; a collapsible frame and a canvas cover gave these six passengers little protection from the elements and none against enemy fire. Captured STZ Komsomolets were designated in the German force as 1.gp. Art.S 630 (r).

*Artillerie Schlepper CT3–601 (r), captured Russian full-track tractor*

*Russian tractor STZ Komsomolets*

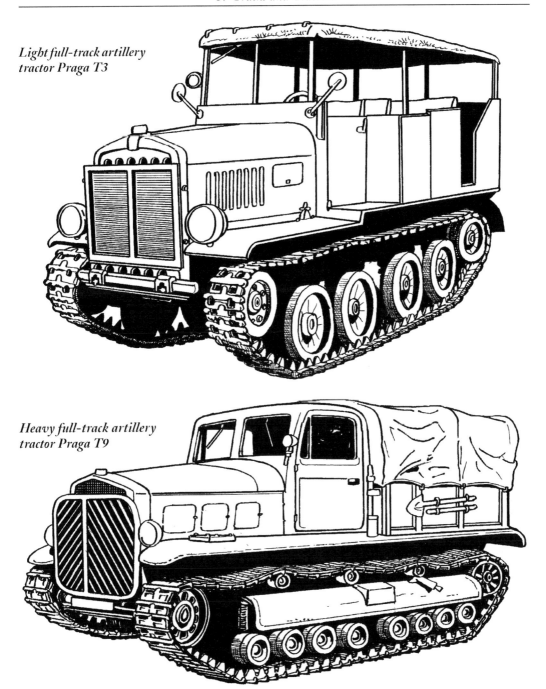

*Light full-track artillery tractor Praga T3*

*Heavy full-track artillery tractor Praga T9*

## PRAGA T3

The Czech full-track light tractor *Praga T3*, known by German armored troops as the *leichter Raupenschlepper Praga T3*, had a 6-cylinder, 77 bhp engine, a maximum speed of 50 km/h, a crew of six, a payload of 600 kg and a towing capacity of 3 t. Length was 4.1 m, width was 2.3 m, height was 2.3 m and weight was 4,650 kg.

## PRAGA T9

The Czech full-track heavy *artillery tractor Praga T9* had a V8 140 bhp engine. Its length was about 6 m, width 2.4 m,

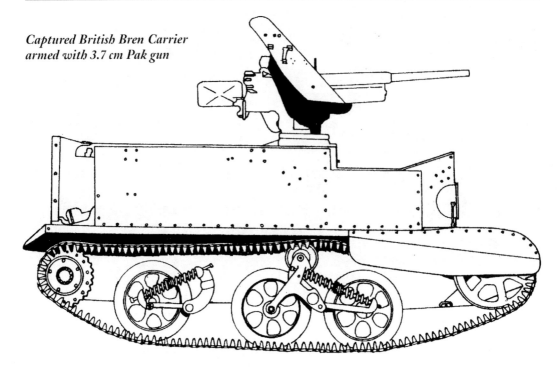

*Captured British Bren Carrier
armed with 3.7 cm Pak gun*

height 2.5 m and weight 10,100 kg. It could tow a load up to 7.5 t.

## BREN CARRIER

A few British *Universal Bren Carriers* were captured after the evacuation of Dunkirk in 1940 and later in the desert war in North Africa. The *Universal Carrier* was designed for a mobile role with stress on high speed at the expense of weight and thus a relatively thin armor. Some were converted by the Germans as artillery tractor or as combat vehicle mounting a 3.7 cm Pak gun. In this role, the anti-tank vehicle was renamed *Panzerjäger Fahrgestell Bren (e) mit 3.7 cm Pak.*

# 4

# Half-Tracks

## Early half-tracked vehicles

The basic concept of the half-tracked vehicle was an attempt to improve cross-country efficiency for wheeled vehicles by adding a movable track bogie: the theory of the traction wheel was that a wheel should be surrounded by a linked series of small tracks that would, as they revolved with the wheel, serve as a self-contained roadway along which the vehicle could travel, regard-less of the rough surface of the ground. During the First World War (1914–1918), the harsh conditions on the frontline prompted military authorities and auto-motive manufacturers to consider ways of fitting tracks to existing road vehicles, thus giving an off-road capability without the huge development costs needed for purpose-built tractors. Perhaps the first mil-itary half-track was the French Lefebvre Tractor of 1914; this tractor had steel wheels

*An early form of half-track: the German Benz-Gaggenau Kraftprotze from 1918*

for normal running and carried crawler tracks at the rear that were arranged to run round small bogie wheels attached to a pivoted frame structure; the front end of the frame could be raised or lowered by worm gearing from handles adjacent to the driving position. Though intended for agricultural use, the Lefebvre tractor was examined and evaluated for military duty, but the design faded into oblivion. By the end of World War I semi-tracked vehicles or half-tracks were first tested by the British and the Americans (e.g., the Holt 75 hp Gasoline Tractor) to tow artillery. This kind of cross-country vehicle, combining wheeled front steering with tracked drive, was particularly well suited to haul and position artillery in the field. In 1918, the Germans experimented with a form of half-track, known as the *Benz-Gaggenau Kraftprotze*, with a 45 bhp engine and primitive track system.

After World War I the concept of wheel-and-track was reintroduced. It must be borne in mind that the late 1920s and 1930s were a period of experimentation in military vehicles, especially on the problem of preserving track life, with wheels being used for road running and tracks for across country and muddy or soft ground. Alternative wheel-and-track propulsion was postulated by several companies, notably in Britain by the firm Vickers-Wolseley. In Germany the Krauss-Maffei company from Munich carried out several experimentations of such vehicles. The concept of the half-tracked vehicle was greatly improved in France by the Renault and Citroën companies at the beginning of the 1920s. The modern method of suspension track was invented by the Frenchman Adolphe Kégresse and tested with success in the Alps in 1922. The Citroën-Kégresse enjoyed large publicity when an expedition equipped with semi-track vehicles made the first crossing of the Sahara desert in 1923. The Citroën-Kégresse vehicles were historically the inspiration for the military half-tracks of the prewar period and World War II. As early as 1923, the French army developed a

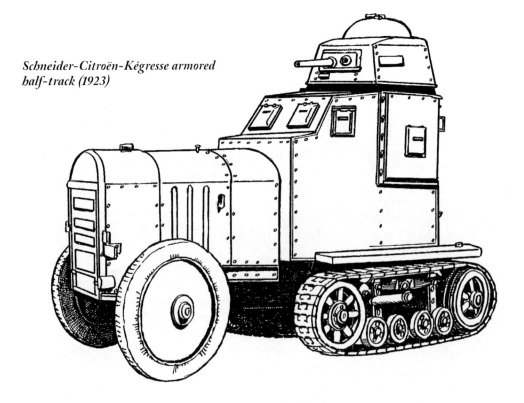

*Schneider-Citroën-Kégresse armored half-track (1923)*

*Citroën-Kégresse military half-track 1925*

Schneider-Citroën-Kégresse armored half-track armed with a 37 mm gun. This kind of vehicle was further developed by the British army in the late 1920s (e.g., the Burford-Kegresse artillery tractor, the Morris-Roadless 1-ton truck and the Guy-Roadless 1-ton truck, all from 1926). The prewar French army also adopted several types of half-track tractors (e.g., the Citroën P14 and P17 from 1931).

The success of the idea of the military half-track might be explained by several advantages. In spite of all the expensive refinements, the half-track remained cheaper than any fully tracked vehicle because it was steered by the front wheels like a motor car, instead of a complex system changing the speed of either track as in tank steering. A half-track vehicle caused far less damage to the public road surface and was only marginally less efficient moving cross-country than a fully tracked tank. The main disadvantage was that anything towed behind a half-track drastically reduced the cross-country capability.

## German experimentations

After the armistice of November 1918, the Treaty of Versailles stipulated a drastic reduction of German military war equipment including vehicle development. In the twenties, when much effort was devoted in Great Britain and France to developing half-track vehicles for military use, a few types of half-track tractors were secretly produced in Germany under the disguise of agriculture and forestry vehicles in order to evade the restrictions imposed by the Versailles Treaty. These early machines were mostly wheeled machines fitted with conversion kits, but they demonstrated the value of this type of vehicle. A discreet scheme was drawn up to develop a range of half-track trucks of varying sizes to fulfill the many military requirements. In German a half-tracked vehicle is called a *Halbketten-Zugkraftfahrzeuge*.

Research began in the 1920s under the hands of private companies, and in 1926 an extensive trial was developed to determine the design of artillery tractors.

### KRAUSS-MAFFEI RK

The *Maffei Räder-Ketten-Schlepper mit Wechsellaufwerk* (KM-RK, changing wheel-and-track system tractor) was designed in October 1930. It had track assemblies running in vertical guides; when driving on soft ground the tracks were lowered from a

*Krauss-Maffei RK-tractor. The tractor is shown here in wheel/road position. For cross-country the tracks were lowered.*

*Krauss-Maffei MSZ 201*

power takeoff using bell-crank arms. The vehicle was powered by a 4-cylinder, Magirus V 100 engine giving a maximum speed of 57 km/h on road in the wheeled position. Only three KM-RK prototypes were ever manufactured and proposed to the Reichswehr as *Selbstfahrlafetten* (self-propelled guns) in 1933. The vehicle caused a sensation but soon proved to be complicated, impractical and unstable; the project was refused and then abandoned. A similar unsuccessful design had been made in 1926 in Britain by the firm Vickers-Wolseley.

## KRAUSS-MAFFEI MSZ 201

Another project of Krauss-Maffei was the *MSZ 201, Rad-Zugmaschine mit Hilfs-*

*kettenantrieb* (wheeled vehicle with additional track). The vehicle was intended as a troop transport (carrying 10 soldiers including the driver). The track/wheel MSZ 201 could also be used as a tractor towing a load of 6 t. As a cargo carrier it had a payload of 1 t. The vehicle had a Magirus 4-cylinder engine, it weighed 5.4 t and maximum speed on wheel was 50 km/h. Twenty-four units were purchased by the German Reichswehr and the Austrian army. A few MSZ 201 were also bought by the Zeppelin company as tractors for towing airships in and out of the hangar. There was a variant with improved track system known as MSZ 203.

There was another variant designed as an *Attrape* (dummy) training armored car with one machine gun placed in a small turret, known as the ZM10, of which 30 units were produced.

## Austro-Daimler ASMK

The Austrian *Austro-Daimler Motor Karette (ADMK)*, also known as *Mulus*

(mule), was a wheel-and-track machine gun carrier. It was a curious small vehicle fitted with four wheels and two tracks. When running on tracks, the rear wheels were completely removed and stowed on brackets adjacent to the rear-mounted engine. The front axles and wheels swung forward and up to clear the ground. Maximum speed was 45 km/h (on track only 15 km/h). It could carry a load of 570 kg. Fuel consumption was 17 liters/100 km on road and 30 liters/100 km cross-country. A shield for the machine gun was carried at the front where the two crewmen rode. About 334 of these slow, ill-protected and unarmored vehicles were ordered and produced in 1935. They equipped machine-gun companies of the Austrian army until 1938. Later variants were built as personnel carriers with enclosed armored bodies and four doors. After 1938 a few ADMK were used in the German army, but none of them ever saw action.

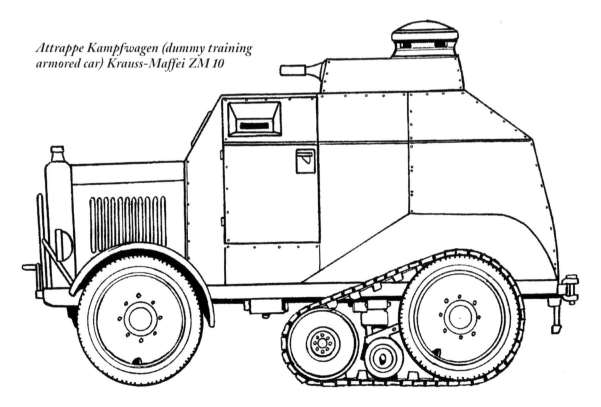

*Attrappe Kampfwagen (dummy training armored car) Krauss-Maffei ZM 10*

*Austro-Daimler ADMK*

## SAURER RR 7/2

The Saurer RR 7/2 was a wheel and track *Panzer-Beobachtungswagen* (armored observation vehicle). Designed in 1936, it had a Saurer CRDv 4-cylinder, 70 hp, diesel engine giving traction to both wheels and tracks. The vehicle weighed 6,420 kg in combat conditions, length was 4.5 m, width was 2.33 m, and height was 2.47 m. It had a speed of 60 km/h on wheels and 30 km/h on tracks. Fuel consumption was 30 liters/

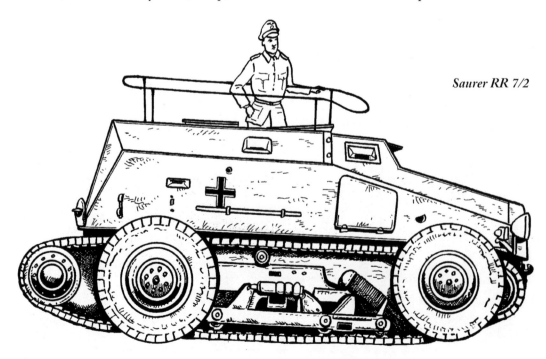

*Saurer RR 7/2*

100 km on wheels and 80 liters/100 km on tracks. Range on wheels was about 500 km. Armor was 10 mm thick at the front and 3 mm at the sides. It was equipped with a wireless radio set and an overhead antenna. It was armed with one 7.92 mm machine gun, and the crew included five men. Wheels were used on roads and tracks for cross-country, and the change over from wheels to tracks could be carried out while the vehicle was traveling at slow speed. It was the only *Räder-Raupen-Fahrzeug* (wheel-and-track vehicle) ever serving in the Wehrmacht. Some 12 units were built for the Austrian Army, and another 140 units were built for the German Wehrmacht and designated SdKfz 254. Although the Waffen SS expressed an interest in this odd machine, it did not go into series production. The design was indeed not satisfying; the vehicle was complicated and difficult to steer and handle, and only a few vehicles of that type were used at the front in 1940, after which they were withdrawn.

## German developments

In the late 1920s and early 1930s, when the Germans made serious but still secret plans for rearmament, contracts were placed with different automotive companies—amongst which were Büssing-NAG, Krauss-Maffei AG and Daimler-Benz, acting under military guidance. Each firm was entrusted to produce a half-track prototype in the 1-ton, 3-ton, 8-ton, 12-ton, and 18 ton classes, respectively. Six cylinder or V12 engines were specified according to size, the tracks were to be as long as possible relative to the chassis (which distinguished half-tracks from tracked lorries such as the *Maultier* series), and rubber track pads were to be standard so that the vehicles could drive on public roads. Overall design was in the hands of the *Waffen Prufamt 6*, the combat vehicle design section of the Army Ordnance Department. A talented engineer named Kniepkampf did most of the work on design and in particular evolved the distinctive overlapping arrangement of the bogie wheels. The first two prototypes completed were those in the 3-ton and 8-ton classes.

The 3-tonner was manufactured by the firm Hansa-Lloyd-Goliath, the well-known Bremen company, and was referred to as the model Hl Kl 2. The *leichter 3-ton Zugkraftwagen Hl Kl 2* was designed to tow artillery; it had a four-cylinder, 3.5-liter engine and

*Daimler-Benz Type Z D 5 1931. This early German half-track, produced in 1931 by the Daimler-Benz company from Berlin-Marienfeld had a 150 bhp engine.*

*3-t light half-track Hl KL2 (1932)*

*Experimental half-track KMZ 100 (1934). This vehicle was designed by the firm Krauss-Maffei from Munich.*

a standard truck-type hood and front wheels. There was also an armored version intended to carry a 7.5 cm L/40 gun, known as Hl Kl 4 H. The Hl Kl 2 was the forerunner of the numerous German half-tracks used in World War II, it was mainly used for trials and later developments over the next few years led to the standard SdKfz 11 half-track.

Half-tracks were developed by the army and therefore were allotted a *SdKfz* number (*Sonderkraftfahrzeuge* "special trucks," *SdKfz* in short).

By 1935 Hitler had totally repudiated the limitations of the Versailles Treaty, and by 1936 the various German half-track models had begun to take the general shape they would retain until their production tailed off as war progressed.

With half-tracked prime movers and armored personnel carriers, the Germans have excelled. In this class they produced

*Hl Kl 4 H half-track with 7.5 cm L/40 gun. This armored armed prototype would have compared favorably with the later SdKfz 251/9 half-track.*

vehicles that gave excellent service and that were unrivaled for cross-country perform-ance. The half-tracked *Zugkraftwagen* formed a large family of standardized vehi-cles, and they existed in various types with up-rated engines and different speed, tow and load capacities. There were many vari-ants, some armed with guns or adapted to specialized military roles. Distinguishing and common features to all German half-tracks included the following:

• A Maybach power plant, 6 cylinder or V12 equipped with an inertia-type starter, varying in output from 90 to 239 bph

• Spoked front wheels

• Caterpillar tracks running almost three-quarters of the length of the vehicle giving increased traction and excellent cross-country performance but which were complicated and required constant main-tenance

• Needle roller-bearing tracks with detach-able rubber track pads

• Tracks suspended by torsion bars on all but the front wheels (a torsion bar was a flexi-ble rod anchored to the vehicle's hull, the opposite end carrying a sprung crank, at the end of which was a suspension bogie or wheel; movement of the wheel and crank twisted the rod)

• Large double and overlapping rubber-tired bogie wheels that carried the top run of the track (the rear unpowered idle wheel was often adjustable and worked as track tensioner)

• Rubber-padded sprockets driving through rollers instead of the more usual teeth (a sprocket is a driving wheel that transfers power from the gearbox output to the tracks)

• A "Clerac"-type geared differential steer-ing combined with normal steering of the front wheels for road work (the differential is an arrangement of gears enabling driving wheel or tracks to revolve at different speeds when the vehicle is turning a corner)

• Two, three or four rows of seats for six to thirteen gunners or infantrymen arranged in charabanc-fashion (the rear row could be replaced by an ammunitions or tool locker)

• Canvas side screens later to be replaced by steel doors

• Open vehicles with a tourer type canvas folding top

The World War II German army's half-tracks were brilliantly engineered, strong, reliable, robust and long lasting, but they were labor intensive and expensive to manufacture. Just as easily destroyed in battle, they were always in short numbers, and—as in many other areas of German production—fell short of requirements. They ranged from 1-ton light vehicles towing light artillery to 18-ton monsters designed to pull the heaviest loads. In appearance the German half-tracks looked quite the same, and—at first sight—it is often difficult to distinguish a 5-ton SdKfz 6 from an 8-ton SdKfz 7. The only visual difference was the size and the number of wheels in the track. To be clear, World War II German half-tracks can be divided into six sorts making three main categories depending on the load that could be towed:

• *leichter Zugkraftwagen*, light half-track including the light 1-ton SdKfz 10 (built by Demag) and the light 3-ton SdKfz 11 (Hansa-Lloyd-Goliath)

• *mittlerer Zugkraftwagen*, medium half-tracks including the medium 5-ton SdKfz 6 (Büssing-NAG) and the medium 8-ton SdKfz 7 (Krauss-Maffei)

• *schwerer Zugkraftwagen*, heavy half-tracks including the heavy 12-ton SdKfz 8 (Daimler-Benz) and the heavy 18-ton SdKfz 9 (FAMO)

*Light half-track Adler HK 301. The light personnel and prime mover Adler HK 301 accommodated eight soldiers including the driver. It had a Maybach 4-cylinder, 95 bhp engine with a speed of 75 km/h. Only five were produced in 1941. Further orders for 50 units were later cancelled, and the HK300 series was discontinued.*

In addition there were numerous variants of those basic designs especially converted to combat vehicles.

The original manufacturer might not be the exclusive maker of the particular vehicle, for certain types were built by other firms and sub-contractors.

## Light half-tracks

Light half-tracks could tow up to 3-ton loads. Several light half-track prototypes were designed by the firm Adler, including the personnel and prime mover Cabrio-Limousine with convertible body (HK 300), but these were never mass-produced and the project series HK 300 was discontinued.

### 1-TON DEMAG D7 SDKFZ 10

The 1-ton class was designed in 1934 and built until the end of the war by the Demag company, but similar vehicles were also manufactured by other firms, for example, Volvo from Sweden. The first produced

was the light 1-ton half-track *Demag DII3* with a 6-cylinder, 42 bph BMW motor. This was the predecessor of the *Demag type D6* that was produced between 1937 and 1939. This was followed by an improved version known as the *Demag D7 SdKfz 10*, which became one of the most numerous half-tracks of the German force during World War II. The *Demag D7*, produced from 1939 to 1945, had a 6-cylinder 100 bph Maybach HL 42 TRKM gasoline engine and a Maybach pre-selective, semi-automatic gear box. The braking system was hydraulic, and the handbrake worked mechanically on the steering brake. Suspension was by means of full torsion-bar; the idler was not sprung but fitted with a shear-bolt safety device. The small vehicle had a low silhouette, was 4.75 m in length and 1.93 m in width, weighed 3,400 kg, had a payload of 1,500 kg, could tow a load of 1,000 kg, and had a maximum speed of 65 km/h on good road. Fuel consumption was 38 liters/100 km on road and 67 liters/100 km off-road. Range was 300 km on road and 170 km cross-country. Officially the Demag D7 could accommodate a crew of eight

*1-ton half-track Demag 7 SdKfz 10*

including the driver. It was intended to carry troops, ammunitions and supply, as well as to tow small guns into combat zones. The Demag D7 had several official versions: The SdKfz 10/1 was a sensing vehicle; the SdKfz 10/2 was a decontamination vehicle; the SdKfz 10/3 was a sprinkler. (The terrible use of combat gas in World War I contributed to the terror of this weapon in the minds of the populace, soldiers and politicians, with impact on strategic consideration and deterrence. Undoubtedly it was fear of retaliation that deterred the use of gas in World War 2, despite the availability in Germany of deadly combat gasses.) The SdKfz 10/4 was armed with a 2 cm Flak 38 anti-aircraft gun, and the SdKfz 10/5 was used for various light gun mounts. There was also an armored and armed variant for frontline combat. In this role—as discussed further below—the D7 was known as the *SdKfz 250.*

### 3-TON HANSA-LLOYD-GOLIATH SDKFZ 11

The light 3-ton series was mainly produced by Hansa-Lloyd-Goliath (later Borgward company) and by Hanomag. The latter company became chief producer of the 3-ton series and turned out 6,170 units (including armored versions). The vehicle was the light 3-ton *SdKfz 11*, and—when

armored and armed—was referred to as the *SdKfz 251.* It was also produced by Adler, Auto-Union/Wanderer, Hanomag and Skoda. The 3-ton SdKfz 11 had an NL 38 Maybach engine, a normal 4-speed type gearbox, a servo-assisted footbrake, and a full torsion-bar suspension. The vehicle could carry eight troops, weighed 5,550 kg, had a payload of 1,550 kg, could tow a load of 3,000 kg, and had a maximum speed of 52 km/h on good road. Fuel consumption was 45 liters/100 km on road and 75 liters/100 km off-road. Range was 240 km on road and 140 km cross-country. It was 5.55 m in length and 2 m in width.

The light 3-ton half-track SdKfz 11 was used in many roles. As artillery tractor it was often paired with a *le. Feldhaubitze 10.5 cm* (light 10.5 cm field howitzer) and, by the end of 1941 onwards, as prime mover for a 15 cm and 21 cm *Nebelwerfer* rocket launching system placed on a two-wheeled trailer. This half-track had several official versions: The SdKfz 11/1 was a fog and smoke laying vehicle; the SdKfz 11/2 was equipped with gas decontamination devices; the SdKfz 11/3 was a sprinkler; the SdKfz 11/4 was another fog laying vehicle; and the SdKfz 11/5 was an ammunition carrier for the 36-round Nebelwerfer 41 rocket system. Worthy of mention is a very specialized conversion of a few *3-ton Hanomag SdKfz 11.* This included a standard chassis with a

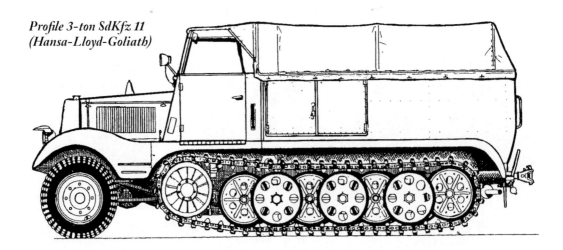

*Profile 3-ton SdKfz 11 (Hansa-Lloyd-Goliath)*

*Light half-track 3-ton SdKfz 11. The SdKfz 11 existed in several variations including troop transport, cargo carrier, artillery tractor and this one with an enclosed cab for driver and troops plus a load area at the rear.*

closed caravan-type body added equipped as an ambulance. This vehicle was intended for the rescue of airmen who had been shot down during the Battle of Britain in the summer of 1940. The half-track configuration was chosen due to its suitability for operating on the beaches and dunes of Holland, Belgium and northern France. The ambulance—manned by a rescue and medical team—patrolled the coast often in collaboration with a light Fieseler Storch spotter plane.

There was, however, an overlap between the 1 and 3 tonner, the former being rather too small for certain tasks (e.g., to transport troops) and the latter too large (e.g., to carry a mortar). In an effort of rationalization to merge both these categories, it was decided (under the injunction of Hitler himself) to create a unique type,

*Front view SdKfz 11 (3-ton light half-track)*

known as the *leicher Wehrmacht Schlepper* (leWS, light army tractor); several unsatisfactory designs were made during 1943 resulting in the discontinuation of the project.

Although Hitler decided to replace the 3-ton *SdKfz 11* with the newly designed *schwerer Wehrmacht Schlepper* (sWS, heavy army tractor), it remained in service in the German army until 1945.

## Medium half-tracks

Medium half-tracks could tow 5- to 8-ton load. Büssing-NAG and Krauss-Maffei received the contract for the half-track in this class and produced the prototype vehicle in 1934. This, the 5-ton *SdKfz 6*, had a Maybach NL 35 six-cylinder engine and followed the same layout as all vehicles in the half-track range. The 5-tonner had a front axle and wheel with the usual Ackermann-type steering and transverse leaf springs. The main weight was carried on the tracks, which stretched the full length of the vehicle aft of the hood. The tracks were of the highest quality, with each shoe cast and then drilled out to reduce weight. Centerline guides were cast in to engage the bogie wheels, and a rubber pad was fitted on each shoe for road running. All shoes were linked by lubricated needle bearings. A drive sprocket was carried at the front of the bogie assembly, and the gearbox was situated between the engine and a short shaft to the differential and final drive. There was a dry twin-plate clutch, and on all models, there was a total choice of eight forward gears and two reverses, since there were alternative selections for each of the normal four gears and reverse. The steering wheel operated the front wheels in the normal way for small changes in direction, but a second drop-arm was fitted in the steering box that acted after the wheel had turned a certain distance to operate the track brakes fitted at either side of the differential. So for sharp turns the appropriate track was braked to assist steer-

ing. Hand and foot brakes were fitted in the normal way and operated the track brakes and sprocket brakes respectively. The road or bogie wheels were pressed steel discs, four pairs each side on early models, later increased to six, all carried on torsion bars. Idlers wheels at the rear completed the suspension, and these could be adjusted to tension the track.

### 5-TON BÜSSING-NAG SDKFZ 6

Designed by the Büssing-NAG company, the 5-tonner was intended to be an artillery tractor or assault engineer vehicle. In the latter role it had four rows of seats arranged charabanc-fashion, while, as a 10.5 cm howitzer tractor, the rear row of seats was replaced by ammunition lockers opening up the sides. Büssing-NAG designed four 5-ton types: model BN L5 produced in 1935, BN L7 produced in 1936–1937, type BN L 8 produced in 1938, and the improved wartime type BN L 9 manufactured from 1939 to 1943. The wartime 5-ton Büssing-Nag *SdKfz 6* (BN L9) was 6.325 m in length and 2.26 m in width. It weighed 8,900 kg, had a payload of 1,550 kg, could tow a load of 5,000 kg, and had a maximum speed of 50 km/h on good road. Fuel consumption was 60 liters/100 km on road and 120 liters/100 km off-road. Range was 310 km on road and 150 km cross-country. It could carry 10 gunners (artillery version known as SKfz 6/1 towing a FH 18 field howitzer). The engineer version could carry 15 troops with their equipment. There was also a version known as the SdKfz 6/2 armed with a 3.7 cm Flak gun. The Krauss-Maffei and Daimler-Benz companies also built these vehicles. After Czechoslovakia was occupied in 1939, the firm of Praga also built this important type. Later production models differed in detail and had up-rated engines but were otherwise similar. Although Hitler decided to replace the 5-ton *SdKfz 6* with the newly design *schwerer Wehrmacht Schlepper* (sWS, heavy army trac-

*Medium 5-ton Büssing-NAG SdKfz 6*

tor), it was a major vehicle in German service until 1945.

## 8-TON KRAUSS-MAFFEI SDKFZ 7

The medium half-tracks in the 8-ton class—known as *SdKfz 7*—were developed by the Krauss-Maffei company from Munich. Early productions from 1933 on were rather similar in appearance to the Büssing-NAG H1 KL 2 but larger. The Krauss-Maffei company made four designs with increasing improved performance: the type KMm8 from 1934–1935; the model KMm9 from 1936; the type KMm10 from 1937, which was standardized and intended for hauling 15 cm or 10 cm field guns; and the wartime type KMm11, which was most famously paired with the dreaded 8.8 cm 18 or 36 Flak/anti-tank gun. The KMm 11 gave a very high "go anywhere" standard of mobility, which was used to good advantage in the fast deployment of the notorious "eighty-eight" anti-tank gun that proved deadly against Allied tanks. The large wartime 8-ton *SdKfz 7* (KMm11) was 6.859 m in length and 2.35 m in width. It weighed 9,750 kg, had a payload of 1,800 kg, could

*Medium Zugkraftwagen 8-ton SdKfz 7*

tow a load of 8,000 kg, and had a maximum speed of 50 km/h on good road. Fuel consumption was 80 liters/100 km on road and 160 liters/100 km off-road. Range was 250 km on road and 120 km cross-country. The engine was a HL62 TUK Maybach 140 hp, six-cylinder unit. The suspension included bogies with leaf-springing in pairs, and after 1942 some models had full torsion-bar. It had seats for twelve gunners and a locker for ammunition.

In 1940 the Krauss-Maffei company was commissioned to design a new 9-ton half-track. The result was a prototype known as the HK 901, but the project was canceled.

More than 3,000 *SdKfz 7* were produced (also built by Büssing-NAG and

Daimler-Benz) in total, making this model one of the most familiar of all the German half-tracks used by the Wehrmacht during World War II.

So successful was the Krauss-Maffei 8-ton SdKfz 7 that the British made a copy of it; this vehicle—designed by the Vauxhall Motors Ltd company from Luton—was designated as the *Bedford Tractor* (BT) and code-named *Traclat* for Tracked Light Artillery Tractor; it was intended to haul 17-pounder, 25-pounder and Bofors guns with ammunitions and crews. The BT was powered by two Bedford engines mounted side by side and geared to a common drive shaft. Quite similar in appearance to the SdKfz 7, the British copy was, however, superior to the German original design particularly in its stowage arrangements (lockers were accessible from outside the vehicle) and the automatic steering system. Six prototypes were produced in 1944 for test, and they gave excellent performance, but the war ended before mass production would start. There were also Italian exact copies of the German medium 8-ton SdKfz 7 built in the period 1942–1944: they were known as the semi-track artillery tractor *Fiat 727 SC* and *Breda Tipo 61.*

## Heavy half-tracks

Heavy half-tracks could tow 12- to 18-ton loads. The heavy half-tracks were designed and produced by Daimler-Benz, and Fahrzeug- und Motorwerke (Famo).

*Front view 8-ton SdKfz 7 (Krauss-Maffei)*

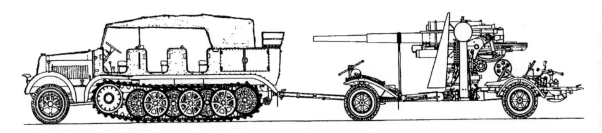

*SdKfz 7 towing a 8.8 cm Flak gun*

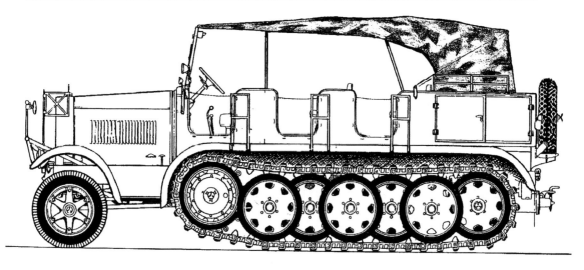

*Profile heavy half-track SdKfz 8 12 t.*

## 12-TON DAIMLER-BENZ SDKFZ 8

The 12-ton SdKfz 8 was designed and manufactured by the Daimler-Benz company. The first models, the *DB 7*, *DB 8* and *DB 9* were in production from 1934 to 1939. They were later superseded by a better type that was similar in appearance but had an upgraded Maybach HL 85 TUKRM V12, 185 bhp, gasoline engine. The result was the standard wartime German heavy half-track 12-ton *SdKfz 8 DB10*, which was in production from 1939 to 1944. This heavy tractor was 7.35 m in length and 2.5 m in width. It weighed no less than 12,700 kg, had a payload of 2,000 kg, could tow a load of 14,000 kg, and had a maximum speed of 51 km/h on good road. Fuel consumption was 100 liters/100 km on road and 220 liters/100 km off-road. Range was 250 km on road and 110 km cross-country. It could accommodate 11 soldiers including the two-man crew. One of the most important of German artillery tractors, it was intended to haul the heavy 21 cm mortar, the heavy 15 cm field gun for which it used a limber to support the trail, or the heavy 10.5 cm anti-aircraft gun. Ammunition was carried in the rear locker, and a second vehicle carried extra rounds. Production of the 12-ton SdKfz 8 ceased in 1944.

## 18-TON FAMO SDKFZ 9

The largest and most powerful German half-track was the impressive heavy 18-ton *SdKfz 9* produced by Fahrzeug- und Motorwerke company (Famo in short) from Breslau. Its origins were in a 1936 requirement for a vehicle to support the armored divisions and act in a recovery role. Two types were designed: the model F2 produced in 1938 and the wartime F3 produced from 1939 to 1944. The 18-ton SdKfz 9 Famo F3 had a Maybach V12 250 bhp gasoline engine. It was 8.325 m in length, almost 3 m high and weighed 15,200 kg. The heavy half-track SdKfz 9 had a maximum speed of 50 km/h on good road and could tow a load of 18,000 kg. Fuel consumption was 120 liters/100 km on road and 270 liters/100 km off-road. Range was 240 km on road and 100 km cross-country. The huge vehicle could accommodate a crew of 8 (artillery version) and 13 (recovery version). Few were built, however, with artillery prime-mover bodywork to tow heavy pieces such as a 15 cm gun, a 21 cm mortar or a large tank-transporter trailer. They were mainly used as specialized tank retrievers (often in tandem, or even three of them if a Tiger tank had to be towed) and recovery vehicles. In this role they were important assets on and

*Heavy half-track 18-t SdKfz 9 Famo. The large dimensions of the vehicle are clearly shown by the size of the soldiers.*

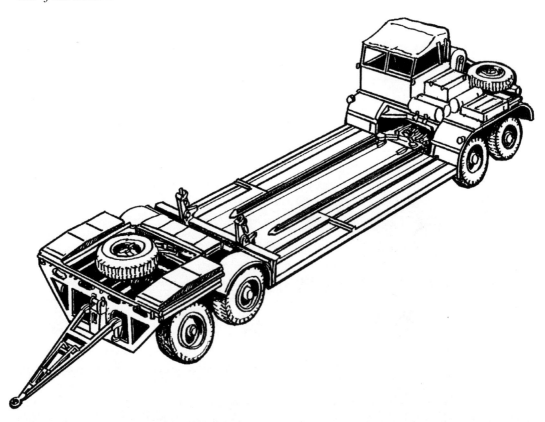

*Tank transporter Sd.Ah. 116. The Sonderanhänger 116 (Sd.Ah, special heavy trailer), which was never produced in sufficient numbers, was towed by a heavy 18-ton Famo SdKfz 9 for transporting medium tanks up to the PzKpfw III.*

off the battle field. Tanks were not only damaged by mechanical breakdowns or combat actions, but they also often got bogged down in muddy and soft ground. After 1943 recovery of disabled tanks became critical for the Germans as frontline losses decimated their available strengths. Indeed, tanks were precious and costly vehicles that no commander might afford to abandon. For this purpose, the heavy recovery half-tracks were equipped with suitable tools and stores, winches, and various forms of cranes including a 6-ton Bilstein crane (the vehicle being then designated SdKfz 9/1) or a 10-ton gasoline-electric crane (SdKfz 9/2) with all-round power traverse and counterweight-ballast boxes for a lifting capacity. By 1943, the huge *Famo SdKfz 9* was made obsolete as a tank recovery vehicle due to the ever increasing tonnage of the late World War II German tanks. Production was thus halted in 1944, and by that time heavy half-tracks were superseded in the recovery role by powerful full-tracked recovery tanks such as the *Bergepanzer Panther (SdKfz 179)* or the *Bergepanzer Tiger Ausf. E (SdKfz 185)*.

Tanks had comparatively limited mileage due to track and suspension breakages when making long runs. To conserve their tracks as much as possible, to speed their deployment to the fighting zone, and also to reduce fuel consumption, tanks were transported by rail and by road on special trailers towed by heavy 18-ton *SdKfz 9 Famo* half-tracks.

## Combat half-tracks

Half-tracks were originally designed as artillery tractors towing light, medium or heavy guns in the forefront of the battle, but they were not designed as vehicles from which to fight. This was soon changed, and half-tracks were adapted to a multitude of combat roles. They were used to bring heavy mortars, machine guns and ammunitions to the front. Eventually they became preferred vehicles of reconnaissance replacing wheeled armored cars. Their versatility enabled other functions such as recovery vehicle, engineering vehicle, field ambulance, artillery observation post or mobile armored command station. Under the pressure of the war, desperate times evoked drastic responses. A major wartime development was the transformation of the standardized artillery tractors into self-propelled guns. Indeed, it was fully recognized that towing a gun behind the half-track drastically reduced its cross-country capability. For this reason experts and front soldiers alike agreed that the weapon had to be installed inside or on top of the vehicle itself. In these conversions, the seats were removed and replaced by a platform for mounting a weapon system. The German armies were fighting increasingly defensive operations on every front after the end of 1942 and had to be more mobile than ever to fill the breeches wherever they occurred in the line. For this purpose half-tracks were partly or fully armored and converted to combat vehicles and weapon-carriers equipped with smoke generators, flame-throwers, heavy mortars, anti-aircraft guns, as well as *Würfrahmen* and *Würfkörper* (rocket launchers). These weapons could also be carried by converted armored *Maultier* trucks.

### COMBAT VERSIONS OF THE LIGHT 1-TON SDKFZ 10

The light 1-ton SdKfz 10 was used as the basis for the following conversions:

• The very specialized *SdKfz 10/1* was fitted with anti-gas equipment.

• The *SdKfz 10/2* was fitted with gas decontamination equipment.

• The *SdKfz 10/3* was fitted with a gas spraying device.

• The *SdKfz 10/4* was a light half-track Demag D7 used as a self-propelled anti-

*Demag 7 SdKfz 10/4 with 2 cm Flak 30 gun*

aircraft mount. It was generally armed with a 2-cm Flak 30 that could fire 120 rounds per minute (6 magazines each containing 20 shells) to a maximum range of 4,000 m. The cab was lightly armored, but no protection was offered to the crew (three or four gunners) who operated on the rear open platform.

## COMBAT VERSIONS OF THE LIGHT 3-TON SDKFZ 11

The light 3-ton SdKfz 11 served as the basis for the following conversions:

• The *SdKfz 11/1* was a *Nebelkraftwagen* armed with rockets.

• The *SdKfz 11/2* was fitted with gas decontamination equipment.

• The *SdKfz 11/3* was fitted with a gas spraying device.

• The *SdKfz 11/4* was another *Nebelkraftwagen* (rocket launcher).

• The *SdKfz 11/5* was a weapon carrier especially intended to launch 15 cm *Panzerwerfer 42* rockets.

## COMBAT VERSIONS OF THE MEDIUM 5-TON SDKFZ 6

The medium 5-ton half-track SdKfz 6 had one official armed conversion designated *SdKfz 6/2*; this was armed with an anti-aircraft gun (usually a 2 cm Flak 30 or a 3.7 cm Flak 36).

There was another unofficial conversion known as the *Panzerjäger Selbsfahrlafette SdKfz 6/2 "Diana"* (self-propelled anti-tank gun). This was a medium 5-ton SdKfz 6 half-track with a large box-type armored superstructure with hinged doors, housing a captured Russian 7.62 cm Pak 36 (r) anti-tank gun. The *Panzerjäger* (tank hunter) Diana had a crew of five and weighed 10.5 tons; maximum speed was about 50 km/h, range was 225 km on road, and armor was between 3 and 5 mm thick. The gun house was 3 m in height and carried 64 rounds; additional ammunitions (about 200 rounds) could be stored in a trailer. Only nine Dianas were converted and engaged in combat in March 1942; assigned to the 90th light armored division in North Africa, they proved quite effective against Allied Grant/Stuart M5 A1 light tanks.

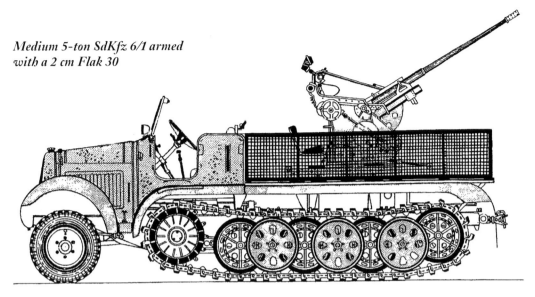

*Medium 5-ton SdKfz 6/1 armed with a 2 cm Flak 30*

*Medium SdKfz 6/2 Panzerjäger Diana*

## COMBAT VERSIONS OF THE MEDIUM 8-TON SDKFZ 7

The medium 8-ton SdKfz 7 had the following armed or specialized conversions:

• The *SdKfz 7/1* was armed with a quadruple anti-aircraft gun (2 cm Flak-Vierling 36 or 38). This powerful weapon—served by a crew of ten—had a rate of fire of 800 rounds per minute. The side rails round the platform were covered by light wire mesh and opened sideways when the weapon was cleared for action.

• The *SdKfz 7/2* often had an armored cab and hood and was armed with an anti-aircraft gun (often a 3.7 cm Flak 36). Both SdKfz 7/1 and 7/2 provided air defense to units in the field and reflected the increasing dominance in the air of the Allied air forces on all fronts as the war progressed. The rapid-firing cannons could also be

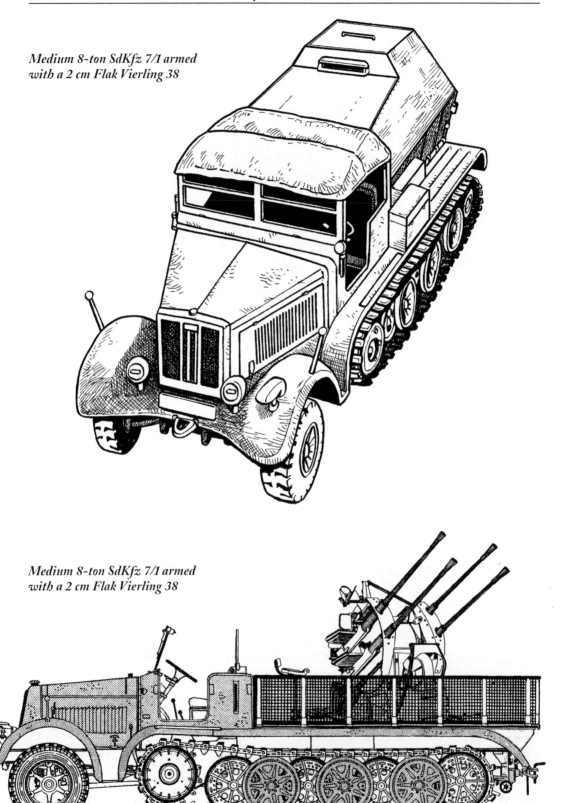

*Medium 8-ton SdKfz 7/1 armed with a 2 cm Flak Vierling 38*

*Medium 8-ton SdKfz 7/1 armed with a 2 cm Flak Vierling 38*

used against ground targets with devastating effects. Both vehicles could be fitted with an armored driver's cab extending rearward to cover the gunners bench, armored shield for the radiator, and wooden (or metal) dropsides replacing the tubular side rails of the earlier models.

• The *SdKfz 7/6*, issued in 1937, was a *Flakmesstruppwagen*—an anti-aircraft survey vehicle that carried the crew responsible for selecting and preparing sites for Flak gun emplacements. The special feature was the extra large locker used to stow surveying equipment and tools. Another vehicle, also designated *SdKfz 7/6*, was a *Feuerleitfahrzeuge für V2*, a very specialized armored version housing mobile control for the firing of V2 missiles.

COMBAT VERSIONS OF<br>THE HEAVY 12-TON SDKFZ 8<br>AND HEAVY 18-TON FAMO SDKFZ 9

The heavy 12-ton SdKfz 8 had a few conversions armed with heavy anti-aircraft guns, generally an 8.8 cm Flak gun mounted on a platform at the back of the vehicle. Known as *Selbstfahrlafette Zugkraftwagen 12* (self-propelled gun 12), this conversion was produced in limited numbers during 1940; the 12-ton semi-tracked artillery tractor SdKfz 8 was given front armor and mounted the famous 8.8 cm heavy anti aircraft gun, which could be also used in an anti-tank role. The same weapon—with dual roles of Pak and Flak—could also be mounted on a heavy 18-ton Famo SdKfz 9. Both vehicles were fitted with hinged sides that could be lowered to form a larger firing platform for the crew of seven gunners. The cab and engine of the half-track were armored with 14 mm steel plates. Jacks or outriggers were attached to the vehicle sides; these were lowered when the gun was in action to increase the stability. Spare ammunition was carried in a towed, two-wheel limber.

## Combat armored troop-carrier half-tracks

Trials and experience had proved the advantages of semi-tracked vehicles for

*Pak/Flak 8.8 cm mounted on a heavy 18-ton SdKfz 9. The depicted vehicle is shown here in firing position. The sides of the rear structure are folded down to provide an operating platform for the gun crew. The outrigger arms are deployed for stability.*

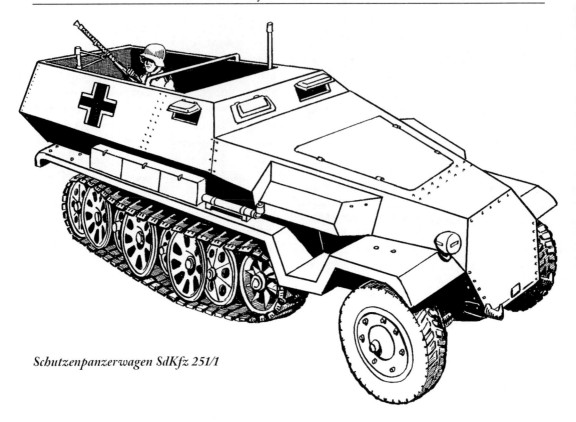

*Schutzenpanzerwagen SdKfz 251/1*

frontline combat roles. In the early years of the *Blitzkrieg* in 1940, a new type of half-track appeared: the armored personnel carrier (APC). In this role, they were called *Schützenpanzerwagen* (*Schtz.Pz.Wg* or *SPW* in short) or "infantry armored carriers." For this purpose, they were provided with armor slopes on all sides to deflect hits. Armored infantry carriers were one crucial component of the Panzer divisions. They improved the quality and the efficiency of the armored divisions. Alongside the tanks, they carried *Panzergrenadiers* (motorized infantry) in relative safety through enemy fire to the point at which dismounted action began; the vehicles had a twin rear door, and the top was open to enable infantrymen to jump out quickly. However, the open top made them vulnerable to grenade or air attack, and the comparatively thin armor only protected against small arms fire. Each SPW vehicle could transport a *Gruppe* (squad of ten riflemen), four half-tracks carried a *Zug* (platoon) and ten vehicles moved a *Kom-*

*panie* (company). Half-tracked *Schützen-panzerwagen* were armed with one or two machine guns for close range defense and attack support. SPWs proved useful in North Africa, where the blistering desert meant that infantry could not follow the armored forces on foot. Rommel's forces, designated *Deutsche Afrika Korps* (DAK), were composed wholly of motorized units. Half-tracks and armored wheeled-cars were widely employed for the bold hit-and-run tactics and sweeping flank maneuvers favored by Germany's most celebrated commander.

There was, however, a major problem with German half-track personnel carriers: there were never enough of them. The numbers built fell always far short of the quantity needed to equip every unit. In general only one of the four *Panzergrenadier* battalions in a Panzer division would be equipped with them, and the bulk of the motorized troops went to combat zones in "soft skin" trucks vulnerable to enemy fire and with limited cross-country mobility. It was a lucky German soldier who even got a ride in an armored troop-carrier, particularly after 1943, when the number of motor vehicles was decreased, heavy equipment and artillery were horse-drawn and infantrymen just had to walk.

Two standardized half-track designs were converted to the role of armored personnel carrier: the light/medium 3-ton SdKfz 11 (re-designated SdKfz 251) and the light 1-ton Demag D7 SdKfz 10 (re-designated in this role SdKfz 250).

## HALF-TRACK SDKFZ 251

In the late 1930s, the Hanomag firm, who was responsible for the manufacturing of the light/medium 3-ton *SdKfz 11*, was instructed to produce an armored personnel car-

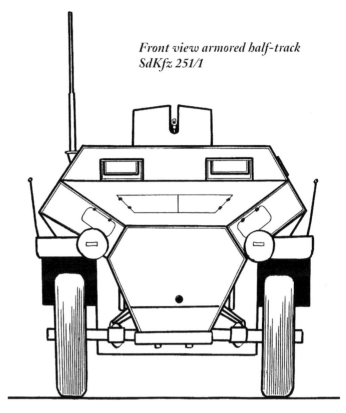

*Front view armored half-track SdKfz 251/1*

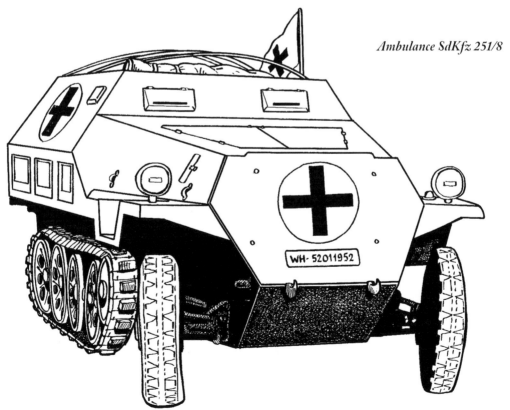

*Ambulance SdKfz 251/8*

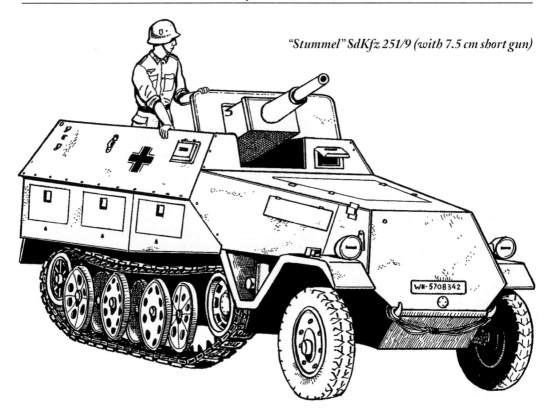

*"Stummel" SdKfz 251/9 (with 7.5 cm short gun)*

rier version. This vehicle, with the distinguishing symbol H.kl.6p. and the ordnance designation *SdKfz 251 mittlerer Schützenpanzerwagen*, was introduced into service in 1940 for use by armored infantry and armored engineer units. Various modifications were added to the original 3-ton design concerning its superstructure and its sloping armor, resulting in four main *Ausführungen* (*Ausf.*, marks): *Ausf.* A, B, C and D.

The *Schützenpanzerwagen SdKfz 251/ 1Ausf. A* was the very basic design and the German standard medium troop carrier. Designed in 1938, by Hanomag for the chassis and by Büssing-NAG for the armored body, the *SdKfz 251/1* was often referred to as *Hanomag* by the Allies during the war. The vehicle had a Maybach 100 hp, six-cylinder gasoline engine placed at the front giving a maximum speed of 53 km/h. The engine drove to the tracks at the rear, the front wheels being to aid steering and for suspension. The rear track assembly used

was the overlapping form of road wheels and torsion bar suspension, which were well tested on this type of vehicle, before eventually being used successfully on late World War II German tanks. Weight (unloaded) was 8.5 t, length was 5.8 m, width was 2.1 m, height was 1.75 m and range was 300 km. Sloping armor was 14 mm thick at the front and 12 mm at the side and rear. The armored personnel carrier SdKfz 251 was generally armed with two machine guns, one at the front protected behind a small armored shield and the other placed at the rear on a high-angle mounting. The vehicle had a crew of two (driver and co-driver/ navigator/machine-gunner) and—officially— it could carry a *Gruppe* (group of ten/twelve infantrymen) who could be brought forward at the same speed as the armored force and cover the dangerously exposed flanks of the tank formations. As a matter of fact, the SdKfz 251 rarely did transport twelve soldiers, as there was barely room in the open troop compartment for eight or ten men in

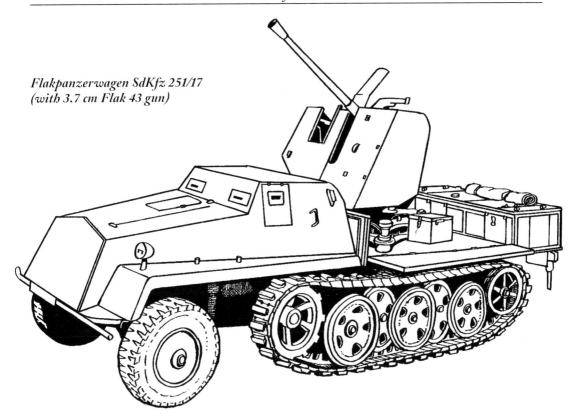

*Flakpanzerwagen SdKfz 251/17
(with 3.7 cm Flak 43 gun)*

full combat gear. The SdKfz 251 was under-powered and difficult to handle, especially in cross-country. It was difficult to steer due to the slope of the steering wheel, but—on the whole—it was an effective and useful vehicle for the armored support role.

Intended originally as a personnel carrier, the SdKfz 251 was later used by other arms of the Wehrmacht and eventually appeared in different variants. A total of 15,250 SdKfz 251 (*Ausf.* A, B, C and D) were built in no less than twenty-two variants. The official variants of the SdKfz 251 were as follows:

• The *SdKfz 251/1* was the basic personnel carrier.

• The *SdKfz 251/2* was armed with an 8.1 cm mortar, with the seats removed to make room for the ammunition.

• The *SdKfz 251/3* was a radio/command vehicle with a radio frame aerial. This armored half-track was intended to replace

the eight-wheeled heavy armored car type SdKfz 232 Fu (see Part 5).

• The *SdKfz 251/4* was an artillery tractor, generally intended to tow a 7.5 cm Pak 40 anti-tank gun or a 10.5 cm infantry gun or a 5 cm Pak 38 anti-tank gun. A sub-variant was an ammunition carrier for light infantry artillery.

• The *SdKfz 251/ 5* was a *Pionerpanzerwagen* (assault engineering armored vehicle), carrying an engineering squad and various loads such as heavy equipment, pneumatic boats or demolition materials.

• The *SdKfz 251/6* was a *Kommandopanzerwagen* (a command vehicle) equipped with a powerful radio set with a large radio-frame on top of the open compartment, a high telescopic aerial at the rear, and panels for maps. It was also intended to transport senior officers in combat zones as safely as possible.

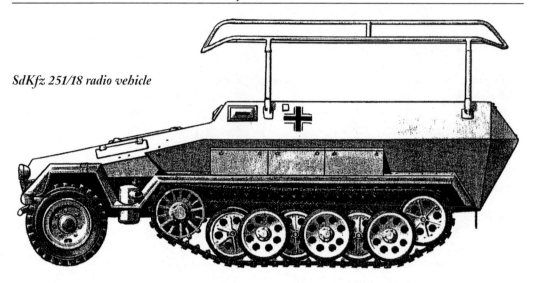

*SdKfz 251/18 radio vehicle*

- The *SdKfz 251/7* was another *Pionerpanzerwagen*, a pontoon/bridge layer used by assault engineering troops. It carried equipment such as light, removable assault bridge sections that were slung along the top of the hull. It could also be armed with an anti-tank Pak 3.7 cm gun in lieu of the usual MG 34 machine gun.

- The *SdKfz 251/8* was a *Krankenpanzerwagen* (an armored ambulance). This version was unarmed, of course, and the hull was painted white with large red crosses. It could transport four wounded on stretchers or eight sitting casualties. The top of the hull was often fitted with curved frames supporting a large canvas to protect casualties against adverse weather conditions.

- The *SdKfz 251/9*, issued in 1942, carried a short 7.5 cm StuK 37 L/24 assault gun for close infantry support. It was a self-propelled mounting nicknamed by the troops *Stummel* (short, clay pipe or cutty).

- The *SdKfz 251/10*, introduced in 1940, was armed with one anti-tank gun—most usually a Pak 36 L42 3.7 cm. It was also intended to serve as a command vehicle.

- The *SdKfz 251/11* was a telephone cable layer, used by engineers.

- The *SdKfz 251/12* was a survey section instrument vehicle for artillery observation equipped with range finder and optical equipment; a gun or a battery of guns or a group of tanks, when firing, threw up smoke and dust obscuring vision; hence observation and correction of firing were often done from such a vehicle posted to a flank where observers were unaffected by obscuration.

- The *SdKfz 251/13* was a sound recording vehicle, a version equipped with sound detecting devices for artillery (non-frequent).

- The *SdKfz 251/14* was a sound ranging vehicle equipped with photo camera and various devices to aid field artillery.

- The *SdKfz 251/15* was a flash and shot spotting vehicle for artillery observation; it was equipped with devices detecting, ranging and measuring enemy artillery fire.

- The *SdKfz 251/16* was a *Flammenpanzerwagen*, a formidable weapon system armed with one machine gun and two flame throwers; introduced in 1943, the machine stowed 700 liters of fuel, fired from flame throwers placed at either side of the fighting compartment. Each weapon could throw 80 sprays of flame of 2 seconds with a range of 35 meters.

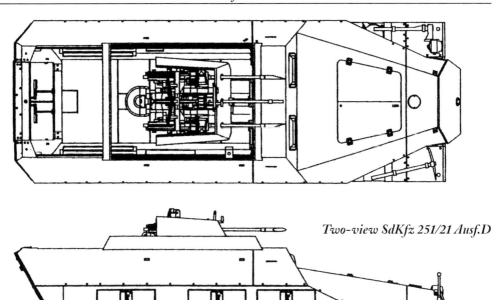

*Two-view SdKfz 251/21 Ausf.D*

• The *SdKfz 251/17* was a self-propelled *Flakpanzerwagen* fitted with a 2 cm Flak 30 or 38 anti-aircraft gun, or a 3.7 cm Flak 43. These weapons could be engaged as much against aircraft as against ground targets; largely employed by both the Luftwaffe and the Heer, it had sides that folded down when deployed for action, providing room for the gun and its 4- to 6-man crew.

• The *SdKfz 251/18* was a radio vehicle for senior officers and also intended for artillery observation.

• The *SdKfz 251/19* was a telephone exchange vehicle equipped with switchboard and communication devices.

• The very specialized *SdKfz 251/20 Uhu* (owl) carried a *Beobachtungsgerät 251*, an experimental infrared searchlight for night vision. The *251/20 Uhu* was used to support Panther tanks operating at night. By the end of the war, the Germans had a considerable advance in night vision wea-

pons. The introduction of genuine night sights based on infrared transmission was only in its infancy in 1945, but the Germans appeared to have developed "passive" systems in which the use of infrared radiation relied on the natural emission of infrared beams from the target itself as, for example, a tank engine exhaust or the heat of the human body. In spite of the many experimental devices produced, including *Obi* (detecting bomber plane exhaust), *Donau 60* (detecting ship funnels for coastal artillery fire), *Spanner* (fitted to fighter aircraft to enable them to home-in on bombers at night), and *Vampire* (rifle sight), few practical results were achieved in combat.

• The *SdKfz 251/21*—introduced in late 1944—was another Flak armored vehicle, with a mount of three 1.5 cm Mauser MG 151 heavy machine guns capable of firing 750 rounds per minute each, or three 2.0 cm automatic rapid-fire anti-aircraft guns; the weapons were electrically operated,

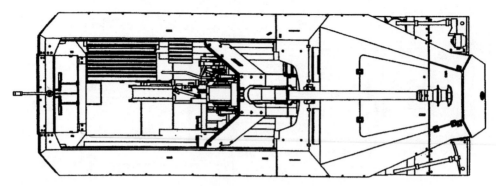

*Two-view SdKfz 251/22 Ausf.D with Pak 40*

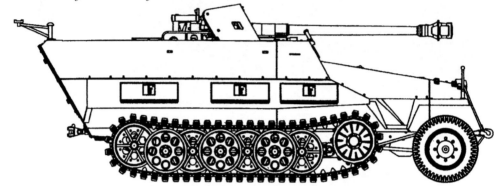

*Front view medium Pakwagen SdKfz 251/22 Ausf.D*

and the vehicle electrical supply could be used. The heavy machine guns were protected with a shield. The vehicle carried 3,000 rounds in readiness, and it, too, had folding sides providing room for weapons and crew.

• The *SdKfz 251/22* was a *mittlere Pakwagen* (medium anti-tank self-propelled mount). Ordered by Hitler himself to increase the German anti-tank arsenal, it was fitted with an L/46 7.5 cm Pak 40 anti-tank gun, a typical expedient in the same class as the eight-wheeled SdKfz 234/4 (see Part 5).

In addition to these "regular" variants, there were several other unofficial conversions more or less improvised by troops in the field, including the mount of a *Flakvierling* (four 2 cm anti-aircraft guns) as well as discarded tank turrets armed with various guns and machine guns. Amongst others, a weapon carried by the SdKfz 251 was the *schwere Würfrahmen* 28 or 32 cm heavy rockets. The rockets were mounted and

*Armored SdKfz 251 armed with Nebelwerfer rockets. This conversion was an attempt to marry firepower and mobility with six Nebelwerfer rockets mounted on the sides of the vehicle.*

fired from their carrying crates, which were fitted in frames, three launcher frames on each side of the half-track's hull. Six rockets could be launched in 10 seconds with devastating fire for which the weapon system was nicknamed *Stuka zum Fuß* (land *Stuka* or "infantry dive-bomber"). The weapon system was also carried on armored Opel Maultier. Rockets were extremely powerful, but imprecise, and were therefore only used at relatively short range against fixed or area targets.

## LIGHT HALF-TRACK SDKFZ 250

The light *1-ton Demag D7 SdKfz 10* design was used as the basis for the armored personnel vehicle under the designation of *leichter Schützenpanzerwagen* (light personnel carrier) *SdKfz 250*. This vehicle was

*Half-track SdKfz 250/1*

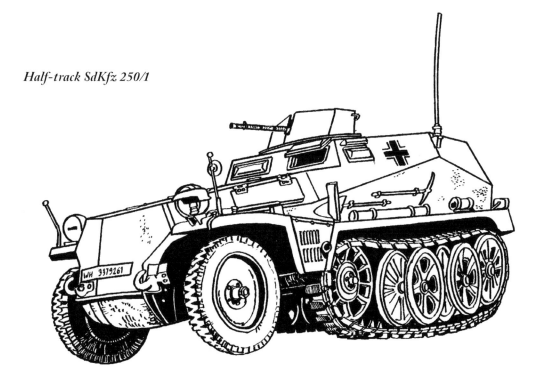

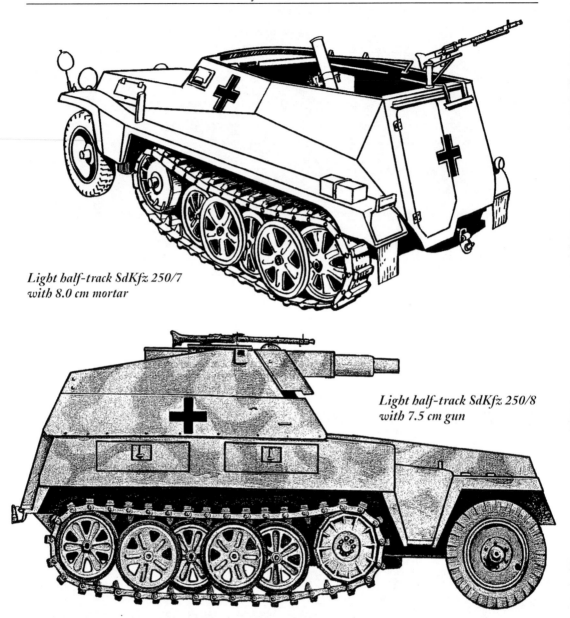

*Light half-track SdKfz 250/7
with 8.0 cm mortar*

*Light half-track SdKfz 250/8
with 7.5 cm gun*

developed following a mid-1930s requirement for a 1-tonner half-track to provide
mobility for infantry and other units operating with the armored divisions. The
SdKfz 250 was obviously smaller than the
SdKfz 251 and formed a more mobile
complement to the medium armored half-
tracks. First seeing action in 1940, production by Demag, Evens & Pistor from Hilsa
and Büssing-NAG continued until 1944.
Length was 4.26 m, width was 1.95 m,
height was 1.66 m, weight (unloaded) was

5.8 tonnes, and maximum speed was 65 km/h.
Front armor was 14.5 mm, sides and rear 8
mm. The engine was a 6-cylinder Maybach
HL 42 TRKM. As in all other half-tracks,
the drive from the engine, positioned at the
front, was to the tracks only, the pair of front
wheels being to aid steering and for suspension. Many improvements and modifications were added to the original design,
mostly intended to rationalize the armor
and redesign hulls in order to facilitate mass-
production and cut down on the amount of

raw materials required. As already mentioned, the chassis was a shortened version of the 1-ton unarmored SdKfz 10 artillery tractor, with one road wheel less on each side. The hull form varied somewhat between different models, hoops could be fitted for a canvas tilt, and modified armor resulted in two main variants: the *SdKfz 250 alte Ausführung* (old design) and the *SdKfz 250 neue Ausführung* (new model that was cheaper and had a re-cut armored compartment). The light vehicle could carry only six soldiers instead of the ten/twelve men of the medium SdKfz 251, but it had better performance. The SdKfz 250 had a good power/weight ratio, and it was fast, but the armor was only protection against small arms and splinters. Cross-country performance was good, but poor in muddy conditions. Though costly to manufacture and demanding constant maintenance, some 13,000 SdKfz 250 were built. Fast, reliable and robust, the light SdKfz 250 was highly popular both with troops and commanding officers. The chief of the famous Afrika Korps, Erwin Rommel, used one of them (named *Greif*, "griffon") as a command and communication vehicle during his campaigning in North Africa.

The standard armored personnel carrier SdKfz 250 was adapted to twelve official functions listed below.

• The *SdKfz 250/1* was the basic SPW model intended to transport personnel, generally six soldiers plus the driver and his assistant; as required, two other soldiers could be carried, but the open compartment became then really crowded. The basic vehicle was usually armed with two machine guns for close-range defense or assault support fire.

• The *SdKfz 250/2* was a telephone cable layer used by engineering troops.

• The *SdKfz 250/3* was a radio/command car equipped with a wireless device and a large metal radio aerial grid frame placed on top of the open compartment.

• The *SdKfz 250/4* was an air support vehicle intended to be used by the Luftwaffe

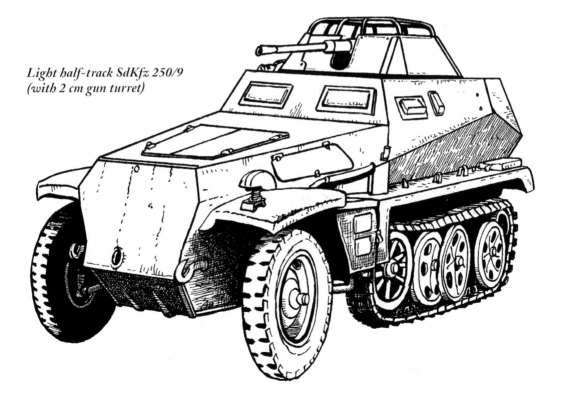

*Light half-track SdKfz 250/9 (with 2 cm gun turret)*

*SdKfz 250/11 with Panzerbüchse 41 (anti-tank gun)*

as an anti-aircraft self-propelled gun, but the project was discontinued.

• The *SdKfz 250/5* was an artillery observation vehicle.

• The *SdKfz 250/6* was an ammunition/cargo carrier.

• The *SdKfz 250/7* was armed with an 8 cm mortar and one machine gun.

• The *SdKfz 250/8* was a self-propelled mounting fitted with a short 7.5 cm field gun.

• The *SdKfz 250/9* was equipped with an anti-aircraft, 2 cm Flak gun placed in a small turret similar to that of the 4 x 4 SdKfz 222 light armored car. Owing to its great mobility, the 250/9 could also be used as a *Panzerspähwagen* (armored reconnaissance car).

• The *SdKfz 250/10* was a self-propelled mount armed with a Pak 3.7 cm anti-tank gun.

• The *SdKfz 250/11* was another self-propelled mount carrying a *Panzerbüchse 41* light anti-tank tapered bore gun.

• The *SdKfz 250/12* was a survey section instrument vehicle arranged as an artillery range-finder.

In addition there were two other specialized variants, which curiously had different SdKfz serial numbers.

• The *SdKfz 252 (Demag D7p.)* was mechanically similar to the 250; it was a *leichter gepanzerter Munitiontransportwagen* (ammunition carrier).

• The *SdKfz 253* was another variant of the 250; it was a *leichter gepanzerter Beobachtungswagen* (light armored observation vehicle) with armored closed roof with hatch and magnifying vision devices.

# Markings and camouflage

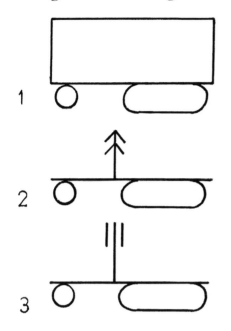

1

2

3

*LEFT: Tactical markings on half-tracks. (1) Motorized infantry in half-tracks, (2) Engineer units in half-tracks, (3) Anti-aircraft gun (Flak) mounted on half-tracks.*

Concerning markings and camouflage, everything previously mentioned about vehicles in Part 1 can be applied to half-tracks.

## Other German half-tracks

In addition to the standard series of medium and light armored combat half-tracks, a number of other armored semi-tracked vehicles were designed at various times from 1935 to 1945. In most cases prototypes only existed. Some of these prototype vehicles were put into frontline service during World War II, including the self-

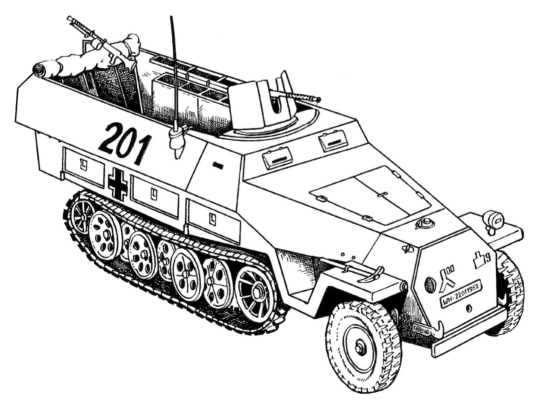

*Markings on troop carrier SdKfz 251/1. On the side: the national identification black cross and the tactical markings (three-digit number) indicating company, platoon and place in the platoon. At the front: the number plate, the divisional emblem and tactical marking.*

*Maultier with Panzerwerfer 42*

*Captured French half-track Somua MCG 5*

propelled mounting for a 7.5 cm KwK L/ 40.8 on a half-track vehicle with engine at the rear. Two other rear-engined types, built in 1935–1936, were the HL kl 3 (H) with a 3.7 cm KwK L/70 tank gun and the HL kl 4 (H) with a 7.5 cm KwK L/40.8 tank gun. Only the Maultier series and the

sWS reached the stage of full production. As already mentioned, the *Maultier* (Mule) series consisted of Opel, Ford and Klöckner-Humboldt-Deutz trucks rated for 2-ton loads and a Mercedes-Benz rated for 4.5 tons, with tracks replacing the rear wheels. These were developed in 1942 after

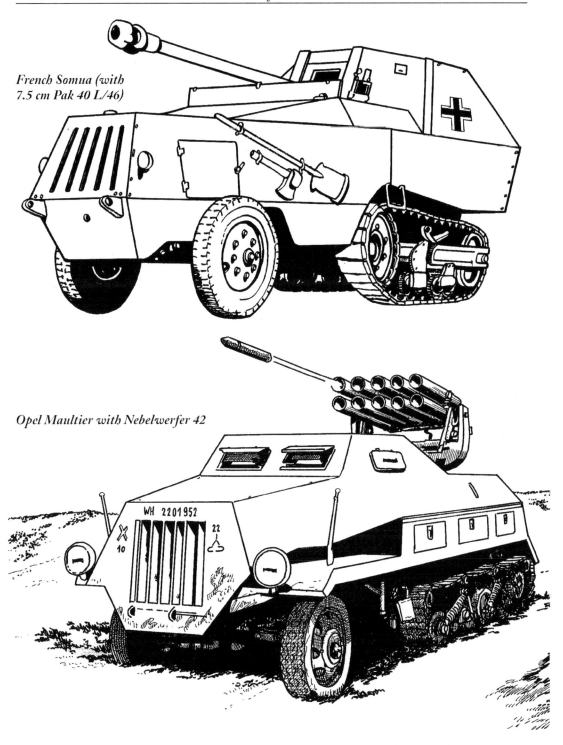

*French Somua (with 7.5 cm Pak 40 L/46)*

*Opel Maultier with Nebelwerfer 42*

experience had shown the uselessness of conventional wheeled vehicles in Russian terrain. The *schwerer Wehrmacht Schlepper* (sWS, heavy military tractor), as already mentioned, was a new half-track design for re-equipping the German force in 1944; simplicity of production and maintenance were aimed for in the designs.

Several types of foreign captured vehicles were also used. Before World War II broke out, France was the main manufacturer of half-tracks, and the French army was equipped with vehicles produced by the Unic and Somua companies. After the victory of June 1940, the German army employed captured French 3-ton semi-track artillery tractors. The *Somua MGC 5*, for example, was a light semi-track artillery prime mover, and its German designation was *le. Zgkw. S (f) Typ MGC*; it was also referred to as *D 50/12 (f)*. Another French prime mover was the *Somua MCL6*, which was designated *Zgkw. S 303 (f)*. Another, the *Unic TU1*, was known as *Zgkw U (f) Typ P107*. Several French armored Somua half-tracks were used by the Germans as self-propelled mounting armed with 7.5 cm Pak 40 L/46 guns or armed with a battery of sixteen 8.1 cm mortars or with the rocket launcher Panzerwerfer 42.

# Demolition vehicles

The idea of a small, remote controlled, demolition explosive carrier vehicle seemed to originate from a French experiment designed by the Kegresse company in 1940. After examination of the captured small machine, the German army further developed the concept and during World War II made three main designs: Goliath, Borgward IV, and Springer. These armored tracked weapons were intended to destroy bunkers, strong points, large concrete obstacles, buildings, mine fields, and even tanks from a safe distance under the remote control of combat engineers.

Demolition vehicles were considered failures on the battlefield due to their vulnerability, mechanical deficiency, comparatively light explosive charge, short range and lack of speed compared to their very high cost. The concept was, however, tactically interesting, and the World War II German demolition vehicles represent the foundation of modern military robotic systems.

## SdKfz 302 and 303 Goliath

In November 1940 the German military authority contracted with the Borgward company for the development of a small, experimental, remotely controlled vehicle. The first design was a small robot, designated *SdKfz 302 leichte Ladungsträger E-motor* (light charge carrier with electric engine), also called *Gerät 67* or *Zerstörer* (demolisher), but better known as *Goliath*. The small, tracked vehicle, manufactured by Borgward and Zündapp, weighed 370 kg, had a length of 1.5 m, a width of 0.85 m, and a height of 0.56 m. It was equipped with two Bosch MM/RQL electric engines, each delivering 2.5 KW (3.35 hp). It carried an 80 kg load of high explosives and was brought into position by a two-wheeled trailer towed by two men; on the rear there was a drum carrying the command wire; this was of the three-strand type with two used for control of the vehicle and the third for detonation of the explosive charge. In action Goliath was thus remote controlled by the cable up to 800 m (875 yd.) in range and driven to a speed of 10 km/h in direction of the enemy target where it was brought to explode. Allocated to especially trained engineer companies, some Goliath were tested in combat in 1943 during the battle of Kharkov (Russia) and during the Allied landing at Anzio (Italy). But, vulnerable to small-arms fire and often breaking down, they proved very inefficient and extremely costly. As a result, the program of electrically powered Goliath was abandoned in January 1944. As early as November 1942, a cheaper version had been designed by the Zündapp and Zachertz firms. Known as the *Goliath SdKfz 303 V-Motor*, this new robot was a more capable variant. It had an internal combustion Zündapp 12.5 bhp gasoline engine with a raised air inlet cowl on top of the hull, longer range (about 6 km = 3.7 mi.), a 10 mm armor, and a payload of 70 kg of explosives. An improved version, slightly larger and heavier, known as *Goliath*

*Goliath SdKfz 303*

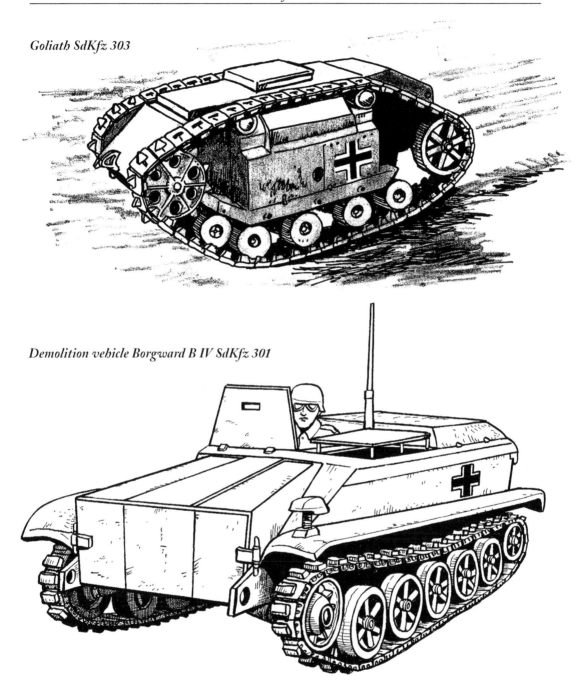

*Demolition vehicle Borgward B IV SdKfz 301*

*SKfz 303b*, was issued in November 1944 with a payload of 100 kg of explosives. Even so, the Goliath 303 remained an expensive and unsuccessful gadget with no tactical significance on the battlefield. When Germany capitulated in May 1945, the Allies found about 4,000 of the unused little vehicles.

## BORGWARD B IV SDKFZ 301

The Borgward firm developed a series of demolition vehicles known as B I, B II, B III, and B IV. The Borgward B I, designed in 1939, was an expandable, remote controlled, mine clearing vehicle; it was pilotless, with a weight of 1,550 kg, a speed

*Demolition vehicle "Springer" SdKfz 304*

of 5 km/h, a length of 1.85 m, a width of 0.8 m, a height of 0.65 m, a range of 18 km, and a 12 mm front plate armor. Later models were bigger, more powerful and carried a larger explosive charge.

There was also an amphibious variant of B II, known as *Ente* (duck); this was propelled on water by a single screw at the rear. It was produced in prototype form only.

The final type that was produced in some number under the designation Borgward B IV SdKfz 301 was a *Schwerer Ladungsträger* (heavy explosive charge layer) also known as a *Funklenkpanzer* (remote controlled armored vehicle). It was a full-tracked armored vehicle equipped with a 500 kg (800 lbs.) explosive charge contained in a large armored box placed at the front; this was intended to be used against a large target (e.g., tank, fortification, obstacles or mine field). The vehicles had a speed of 40 km/h, a weight of 3.6 tons, and an armor between 15 and 20 mm. The vehicle included normal driving controls, and it was steered as near as possible to the target by a driver who dismounted in its vicinity; then the vehicle was remotely controlled by an engineer to the target by wireless control for the final phase of the operation: the explosion of the charge and, hopefully, the destruction of the target. In 1942 some 238 were produced, 651 in 1943 and 304 in 1944,

but—as far as we know—none of them did see actual combat service.

## SPRINGER SDKFZ 304

The *mittlere Ladungsträger Springer SdKfz 304* was an expendable, fully tracked, demolition medium armored vehicle designed as a replacement for both Goliath and Borward carriers. Produced by the NSU company, the *Springer* (Blaster) vehicle shared many components—notably the drive-train, the engine, the overlapping road wheels, and parts of the running gear—with the previously described *NSU Kettenkrad* (heavy motorbike on tracks). The Springer SdKfz 304 weighed 2,400 kg, and it was powered by a 4-cylinder, 1.5-liter, 36 hp Opel Olympia engine. Speed was 42 km/h on good road; length was 3.17 m; width was 1.43 m; height was 1.45 m. Armor was between 8 and 10 mm. The vehicle was driven by a passenger close to the target area. There the driver left the vehicle and remotely directed it further using radio equipment right to the target, where the 330 kg explosive charge carried by the tracked vehicle was exploded by remote control. Only fifty experimental units were built and none ever saw service. There was also a plan to use the vehicle as a small tank armed with a recoilless 10.5 cm IG gun, but this project, too, came to naught.

### KRUPP MINE-CLEARING VEHICLE

In 1994 the Krupp company designed a *schweres Minenraumfahrzeug* (heavy mine-clearing vehicle). This monster vehicle, also known as the *Krupp Raumer S*, weighed 130 t and consisted of two 2-wheeled, articulated sections, each powered by a Maybach HL90 engine. The solid steel wheels were no less than 2.7 m (10 ft.) in diameter as mine demolition was by weight alone; there were different wheel widths at front and rear, so as to sweep a wider path. The super heavy *Krupp Raumer S* existed only in prototype form; the only unit ever built was never used and captured at the end of World War II by U.S. troops.

## Conclusions about German half-tracks

To conclude this section about World War II German *Zugkraftwagen*, one may say that half-tracks were excellent vehicles used in a multitude of roles. Their principal weakness was, however, their comparative vulnerability due to rubber front wheels, thin armor and open top. Even the armored troop carriers were rather vulnerable: indeed, a single grenade could decimate a whole combat group, particularly in urban warfare. For these reasons, there was a project to replace both the SdKfz 250 and 251 by a full-track vehicle with armored roof based on the design of the Czech PzKpfw 38 (t) tank. This project could never be materialized.

The half-track principle was not further developed after 1945 when similar or better cross-country performance could be obtained from multi-wheeled, all-wheel drive vehicles and full-track tanks. Exceptions were a few designs that stayed in service within several armies until the early 1960s. For example, the German armored *SdKfz 251* was produced after the war in substantially the same form in Czechoslovakia and designated the armored personnel carrier *Tatra OT 810*. Another long-lived half-track design was the versatile U.S.-made White M2 and M3, as well as the derivates M5 and M9, which were still used in combat until the 1970s.

# 5

# Wheeled Combat Vehicles

## Armored cars

Nowadays all arms and services are fully mechanized, and no recognized army in the world today, however humble, would consider itself other than a mechanized force. This is the result of a long development. The armored, wheeled car was the earliest form of armored vehicle and predates by far the invention of the fully tracked tank. The first recorded example of an armored fighting vehicle—combining firepower, protection and mobility—dates from about the year 2500 BC at the Sumerian city of Lagash. It consisted of a four-wheel chariot, armored with hides, drawn by donkeys with a crew of two warriors. It is further recorded that chariots were used at war by the ancient Assyrians, Egyptians, Hittites, Romans and Celts. One early suggestion for an armored vehicle that moved

*Vigevano's windmill armored vehicle. The Italian physician Guido da Vigevano designed about 1335 a windmill-driven machine with power transmitted from the sails to the wheels via pinions. The trouble was that such a machine would have depended upon a fair wind and could sail only before the wind and so, since there was no guarantee that the enemy would remain downwind, the idea lacked practical application.*

169

*Austro-Daimler armored car of 1903*

independently of muscular horse power came in 1335 from an Italian physician, Guido da Vigevano, who designed a windmill-driven machine. In 1417, the Hussite leader, Johan Ziska, successfully resisted a force of German knights by forming his heavy wooden farm carts—armed with small cannons and handguns—into a defensive circle and holding the enemy at bay from a *Wagenburg* (wagon barricade). The Hussites moved in columns of horse-drawn, armor-plated carts, the sides pierced with loopholes from which attackers were shot at with firearms. As soon as an assault was repulsed, Ziska's pikemen and cavalry charged to counterattack, sealing the victory. The genius Renaissance artist and engineer Leonardo da Vinci designed, about 1482, a wooden fighting vehicle moved by cranks that drove the road wheels. In 1855,

a certain James Cowan designed a steam-powered, metal-covered vehicle armed with scythes and guns. All these machines were technical speculations ahead of their time and well outside conventional bounds. They were nevertheless impractical, cumbersome, unreliable and terribly slow—if movable at all—because of the low power-to-weight ratio. It was not before the invention of a practical internal combustion gasoline engine late in the 19th century by Gottlieb Daimler and Karl Benz, that the idea of a fully mobile, armored car could be feasible.

By 1900, the automobile was no longer a curiosity, and cars were used for civilian transportation and military purposes in increasing numbers. In 1902 the Englishman F.R. Simms made a four-wheel motorcycle armed with a Maxim machine gun, but the maneuverability of the unprotected

*The French Charron-Girardot & Voigt
armored car (1904)*

vehicle must have left a lot to be desired. The first Austrian/German armored car was the Austro-Daimler from 1903. It had a crew of four (commanding officer, driver, machine gunner and loader); it had a high-set hood concealing the gasoline engine, a square cab for the driver and a box body with revolving turret on top mounting a Skoda machine gun; in 1905 the turret was made larger with a capacity of two machine guns. The driver could see through slits in the front armor or, when conditions allowed, could elevate his seat so as to raise his head through a hatch on the cab top, enabling him an all-round view. The vehicle weighed 3.5 tons and had a maximum speed of 45 km/h (28 mph).

In the very beginning of the 20th century, the Russian empire purchased several armored cars designed by the French firm Charron-Girardot & Voigt; the Charron-Girardot & Voigt armored car had a 4.5 mm thick armor, was armed with one machine gun and was said to have a speed of 30 mph;

they were used successfully for riot control in Saint Petersburg in 1904. In 1909 the major German gunmaker, Krupp, presented what may be considered as the first self-propelled anti-aircraft gun. This consisted of a 7.5 cm gun mounted on the rear of a 50 hp truck, intended to fire against aircraft and balloons. At the same time a similar weapon system was designed by the Rheinische Metallwaaren-und Maschinenfabrik (Rheinmetall), consisting of a 5 cm gun mounted in a turret on an armored car. The first armored car to appear on a battlefield was the Italian 4-ton Bianchi/Fiat, protected by 6 mm of armor in Libya during the Italo-Turkish war in 1912. The American army made wide use of various cars during the Mexican campaign of 1915–1916.

During the First World War (1914–1918), armored cars were designed and operated by the various belligerents. On the Western front, their use was, however, limited since such wheeled vehicles had no or very little cross-country capability and were only useful on good surfaced roads; trench warfare, with its barbed wire encumberment and the morass of no man's land, rendered them impotent. The narrow high-pressure tires of the day were useless on soft ground. On other fronts such as the Middle East, Russia or the Balkans, where large space for maneuvers was available, armored cars proved useful, quick and powerful weapons for reconnaissance, convoy escort and swift hit-and-run raids in enemy territories, although frequently becoming bogged down when operating in loose ground and sand. The famous American car, the Ford Model T, was widely used as a light patrol car and as machine-gun carrier in the North African desert, the western desert and in operations against the Turks in Palestine and Mesopotamia. Armed Ford T cars played a vital part in the Gaza battle of 1917. Similar types—armed with Lewis machine guns—were used by the famous Lawrence of Arabia supporting the "Arab Revolt" against the Turks.

## Early German armored cars

The earliest German armored cars of World War I were, like contemporary British, Belgian and French vehicles, improvisations, mainly based on civilian touring cars fitted with armor plates to give some protection to the crew and engine. They were generally used by *Jäger* (light infantry) battalions of cavalry divisions in the support of horse-mounted units. In 1915 three experimental armored vehicles were built by the Daimler, Ehrhardt and Büssing companies. They had four wheel drive, front and rear driving controls, and solid tires. These prototypes were formed into a unit in 1916 and sent first to the Baltic provinces and then on to the Western front. Conditions in neither area were suited to the employment of armored cars, but the unit performed useful work in Romania where it was sent later

in the year before returning to Germany at the end of 1916. The Büssing and Daimler companies were committed to other types of war production, and so the main orders for further armored cars were given to the Ehrhardt company, which produced twelve improved vehicles in 1917. These were used to equip five new armored units known as *Panzerkraftwagen–MG Züge* (armored machine gun carrier squadrons). Other units were later formed with captured Italian, French, British and Russian vehicles. A further twenty armored cars were ordered from the Ehrhardt company in late 1917. These, together with the earlier cars, were on the whole similar to the 1915 designs, but the weight, which was one of the biggest drawbacks of all the 1915 cars, was reduced to just over 7 tons. Certain improvements in detail were introduced, the most noticeable being revisions to the frontal armor—horizontal, instead of vertical, grills over the radiators and protection for the headlamps—and protective boxes over the rear wheels. Another twenty Ehrhardt cars were produced in the period 1919–1922 for use in maintaining internal security in Germany. Another German wheeled armored vehicle known to have been built during World War I was a Mannesmann-Mulag truck armored as a personnel carrier; this truck was fully enclosed and had provision for weapons for use by the crew, but no turret.

After the Armistice of 1918, Germany was an unsettled state with popular uprising and insecure borders. In this chaotic political background, a number of armored cars were designed for use in maintaining public security. In addition to the Ehrhardt armored cars, already mentioned, thirty so-called *Notwagen* (improvised cars) were built on truck chassis. The Marienwagen was a Daimler truck chassis with the rear wheels replaced by track: the first German half-track. A Marienwagen with hull and turret was designed by the Ehrhardt company too. In 1919 appeared the *Panzerkraftwagen* Daimler DZVR, a conversion of the

*Daimler Panzerwagen (1915). The Daimler heavy armored car from 1915 had a crew of nine, serving three machine guns. Maximum speed was 50 km/h and range was 155 miles. Weight was 8.86 tons, and armor was 7 mm thick. Only one prototype was ever built.*

*Ehrhardt type 21. The heavy armored car Ehrhardt 21 from 1921–1922 had a crew of six. It was fitted with a top-turret armed with two machine guns and weighed 11,000 kg. Maximum speed was 53 km/h and maximum range was 350 km. Known as the Schupo-Sonderwagen (special police car) or Straßen-Panzerwagen (street armored car), thirty-three exemplars were built and allocated to the German police for peacekeeping and anti-riot duty.*

World War I four-wheel drive Krupp-Daimler KD1 artillery tractor, of which about 45 were armored. The terms of the Treaty of Versailles, which became effective in January 1920, limited the German army to 100,000 men and prohibited the use of armored fighting vehicles. However, the use of armored but unarmed, wheeled military personnel carriers was permitted. A total of 105 vehicles was the limit fixed. The vehicles built for this function were designed to carry twelve men each in addition to a crew of three and were known as *gepanzerter Mannschaftstransportwagen* (SdKfz 3-MTW, armored personnel carrier). The designs and development of MTWs was rigidly supervised by the Inter-Allies Military Control Commission and rearward steering, command cupola and even the use of sloped armor were prohibited. The final design of MTW cars was a clumsy vehicle weighing about 11 tons loaded; although it had four-wheel drive, its weight and the solid tires used seriously detracted from its cross-country performance.

A special body of police, known as the *Schutzpolizei*, which was limited to 150,000 men by the Treaty of Versailles, was permitted to have one armored car for every 1,000 policemen. Three types of *Schutzpolizei Sonderwagen* (Special Police Cars) were built in the period 1921–1922 by Daimler, Ehrhardt and Benz. All three vehicles were similar in appearance to the MTW, but all were fitted with twin turrets and command cupolas on top of the hull and had rear steering wheels, as these features were not banned by the Control Commission. A total of 85 special police armored cars were built. Many of them were later taken over by the German army for training purposes or as armored passenger cars for high officials.

## Reconnaissance role

Despite all the obstacles, the motor vehicle began to play an increasingly promi-nent part in military thinking. With the tank reluctantly given a permanent place in the order of battle in the 1930s, the need for cross-country vehicles to support the new weapon in the field became apparent. In the period 1918–1939, the ingredients for change were ready—vehicles driven by reliable internal combustion engines, armor plates, light and compact guns and machine guns, and embryonic radio systems with the potential of imposing close command over troops in the forefront of combat. Cavalry regiments were massively converted from horses to armed motor cars and tanks. The British, the Dutch and the French used their armored cars for colonial policing duty. The Germans—who were forbidden to have tanks by the Treaty of Versailles of 1919—were allowed only a limited number of armored cars primarily for internal security service and police duties, as already mentioned. In the early and mid-1930s, they used them as the start of their modern *Panzerwaffe* (motorized armored force) for medium and distant reconnaissance; armored cars fitted in the concept of a compact and mobile, hard-hitting, fast-moving, reborn army. Experimental models were tested extensively in secret in Germany and, by special arrangement, in Russia.

The easiest type of armored fighting vehicle to produce was the armored car because existing civilian automobile production could be easily adapted to its manufacture. Yet, the armored car had a mixed reception right before the beginning and during World War II. As a fighting vehicle, it suffered a basic defect: it could no longer survive in the face of tanks and anti-tank artillery. But as a reconnaissance vehicle, it still performed a valuable function. Time and efforts spent on reconnaissance were (and still are) never wasted as obtaining intelligence is a vital process in the conduct of war. The reconnaissance units of any army require considerable specialized skills, insight and above all daring as they have the most dangerous task to do: they form the point of the advance, they must probe forward until they encounter enemy forces, and they penetrate enemy deployment where they must remain unseen in order to observe and obtain tactical intelligence; if they are located and attacked, they have to quickly evade. Gathered information such as the enemy's strength, identification, intention, position, speed, direction, and so on, are then transmitted to divisional headquarters who, according to their reports, send other units forward. The information obtained on the organization and strength of the enemy provides the basis for the conduct of the battle.

Reconnaissance may be performed by fighting for information or by stealth. The Germans—during World War II—stressed aggressiveness and often attempted to obtain intelligence by employing force. Often they assigned supplementary tasks to their reconnaissance units, such as reconnoiter routes, sabotage behind enemy lines, harassment, or even limited attack on the opposing party and maintaining the momentum of the offensive.

To a certain extent, motorcycles were suitable for *Spähtruppen* (reconnaissance units), and each *Aufklärung Abteilung* (Panzerdivision's reconnaissance battalion) had a motorcycle company. But obviously motorcycles did not offer adequate protection to soldiers fulfilling this aggressive and dangerous job. A wheeled reconnaissance armored vehicle—called a *Panzerspähwagen*—was actually much more suitable for this purpose.

Compared to fully tracked tanks, wheeled vehicles were less adequate in rough ground and poorly armed, but they presented some advantages such as greater economy in action, higher speed, longer range and relative silence; they were equipped with radio because it was essential for commanders to remain in constant contact with the advance forces. For this purpose, German reconnaissance vehicles were equipped with complete radio sets including transmitter, receiver, power unit and accessories, referred to by the designation *Fu* (short for *Funk*, "radio"). The most common sets installed in reconnaissance cars were the type *Fu 12*, an 80-watt transmitter with a range of 25 km (15.5 mi.) and *Fu.Spr.f.* (with a range of 5 km (3.1 mi.).

By 1940 the Germans had about 600 armored reconnaissance vehicles—enough to give the reconnaissance battalion of each of their twelve *Panzerdivision* (armored divisions) about 50 of them.

As a rule the Germans employed their armored cars for *Gefechtsaufklarung* (battle reconnaissance). An armored car patrol normally was composed of three car one of which was equipped with a long-range radio set. An artillery observer often accompanied the patrol so that in an emergency, fire could be brought down quickly. The patrol was organized either for short reconnaissance or for missions lasting one or two days. Tasks were defined clearly, and nothing was allowed to interfere with the patrol's main objective. If enemy forces were met, action was avoided unless the force was so weak that it could be destroyed without diverting the patrol from its main task. If enemy action was anticipated, the patrol was reinforced with self-propelled guns and occasionally with battle tanks. Engineers and motorcyclists were often attached to the unit, the former to deal with road blocks and demolitions, the latter to collect messages and relay them to the rear.

The German armored wheeled cars performed very well in the western campaigns in 1939–1941 and particularly in the desert war in northern Africa. The famous German *Afrika Korps* was a totally mechanized force campaigning in open desert, which aptly has been described as the tactician's paradise and the quartermaster's hell as transport of supplies was crucial. But from 1942 onwards they proved much less serviceable, since it was all too easy to ambush them or destroy them by light anti-tank weapons or from the sky with tank-hunting aircrafts. The comparatively poor cross-country performance of armored cars has always limited their usefulness. The demand for armored cars was henceforth reduced though they were still used until the end of the war.

During World War II, the Germans designed several types of *Panzerspähwagen.* German armored cars were divided into two main kinds: *leichter Panzerspähwagen* (light cars with four wheels) and *schwerer Panzerspähwagen* (trucks with six wheels and heavy cars with eight wheels).

## Light cars with four wheels

Four-wheel cars were light or medium reconnaissance armored cars called *leichter Panzerspähwagen.* Light open passengers cars with stripped down bodies were used by the Reichswehr in the early 1930s as wireless vehicles and as personnel carriers. Some of these had windshield armor added. They were conventional 4 x 2 drive but with the light, stripped down bodies had a moderate cross-country performance. In 1933 improved cars were developed by the Daimler-Benz and Adler firms. These early vehicles were nonetheless only stop-gap designs, and better cars were developed. In 1938, the special army vehicles SdKfz 221, 222, 223 and 261 were designed and issued to the reconnaissance companies of the armored motorized divisions and took part in all 1939–1940 major campaigns. After the victory of 1940, several types of light scout cars of foreign origin were captured and used by the German army (e.g., the French Renault ADK, Panhard 38 or the British light reconnaissance Beaverette Mark IV Standard, or the Italian AB 40).

Unsuited to rough Russian grounds, the production of the light armored cars series stopped in 1942 when they were replaced by half-tracks. Light cars were then reserved for the purpose of training tank crews or issued to the German police forces for keeping order.

The Germans also designed several types of *Panzerkampfwagennachbildung* (dummy armored vehicle), which were standard army utility cars fitted with wooden plates. These dummy armored vehicles were employed for the purpose of training Panzer crews.

*Captured British
Beaverette Mk IV*

## ADLER KFZ 13 AND KFZ 14

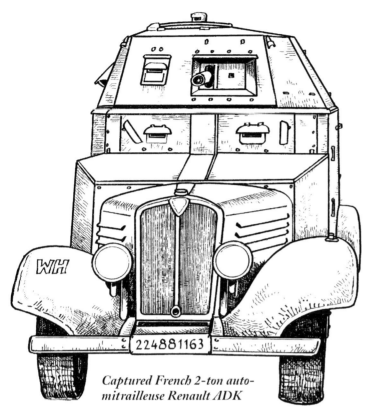

*Captured French 2-ton automitrailleuse Renault ADK*

One of the first armored cars to see service in the German army at the beginning of the 1930s was the 4 × 2 *Adler Standard 6 Kfz 13*. It was merely a conversion of the civilian-type Adler Diplomat. The military adaptation Kfz 13 was produced by Daimler-Benz, and the armor body was manufactured by the Deutsche Edelstahlwerke company from Hannover-Linden. The Adler-Daimler-Benz Kfz 13 had an Adler Standard 2.9-liter, 6-cylinder, 60 hp gasoline engine, a length of 4.20 m, a width of 1.70 m, and a weight of 1,900 kg. Maximum speed was 60 km/h and range was 320 km. Fuel consumption

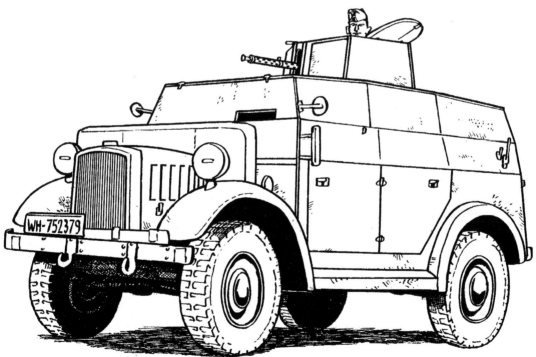

*Panzerkampfwagennachbildung. This dummy armored car, developed from a standard light car chassis fitted with wooden plates, was used for training purposes.*

was 22 liters/100 km on road and 30 liters/ 100 km cross-country. The car could carry 350 kg of load and was armed with one 7.92 mm MG13 (or MG34) machine gun with 1,000 rounds protected by an armored shield. The crew included two men, the driver and the machine gunner; two or three extra passengers could be carried as well. The armor of the compartment did not exceed 8 mm, the top was open (which gave limited protection) and cross-country performance was poor. Because of these deficiencies, this vehicle was more a *Waffenwagen* (armed car) than a proper armored reconnaissance car. From 1932 to 1934 Daimler-Benz produced 147 Kfz 13.

There was also a radio car version, known as the *Funkkraftwagen Kfz 14*, equipped with a long range wireless set and frame aerial with a crew of three, of which 40 were produced. Though some were used during the 1939–1940 campaigns in Poland and France (and even used in combat on the Russian front as late as 1943), the Kfz 13 and the radio version Kfz 14 were only interim solutions with passenger car origin and poor military performance. They were therefore ill-suited for frontline combat duty, but they proved valuable for training purposes.

## MANFRED WEISS-STRAUSSLER 39 M CZABA

The light scout car 39 M—based on the design of the British Alvis AC2—was designed in 1939 by the Hungarian Nicholas Straussler and produced by the Manfred Weiss Company. The armored car had a crew of three and two driving positions, front and back, for making movement in either direction without turning.

It had a 4-cylinder, rear-mounted engine with dual ignition. It had two- or four-wheel steering with steering box at each wheel. Armor was 9 mm thick. Length was 4.52 m, width was 2.2 m and weight was 5,900 kg. Maximum speed was 65 km/h and range was 150 km. The armored car was armed with one 8 mm machine gun and one 20 mm quick-firing cannon, both placed in a rotating turret. It was built originally for the Hungarian army, but many served under the German colors. Sixty-one were produced in 1939 and another forty in 1940. In 1944 the Hungarian Manfred Weiss-Strausser company was acquired by the SS. With this firm as a core, Himmler wanted to construct a steadily expanding SS cartel.

*Leichter Panzerspähwagen Adler Kfz 13*

*Light scout car Manfred Weiss-Strausser 39 M*

## LIGHT ARMORED CAR SDKFZ 221

By the rearmament program of 1935, new designs were made. Built by Horch-/Auto-Union, the 4 x 4 *leichter Panzerspäh-wagen SdKfz 221 (MG)* was introduced in 1936 as a replacement of the outdated Adler Kfz 13 and Kfz 14. It was a four-wheel drive car intended for reconnaissance purposes. It had a crew of three, composed of commander, driver and radio operator, who was also a gunner in the armed version. Devel-

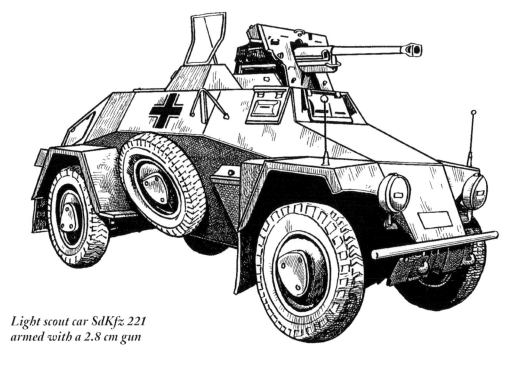

*Light scout car SdKfz 221 armed with a 2.8 cm gun*

oped in 1934 the SdKfz 221 incorporated the use of a standard four-wheeled heavy passenger car chassis with an armored body and turret mounted on top of it. The chassis was often that of the heavy *Einheit* (standard) Horch produced by the Horch company for all armored cars for soft skin and armored bodywork. The hulls were made by separate contractors such as the Weserhutte Company. The vehicle had a rear mounted engine, coil spring suspension and 4-wheel steering. The engine was initially a Horch 3.5-liter V8 engine, but in 1941 this was replaced with a more powerful 3.8-liter engine. This larger engine was a side valve, liquid-cooled gasoline engine that had a maximum output of 90 bhp at 3600 rpm. It had a dry plate clutch with a 5F1R gearbox, giving it all-wheel drive with rear differential integral with the gearbox. Both differentials were lockable. The SdKfz 221 had a weight of 3,750 kg and a 100-liter fuel capacity, giving it a range of 310 km and a maximum speed of 85 km/h. Fuel consumption was 35 liters/100 km on road and 50 liters cross-country. Its armor was rolled armor plates that were 8 mm thick at the front, side and top and 5 mm on the rear hull. This armor could withstand rounds from 8 mm or .30 caliber machine guns. The SdKfz 221 was armed with one machine gun, an MG 34. The vehicle was equipped with an anti-grenade, overhead protection, hinged, wire mesh grille on the open turret. Fast and maneuverable, but with an inadequate cross-country performance, it became the most widely used German light reconnaissance armored car of the first years of World War II. The type SdKfz 221 was issued to *Aufklärung* (reconnaissance) units of light panzer and motorized infantry.

From 1942, some SdKfz 221 mounted a *Panzer Büchse* (anti-tank) 2.8 cm sPZB41 gun; with this armament the vehicle was designated *SdKfz 221 mit sPzB*; this gun had a tapering bore and a high muzzle velocity of 4,600 feet per second.

## SDKFZ 222 AND SDKFZ 223 (FU)

The SdKfz 221 was used as model for other improved versions.

The light, armored 4 x 4 *SdKfz 222* was equipped with the Horch 801 chassis with the V8 3.5-liter engine. It was basically a

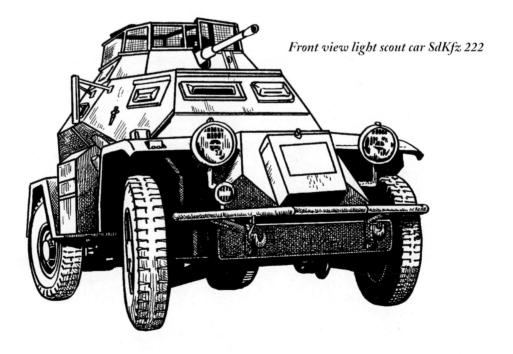

*Front view light scout car SdKfz 222*

*Light armored car SdKfz 222. This version was armed with a KwK 2 cm gun.*

modified version of the Sdkfz 221 with a larger turret designed to carry additional weapons. It was armed with one 2 cm KwK 30 or 38 gun and one 7.92 machine gun. It had a crew of three, weighed 4,300 kg and was fitted with 8 mm armor all round. Fuel consumption was 35 liters/100 km on road and 50 liters cross-country. This vehicle was updated in 1942 to the improved type V chassis and incorporated hydraulic brakes and a bigger 3.8-liter V8 side valve, liquid-cooled gasoline engine. Top speed was 85 km/h, and with a 100-liter fuel capacity, it had a range of 280 km on good road and 200 km off-road. It also had its frontal armor thickened to 14.5 mm at the front and 8 mm at the sides. The 2 cm cannon was mounted coaxially with a MG 34 and could be ele-

vated almost vertically for air defense. It was fast and maneuverable, but cross-country performance was poor, and the chassis was overloaded by the heavier gun and turret mount.

The variant 4 x 4 *SdKfz 223 (Fu)* was basically the same vehicle equipped with radio and fitted with a bulky radio aerial frame. Similar in form to the model SdKfz 222, it had a small turret with only one machine gun, and later versions were fitted with a collapsible, rectangular frame, wireless aerial.

### SDKFZ 260 AND 261

The 4 x 4 *SdKfz 260*, based on the SdKfz 221 chassis and engine, was a radio/

*Light armored car SdKfz 261. This vehicle differed from the SdKfz 221 as it was an unarmed command car equipped with radio and hinged aerial.*

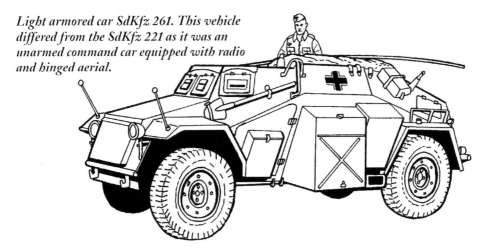

command car with improved performance. Length was 4.75 m, width was 2 m, weight was 4,300 kg, maximum speed was 80 km/h, range was 320 km, and armor was 8 mm thick. This vehicle was deprived of a turret and officially was intended to carry one machine gun, but the bulk of the radio equipment prevented any armament. The type SdKfz 260 was equipped with pole aerials.

The cumbersome radio frame of the *SdKfz 223 (Fu)* was replaced in those models by a hinged collapsible radio mast. The same vehicle with different radio equipment was designated SdKfz 261.

## SDKFZ 247/1 AND SDKFZ 2

These two reconnaissance/radio cars differed only in wireless equipment and in a slight change in the front of the hull. They were generally used as armored staff cars for senior officers. Although front-engined and turretless, they were rather like the SdKfz 221–223 series of light vehicles in appearance.

## PANHARD 38/P240 (F)

The 4 x 4 Panhard 38 *auto-mitrailleuse* (armored car), designed in 1935, was intended for use in the French North African colonies. It saw wide service in the cavalry and reconnaissance units of the armored French army, notably during the Battle of France in May–June 1940. It was a car not unlike the British Daimler in appearance. About 190 French Panhard 38 scout cars were captured by the Germans after the defeat of June 1940, and they attained a certain significance in the German army. The occupiers apparently liked the sound design

*Captured French Panhard 38*

WH 558813

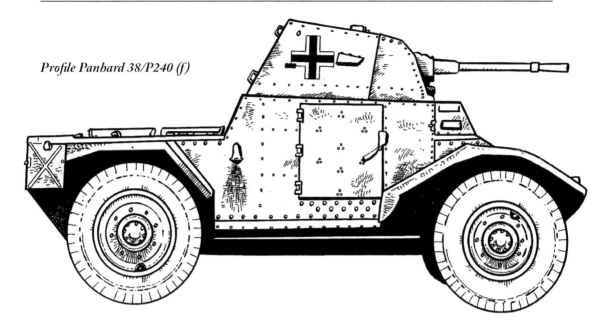

*Profile Panhard 38/P240 (f)*

and decided to adopt them for their own service. Renamed *Panzerspähwagen P240 (f)*, 150 of them were allocated to the Wehrmacht reconnaissance units. The remaining forty were fitted with railroad wheels and used as *Eisenbahndraisinen* (railway patrol cars), the Gothaer Waggonfabrik and Bergisch Stahlindustrie from Remscheid carrying out the railway fittings necessary for these vehicles. Some of these were retained for garrison use in France, but others were later used for anti-partisan operation in the Soviet Union. After the liberation of France, the Panhard 38 scout car was once more put into production with a larger turret armed with a 47 mm gun; known as the Panhard 178, these new vehicles were issued to the French cavalry units and were used for many years after 1945; some saw action in the Indochina War (1946–1954), and it was not until 1960 that the last of them were taken out of active service. The armored car had a crew of four and was powered by a Panhard type ISK 6.3-liter water-cooled gasoline engine, placed at the rear of the vehicle, developing 105 bhp. Weight in full combat condition was 8,300 kg, overall length was 4.79 m, width was 2 m and height was 2.31 m. Maximum speed was 72 km/h (45 mph), fuel consumption was 40 liters/100 km on road and 70 liters/100 km cross-country and maximum range was 300 km (186 mi.). Armor was 20 mm at the front and 7 mm on the sides. Armament included one 25 or 37 mm gun and one or two 7.5 mm machine guns, both placed in the fully rotating top turret.

### AUTO BLINDA FIAT-SPA AB 40

The Italian light Fiat-Spa AB 40 was the World War II standard Italian armored reconnaissance car. Several of them were used by the German army and designated *Panzerspähwagen AB 40 201 (i)*. The vehicle had driving positions at both front and rear, a crew of 4, a 6-cylinder 100 bhp 5-liter OHV engine, and gearbox with 6 forward and 4 reverse. Speed was 78 km/h and range was 400 km on road. Armor was 9 mm thick, length was 5.1 m, and weight was 7.5 tons. Armament consisted of one 20 mm M35 L/65 (i) cannon with 456 rounds placed in the rotative turret and one 8 mm Breda 38 (i) machine gun mounted on the front hull.

In 1943 appeared an improved version known as the *Fiat AB-43* with a speed of 90

*Italian Auto blinda*
*Fiat-Spa AB 40*

km/h, an armor of 8–22 mm, and a 47 mm gun and two 8 mm Breda 38 machine guns.

## Armored trucks with twin rear bogie

Six-wheel reconnaissance vehicles were converted chassis of medium commercial trucks that were fitted with an armored body and a turret. Structurally all these armored vehicles were normal 6-wheeled trucks with three rigid axles on longitudinal leaf springs. Both double-tired rear axles were driven. The front axle was strengthened to take the extra weight, and the radiator surface was increased by about 20 percent for additional cooling water capacity. They were given double steering, and the use of larger and stronger tires was examined. They were intended as a reinforcement to the light, armored four-wheeled vehicles but considered to be only provisional equipment until replacement by modern and better performing 8-wheel types was available. Several models of six-wheel vehicles were produced

for the Reichswehr and the Wehrmacht, and some of them saw action in Poland and France in 1939 and 1940. Six-wheeled vehicles were, however, merely trucks, lightly armed, poorly armored, underpowered with limited performance especially in rough ground and therefore road-bound. After 1941 they were replaced at the front by eight-wheel armored cars and half-tracks, and henceforth only used as training vehicles.

### AUSTRO-DAIMLER ADGZ

The heavy 6 x 4 twin-bogie armored truck *Austro-Daimler ADGZ* had a 6-cylinder 150 bph engine. The truck was 6.3 m in length, 2.16 m in width and 2.5 m in height. Its weight was 7,950 kg. The armament included one light automatic gun and one machine gun placed in the rotating turret and one machine gun in the front hull. Twenty-seven of these reconnaissance armored trucks were produced between 1935 and 1937 and another twenty-five in 1942.

*Heavy armored truck 8 x 8
Austro-Daimler ADGZ*

## STANDARTENWAGEN

The so-called *Standardenwagen* (standardized car) was a 6 x 4 Krupp-Protze L 2 H 143 artillery towing truck, which was fitted with sloping armored plates. This vehicle, produced in the years 1937–1939, was intended to be used as a *Panzerspähwagen* (armored reconnaissance car). Weight was 4,800 kg, maximum speed was 70 km/h on road, and armor was 8 mm thick. Fuel consumption was 28 liters/100 km on road and 40 liters/100 km cross-country. Range was 390 km on road and 270 km cross-country. The vehicle was armed with one machine gun and could accommodate a

*Krupp-Protze L 2 H 143 Standartenwagen*

crew of six, including the driver and the machine gunner or a load of 600 kg. Only a few Krupp L 2 H 143 were converted, and this was not a frequently seen armored reconnaissance truck.

## KRUPP GEPANZERTES RADFAHRZEUG

The chassis of the 6 x 4 light truck type L2H 143 was also used as the basis for a 6-wheel reconnaissance car known as the *Krupp gepanzertes Radfahrzeug* (Krupp armored wheeled vehicle). Designed in 1936, this vehicle was powered by a Krupp 3.3-liter Boxer air-cooled 4-cylinder 60 hp engine; it was 5 m in length, 2.2 m in width and 2.3 m in height; it had a crew of three, a speed of 70 km/h on road, and a range of 450 km on road and 360 km cross-country. The original version was armed with a single machine gun mounted in a small turret, but production models were armed with three machine guns, one in the front and rear hulls, and one in a larger turret. A few

units of the German *Krupp gepanzertes Radfahrzeug* were purchased by the Dutch in 1938. Known as *Wilton-Fijenoord 1938*, they entered service in 1938 in the Royal Dutch Army of the East Indies (today Indonesia) for colonial peacekeeping purposes. The Dutch version had a notable peculiarity: the external body could be electrified to hold attackers at bay.

## ARMORED TRUCK SDKFZ 231 (6-WHEEL)

The *Schwerer Panzerspähwagen SdKfz 231 (6-Rad)*, or 6-wheel heavy reconnaissance truck, was produced between 1930 and 1936. This conversion was based on the chassis of a standardized medium army 6 x 4 truck, either a Magirus type M 206, a Büssing-NAG type G 31 or a Mercedes-Benz type G 3a. The chassis had drive to the four rear wheels only, and the steering was conventionally on the front wheels alone. Some vehicles were fitted with "unditching" rollers placed under the chas-

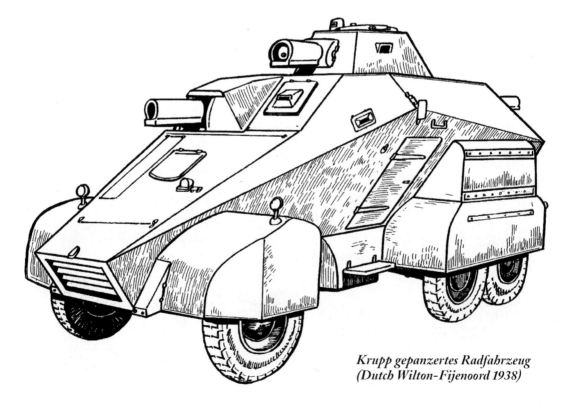

*Krupp gepanzertes Radfahrzeug (Dutch Wilton-Fijenoord 1938)*

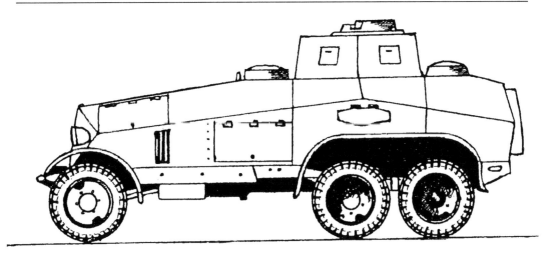

*Daimler-Benz G3P. This prototype, designed in 1930 on a commercial type chassis, was eventually developed into the standard Schwerer Panzerspähwagen SdKfz 231 (6-Rad) type produced in the 1930s.*

*Schwerer Panzerspähwagen SdKfz 231 (6-Rad)*

sis. The truck was fitted with well-designed, effectively sloping armor: 14.5 mm at the front and 8 mm at the sides. The long gap between the front and rear wheels was a noticeable characteristic of the 6-wheeler SdKfz 231. The vehicle was equipped with a rear driving position for quick changes of direction; it thus had duplicate steering positions with alternative controls; the second steering wheel and controls came into action when the reverse gear in the direction box was engaged. There was a crew of four (two drivers/radio operators, one gun-

ner and one commander). Performance and dimensions were, of course, slightly different according to the original chassis and engine. On average, length was 5.6 m, weight was 5,000 kg, maximum speed was 65 km/h, fuel consumption was 35 liters/100 km on road (55 liters/100 km off-road), and range was 200 km cross-country and about 300 km on good road. The armament, placed in a fully rotating top turret, consisted of one 2 cm KwK 30/38 cannon and a co-axial 7.92 mm MG 34 machine gun. The vehicle was in service from 1933 up

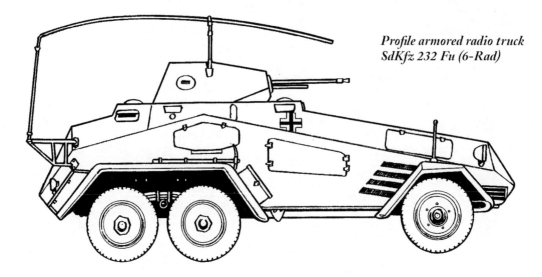

*Profile armored radio truck*
*SdKfz 232 Fu (6-Rad)*

to and including the victorious campaigns of 1939–1940. But its cross-country performance, lacking front wheel drive, fell somewhat below desirable standards, and from late 1940 onward, six-wheelers were gradually replaced by eight-wheelers and later half-tracks in the reconnaissance role.

## RADIO TRUCK
## SDKFZ 232 (6-WHEEL)

There was a variant intended as a radio car, known as a *Panzerfunkwagen SdKfz 232 (6-Rad)*. This, too, was constituted from the chassis of a Magirus type M 206, a Büssing-NAG type G 31 or a Mercedes-Benz type G 3a truck. The vehicle was equipped with a powerful 100-watt wireless radio set. Performance, dimensions, external appearance and armament were slightly the same as the SdKfz 231, but the principal point of difference lay in a large *Rahmenantenne* (antenna framework) placed over the bodywork. This horizontal grid frame aerial for transmission consisted of parallel tubes carried on two outriggers at the back of the vehicle; the frame had a central bearing that rested on a turret support shaped like an inverted U, which allowed the turret to turn beneath the aerial without transmitting any movement to it.

## COMMAND TRUCK
## SDKFZ 263 (6-WHEEL)

Another 6-wheel radio/command truck, based on the *SdKfz 231* design, was the *schwerer Panzerfunkwagen SdKfz 263 (6-Rad)*. Intended as a mobile headquarter/wireless command vehicle, the type 263 differed from the models 231 and 232 in its turret, which was fixed allowing more room inside the vehicle. Armament included only one machine gun, and the radio frame aerial was somewhat larger than that of the SdKfz 232. There was a crew of five (two drivers, one commander and two radio operators).

## Captured six-wheel armored trucks

The Germans also employed captured, six-wheel armored cars and twin-rear bogie trucks, notably those of the Dutch army defeated in May 1940 and Russian 6 x 4 vehicles captured after 1941. As the captured armored trucks were on the whole poor combat machines, they were mainly used as training vehicles by the NSKK (the Nazi Drivers' Corps); a few were converted as command or radio cars. Others were allocated to the *Ordnungpolizei* (Order Police)

*Captured armored truck DAF M-36 (Dutch) seen here in service of the German Ordnung Polizei*

for maintaining the Nazi order in and out of the Reich.

## DUTCH DAF M-38

The Dutch company *van Doorne's Aanhangwagen Fabriek* (DAF, van Doorne's trailer factory) from Eindhoven was created by the brothers Hubert and Willem van Doorne in 1932. In 1936, DAF began to be involved in military vehicles. The results were various armored cars used by the Dutch army in the pre-World War II period. The *M-36 pantserwagen* was introduced in 1936. It had a Daimler-Benz 80 hp gasoline engine, a crew of five, a total length of 5.85 m, a total width of 2.1 m, a total height of 2.5 m, and a weight of 6,100 kg. The Dutch *pantserwagen* was heavily armed with a light Bofors gun caliber 3.7 cm placed in the rotating top turret, and three M-20 machine guns caliber 7.9 cm; one was coaxially placed in the turret, another at the front and the third at the back of the hull. In 1938, the M-36 was improved with a Büssing-

NAG engine, and this variant was known as the *DAF M-38 pantserwagen.*

## RUSSIAN GAZ-BA 32

The *GAZ BA-32* was one of a family of Soviet medium armored vans developed in the early 1930s on the basis of the twin rear bogie light truck *GAZ-AAA* (Russki-Ford) to which armor had been added. The armored truck *GAZ BA-32* had a 4-cylinder 50 bph GAZ M1 engine, a crew of four, a length of 4.65 m, a height of 2.43 m, a weight of approximately 5,000 kg, and a maximum speed of 50 km/h. It was armed with one 4.5 cm KwK gun, and one 7.92 mm machine gun placed in the turret of the T-26 light tank. Another 7.92 mm machine gun was placed in the front hull. The vehicle was not entirely satisfactory as the armored hull, weapons and turret considerably raised the weight for the modest truck chassis; performance suffered and the suspension was overstressed. Nonetheless, the armored truck saw service in the Far

*Captured Russian armored truck GAZ-BA-32*

East in 1937 along the Mongolian border. A part of the production was exported and sold to Turkey, Afghanistan and China in the late 1930s. The most famous foreign user was Spain, where a total of sixty BA armored cars—named *Blindado Ruso* (Russian Armored Car)—were delivered to the Republican forces in 1936; these took part in several of the major battles of the Spanish Civil War including Madrid and Teruel.

After the successful campaign in Russia in the summer of 1941, the Germans seized important stocks of Soviet-made armored trucks, and a few of them continued in service of the Finns well into the 1950s.

## FIAT AUTO BLINDA 611

The 6 x 4 armored car, designed in 1934, was based on the chassis of a Fiat

*Armored truck Fiat Auto Blinda 611*

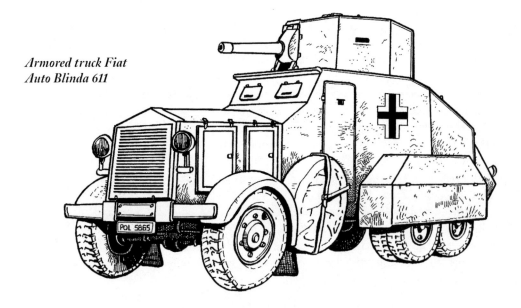

Dovunque truck. The vehicle was powered by a Fiat 6-cylinder 45 bhp gasoline engine. Length was 5.67 m, width was 1.85 m, and height was 2.64 m. It had a crew of five, a speed of 50 km/h, and a range of 280 km. Armor was between 6 and 11 mm. The vehicle was armed with one 47-mm gun placed in the rotating top turret and two Breda 38 machine guns. The Fiat Auto Blinda 611 was used during the war in Ethiopia in 1935. Several of them were captured by the Germans and employed to train their Panzer crews.

## Eight-wheel reconnaissance cars

Of all World War II German wheeled armored vehicles, eight-wheel cars were doubtless the most impressive. Several prototypes were designed in the period 1928 to 1930. The Büssing, Daimler-Benz, Austro-Daimler, and Magirus companies made designs for 8-wheeled troop transport vehicles. These were extensively tested in secret in Germany and at Kazan in Russia to evade the spying eyes of the Allied Control Commission. Two Daimler-Benz prototypes were known as the ARW/MTW *Achtradwagen-Mannschaftstransportwagen*

(8-wheeled troop carrier), a disguise for the true function of armored reconnaissance car. They had 8 wheels and independent suspension on all wheels, and they featured two driving positions: one at the front and another at the back for quick change of direction. The ARW/MTW was intended to have a turret armed with a gun, but this feature was never mounted to conceal the obvious military purpose. The Magirus 8 x 8 design was quite similar and incorporated some of the same features as the Daimler-Benz ARW/MTW. The Büssing-NAG firm made an ambitious design for a *Zehnradwagen ZRW* (10-wheeled armored vehicle); this had all ten wheels equally spaced, duplicated steering controls at both front and rear, and was also turretless and unarmed. With five pairs of wheels, the steering arrangements of the ZRW must have presented considerable design difficulties, although unfortunately details are not available. These early multi-wheel vehicles had very useful features, many of them well in advance of general practice, but they were not further developed at the time. The economic crisis in 1929–1930 prevented more expenditure, and attention was turned instead toward the cheaper 4 x 4 cars and 6 x 4 trucks. The 8 x 8 concept was however reintroduced in 1935 when Hitler repu-

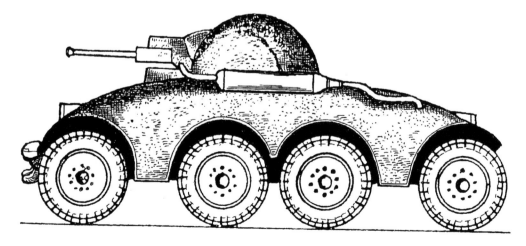

*Daimler-Benz ARW/MTW. The "troop transport" is shown here as it was intended to be: an 8-wheeled armored reconnaissance vehicle with turret and gun.*

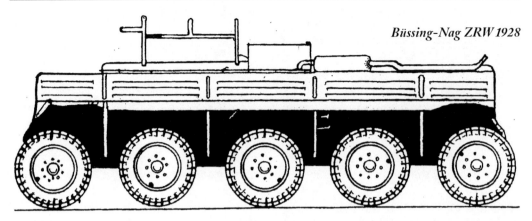

*Büssing-Nag ZRW 1928*

diated the limitations of the Treaty of Versailles and openly rearmed. Owing to knowledge and experience gained between 1927 and 1930 with early 8- and 10-wheeled vehicles, a new eight-wheeled vehicle called the *VsKfz 623 Versuchkraftfahrzeug 623* (experimental vehicle) was designed. This prototype gave birth to a standard model called the *schwerer Panzerspähwagen SdKfz 231 (8-Rad)* or eight-wheel heavy reconnaissance car, which entered service in 1938.

It should be noted that heavy, eight-wheel reconnaissance cars were intended to replace the six-wheel armored trucks whose performance off road could be bettered, and—without consistency for the ordnance pattern—both categories of vehicles were allocated the same *Sonderkraftfahrzeug* (SdKfz) serial number. To avoid confusion, the number of wheels (6-Rad or 8-Rad) was always added.

### HEAVY ARMORED CAR AUSTRO-DAIMLER TYPE ADGZ (8-WHEEL)

The *schwerer Panzerspähwagen ADGZ (8-Rad)* was designed by the Austro-Daimler company in 1935. It was a further development of the previously described twin-bogie armored heavy truck *Austro-Daimler ADGZ*. This turreted version was an unusual and striking beast with 8 all-drive wheels, the center two being twin wheels and the outer two being single. It

had an Austro-Daimler M 612 engine with large louvers. Length was 6.26 m, width was 2.16 m, height was 2.56 m, weight was 12,000 kg, maximum speed was 70 km/h (on road), and fuel consumption was 90 liters/100 km (on road). Armor was 11 mm thick. The crew was composed of six men, and armament included one 2 cm cannon and three machine guns. The *schwerer Panzerspähwagen ADGZ (8-Rad)*—compared to the popular SdKfz 231 (8 wheels)—was not a widely seen vehicle during World War II. A total of 27 units were produced from 1935 to 1937 for the Austrian army. After the annexation of Austria in 1938, these were made part of the Third Reich forces inventory, but as the Wehrmacht did not show interest in these vehicles, they were transferred to the SS forces (Waffen SS and police). Between 1941 and 1942 another twenty-five units were produced and essentially employed by the Waffen SS in Eastern European countries for occupation and peacekeeping services, anti-guerilla actions and police duties. In 1944 the few remaining heavy ADGZ armored cars were in precarious operational conditions. They were gradually removed from frontline service and used for training purposes.

### HEAVY ARMORED CAR SDKFZ 231 (8-WHEEL)

Issued in 1938, the 8 × 8 *Panzerspähwagen SdKfz 231 (8-Rad)* was the first basic

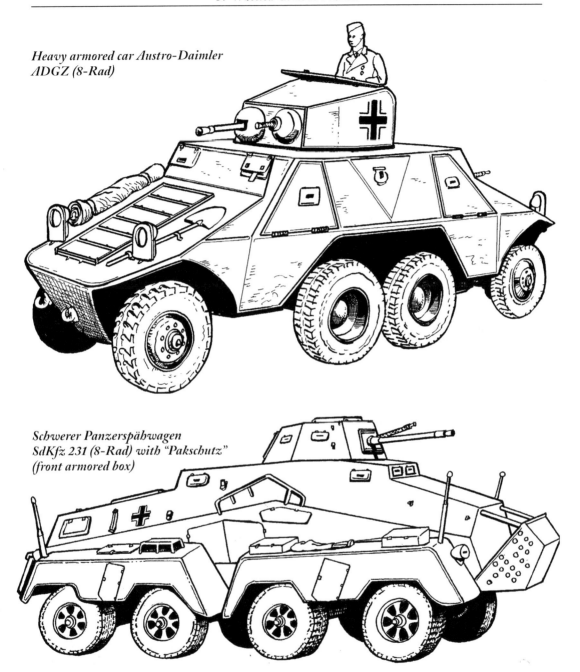

*Heavy armored car Austro-Daimler ADGZ (8-Rad)*

*Schwerer Panzerspähwagen SdKfz 231 (8-Rad) with "Pakschutz" (front armored box)*

type and the most popular of all World War II German 8-wheeled heavy reconnaissance cars.

The vehicle had several features in common with the six-wheeled vehicles from which it took over the SdKfz designation. Although a rear-engined vehicle, the hull form and positioning of the front and rear driving positions was quite like that of the SdKfz 231 (6 wheels), and the armament and the turret were similar too. However the 8-wheeled layout with drive and steering on all wheels gave the new reconnaissance car a good cross-country performance, nearly as good as that of a fully tracked vehicle, but on steep inclines and in soft ground it was at a severe disadvantage. It was impressive and martial-looking but also rather clumsy with a high profile and thus could be easily spotted. The vehicle was manufactured by the Deutsche Werke, Schichau (with the chassis being produced by Büssing-NAG) to replace the early 6 x 4 models and was produced from 1936 to 1943. It was equipped with an 8-wheeled chassis that had steering and drive for all wheels, owing to a rather complicated transmission arrangement. The suspension was independent on all wheels with the use of longitudinal semi-elliptic leaf springs. As with the six-wheeler series, German eight-wheeled reconnaissance vehicles were designed with the knowledge that country lanes were often narrow. They had thus driving positions at both front and back, with two drivers and gears that enabled quick withdrawal, convenient driving and fast speed in both directions. Forward and rearward facing steering controls were fitted for rapid maneuvering, advancing and reversing. The engine was mounted in the rear for protection and an 8 mm armored plate was

welded at the front to give better protection.

The 8 x 8 *Panzerspähwagen SdKfz 231 (8-Rad)* was powered by an 8360 cc overhead valve V8 Büssing-NAG engine giving 155 hp at 3,000 rpm, and this was increased to 180 bhp at 3,000 rpm in later models. This engine drove all 8 wheels via a three speed forward/reverse gearbox and two speed transfer box. It had self-locking differentials. On good road, a speed of 85 km/h (50 mph) was reached. Width was 2.2 m, height was 2.4 m and length was 5.85 m; weight was 7,700 tons. Fuel consumption was 50 liters/100 km on road (90 liters/ 100 km off-road), and range was 150 km cross-country and about 270 km on good road. The sloping armor was well-designed and rather strong: 14.5 mm (later 30 mm) at the front and 8 mm at the sides. Some models were fitted with a so-called *Pak-schutz*, a kind of armored box placed at the front for increasing protection against enemy anti-tank gun fire. The rotating turret was spacious and moved on balls. It was

*Schwerer Panzerspähwagen SdKfz 231 (8-Rad)*

fitted with a periscope and a photo camera. Turret and hull were furnished with vision ports and exit hatches. Firepower was, however, rather poor. Placed in the turret, armament only consisted of one 2 cm KwK 30 or KwK 38 light gun and one coaxially mounted 7.92 mm MG 34 machine gun. The crew of four included a gunner, a commander/gunner, a driver and a radio-operator/second driver. Despite its good cross-country capability and its impressive look, for a vehicle expected to make first contact with the enemy, the *schwerer Panzerspähwagen SdKfz 231 (8-Rad)* as well as its radio and command versions were inadequately armed and armored.

## ARMORED CAR
### SDKFZ 233 (8-WHEEL)

Several variants were based on the *SdKfz 231 (8-Rad)* type. Produced in 1941, the turretless *schwerer Panzerspähwagen SdKfz 233 (8-Rad)* was basically a heavy support version armed with a short 7.5 cm

Stuk/37 L24 gun. The gun was placed not in a turret but in an open combat compartment; its principal drawback was the limited forward traverse. The SdKfz 233 (8-Rad) had a crew of three.

## SDKFZ 232 FUNK (8-RAD) AND SDKFZ 263 (8-RAD)

A similar vehicle was the radio car *SdKfz 232 Funk (8-Rad)*, which was fitted with a large grid frame radio aerial, mounted to permit rotation of the turret. This grid frame was cumbersome, clumsy, vulnerable and fragile, so in later models it was replaced by a simpler type of telescopic pole wireless aerial.

Another radio version, the *SdKfz 263 (8-Rad)* had the rotating armed turret replaced by a fixed raised structure to serve as battalion and regiment radio transmission car. This variant was only armed with one machine gun mounted at the front, although this was not always fitted. Both 232 and 263 carried wireless equipment for

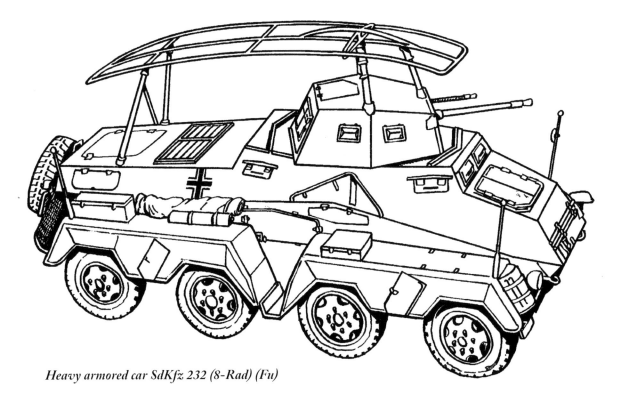

*Heavy armored car SdKfz 232 (8-Rad) (Fu)*

*Schwerer Panzerfunkwagen*
*SdKfz 263 (8-Rad)*

use as a formation command vehicle. After 1941 these cumbersome radio cars were replaced by half-tracks.

## Late development of eight-wheelers

Eight-wheel *Panzerspähwagen* were in service throughout the war on all fronts. They played an important role in the 1939–1941 *Blitz* campaigns and performed very well in North Africa. However, after 1942, they were progressively replaced by half-tracks in the reconnaissance and wireless/command role. They did not disappear, though, and remained in production until the end of the war as artillery carriers.

With operations in hot countries in view, a new version was set in motion as early as 1940, but it was only in late 1943 that a new eight-wheel armored car was produced, known as the SdKfz 234 ARK series. The new version featured longer range, improved suspension and larger tires,

thicker armor, an air-cooled diesel engine, increased speed and powerful armament. Externally the SdKfz 234 ARK series was similar to the earlier models. The most obvious external difference was the mudguards: the earlier 8-wheeled armored cars had a break between the front pair and rear pair of mudguards on each side; the new cars had a single long mudguard on each side containing stowage lockers. The new vehicle, known as the *schwerer Panzerspähwagen SdKfz 234*, was first manufactured in 1941 by the Büssing AG Company, but it was not until late 1943 that the first models were delivered. The chassis specifications of the four ARK series models were identical (apart form the varying weights and height). They were powered by a 14,825 cc V12 air-cooled Tatra diesel engine developing about 220 hp at 2,250 rpm mounted at the rear of the vehicle. This air-cooled engine was suitable for use in very cold as well as hot climates; by that time the Russian and northwest European fronts were all-important. The engine drove all eight-

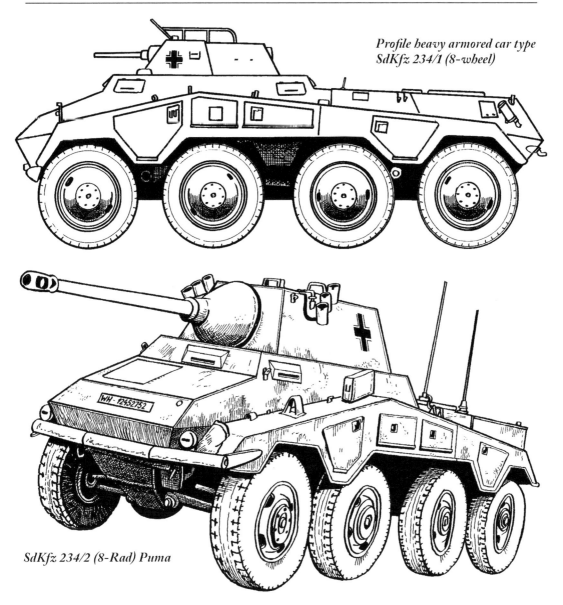

*Profile heavy armored car type SdKfz 234/1 (8-wheel)*

*SdKfz 234/2 (8-Rad) Puma*

wheels via a 3-speed forward/reverse gear-box and 2-speed transfer box. All variants were fitted with air brakes and all-wheel steering with independent suspension with inverted leaf springs. All were fitted with radio (FuG. Spr. Ger. A and FuG. 12). All models had slightly different performances and weight according to their weapons. On average they had a speed of about 90 km/h, a length of 6 m, a width of 2.33 m, a height of 2.1 m, and a weight of 7,700 kg. Fuel consumption was 40 liters/100 km on road, 60 liters/100 km cross-country, and it had a range of 600 km on road and 400 km cross-country. Armor was 30 mm at the front and 14.5 at the sides. The crew included the usual four men. The vehicles of the 234 series, because of their modern design, were among the most advanced armored vehicles to appear by the end of World War II. Four types existed, armed with various caliber weapons as follows:

• The *SdKfz 234/1 (8-Rad)* was armed with one 2 cm KwK 38 gun and one coaxial MG 42 placed in a roofless turret allow-

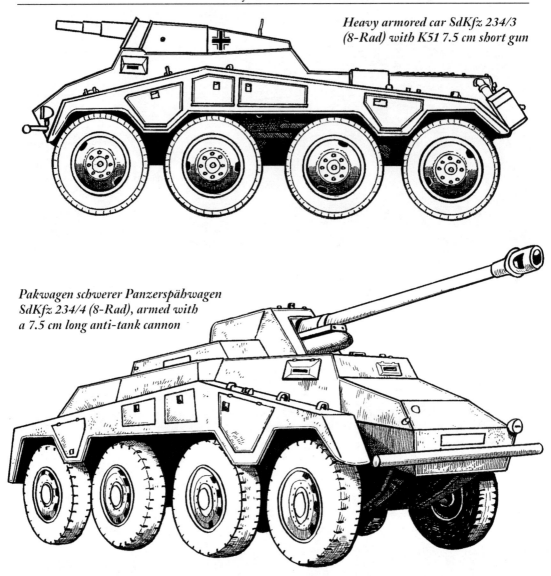

*Heavy armored car SdKfz 234/3 (8-Rad) with K51 7.5 cm short gun*

*Pakwagen schwerer Panzerspähwagen SdKfz 234/4 (8-Rad), armed with a 7.5 cm long anti-tank cannon*

ing both high elevation anti-aircraft and ground fire. This type of turret, which was protected on top by wire netting grilles, helped to reduce the overall height of the vehicle. This mount was made by Daimler-Benz (Berlin) in conjunction with the Schichau Works in Elbing.

• The *Sdkfz 234/2 (8-Rad)* was the most famous of this new generation. Popularly known as the *Puma*, this car had a crew of four, a length of 6.8 m, a maximum speed of 85 km/h on good road, and a range of 800 to 1,000 km. It weighed 11,700 kg, and it was armed with one MG 42 machine gun, six smoke shell launchers and one 5 cm KwK 39/1 anti-tank gun placed in a rotative, oval, fully traversable turret. The *SdKfz 234/2 Puma* could also be armed with a 5 cm L/60 gun (which was also used in MK III Ausf J tanks). It was the only model of this series to have an enclosed fighting compartment in the form of a rotating turret with a full 360-degree traverse. The *Saukopf* (Pig's Head) gun mantlet was built with 100 mm armor. About one hundred *Puma* were built.

• The *SdKfz 234/3* was armed with a 7.5 cm L/24 or a 7.5 cm K 51 short gun that could swing 12 degrees either side. In addition an MG 42 was mounted coaxially. The gun was placed in a turretless open structure giving the crew of four no overhead protection. Frontal armor was 30–40 mm thick, and there was room inside the vehicle for 50 rounds of ammunition. Weight was 10,000 kg, maximum speed was 85 km/h and range was 600 km cross-country and 1,000 km on road. Eighty-eight 234/3 models were produced.

• The *SdKfz 234/4 Pakwagen* was armed with an anti-tank 7.5 cm L/48 Pak 40, which assimilated this vehicle to a *Panz-erjäger* (tank-hunter). This turretless version was intended to replace the 234/3 on account of its armament's lack of power and its strongly curved ballistic trajectory. Although the main armament of the 234/4 was better, the strong recoil had an undesirable effect on the chassis and wheels, and the gun still had only limited sideways movement. Eighty-nine were built.

## Markings and camouflage

Concerning markings and camouflage, everything mentioned about vehicles in the previous section can be applied to reconnaissance cars, but—like tanks—reconnaissance cars had *tactical markings*. Tactical numbers enabled a unit commander to quickly call up one of his vehicles by radio and pick it out more easily across the battlefield. The number was usually indicated by three large stenciled figures placed on both sides of the turret, but they could also be repeated on the turret rear or sides of the hull. There were many variations on the theme, some being in "solid" or outlined form, or red, yellow, white or black according to the turret background color. These rather large numbers were adopted as a result of war experience for better and quicker identification by the commander on the battlefield. The first figure indicated the *Kompanie* (company), the second the *Zug* (platoon) and the third the vehicle's place within the platoon. For example, 121 would mean that the car belonged to the first company, was from the second platoon and was the platoon leader's tank, as the figure one was always reserved for the platoon leader.

Each Panzer division had its own distinctive insignia, and in many cases these signs were placed on the reconnaissance armored vehicles as well.

## Uniforms

The *Panzerwaffe* (armored force) was officially created in 1935, and it was rapidly transformed from an experimental and largely clandestine department into an important fighting branch of the German

*Markings on a turret. The markings on the depicted turret of a Sdkfz 234/2 (8-Rad) Puma included the national black cross with white outline and a three-digit number. The first figure indicated the company within the regiment, the second figure indicated the platoon within that company, and the third figure indicated the individual vehicle within that platoon.*

*The black Panzer uniform (1940)*                    *Captain (Hauptmann) Panzer troop*

army with divisional formations. Armored troops (including armored reconnaissance cars' crews) were newcomers without tradition in the German army, and a special uniform, the *Sonderbekleidung der deutschen Panzertruppen* (special uniform for the German armored force), was designed in November 1934. This special Panzer uniform was a complete departure from the standard issue military uniform in use by that time by the German forces. It was wholly distinctive, original and striking, both in style and color.

The German special tank uniform was black; this color had symbolically and emotionally a strong meaning, but practically, lubricant, oil and grease stains were harder to see on a black item; oil patches were a common hazard for tanks and armored car crews. On the other hand, the black uniform had one major drawback. It was completely unsuitable for camouflage purposes; the wearer became conspicuous when outside his vehicle and it clearly identified the wearer as a tank soldier; so if men in black uniforms were seen at the frontline, there was a good chance that they were undertaking a reconnaissance prior to an armored attack.

*Oberfeldwebel (Staff Sergeant) Panzer troop 1943*

*Totenkopf (Death's Head) worn by armored troops. This was displayed on both collars of the jacket with pink piping.*

The two-piece Panzer uniform was intended to be practical yet also to convey the elite status of the *Panzerwaffe*. It consisted of a jacket and trousers worn with shirt and tie. It was very practical, being especially designed for men having to operate in a confined space and having to easily climb in and jump out of the vehicle.

The Panzer *Feldjacke* was a short hip-length, double-breasted, tight-fitting jacket, having no external pockets or external features that would snag. The buttons on the slanted front closure were concealed. The jacket had a partial lining inside each front with pockets, a small fob pocket and a rear hip pocket. It had a deep fall collar and broad lapels decorated with collar piping. The collar patches were the most eye-catching feature since they displayed a silver/white metal *Totenkopf* (death's head). The combination of black uniform and death's head was dramatic and fearsome. The designers of this uniform were probably influenced by the historical aspect of the old imperial German Death's Head black Hussar uniform. The jacket was normally worn open at the neck with the wide lapels folded back showing the grey shirt and the black tie; if required, it was buttoned across the neck to give extra warmth. By being double breasted, the jacket was intended to provide additional frontal protection to the wearer from wind as well as extra warmth, but military doctors were concerned about the lack of climatic protection it gave to the lower abdomen. The shoulder straps—partly concealed by the lapels—were stitched down onto the jacket to prevent them becoming caught up on any projection inside the tank or armored car.

A general issue was a black leather *Koppel* (waist-belt) with a rectangular *Koppelschloß* (buckle-plate) bearing a raised motif—an eagle and swastika, with folded wings in a circular rib and bearing the legend *Gott Mit Uns* (God With Us). There was also a cross-chest leather belt but—as this could snag on projections inside the vehicle—it was often discarded.

The *Feldhose* (trousers) were the same for all ranks: they were black, full length and slightly baggy. They were fastened around the ankle and usually tucked into the universal *Marschstiefel* (marching jackboots) giving a deep "pull-down" effect. The trousers had two slanting side pockets, both with button down flaps, and a small fob pocket and a hip pocket.

Early in 1941 it was ordered that henceforth the army boots would be replaced by

*Schnürschue* (ankle-length laced shoes) with short *Gamaschen* (canvas gaiters)—an item largely ignored.

A *Hemd* (shirt) was worn under the *Feldjacke*. This could be black or dark grey, with or without breastpockets, with or without shoulder straps, with or without breast eagle/swastika and war decoration. The shirt was often worn with a black *Kravatte* (tie). An alternative was a roll-neck grey or black woolen sweater for bad weather.

Originally the tank and armored car crews were issued with a black beret, consisting of a crash liner fitted with a beret cover called a *Schutzmütze* (protection cap). It was compact, soft, close fitting and rather suitable for wear inside an enclosed armored vehicle. However, it was gradually phased out by 1940 and replaced by various army headgear including peaked and peakless caps as well as the standard army steel helmet.

The black *Sonderbekleidung* was originally intended for wearing only when the crews were on duty with their armored vehicles. A normal *Feldgrau* (field grey) uniform and greatcoat—which retained their specific insignia—were issued for other occasions. However, the black uniform became so popular with the crews and proved attractive enough that they took to wearing it with pride for all military and social functions.

All Panzer crews were issued with a *Drillichanzug* (fatigue uniform). This uniform—usually but not always deprived of insignia, medals and ranks—was white/light-grey and made of unbleached denim material. It consisted of a shapeless buttoned jacket with two patch pockets and a turn down collar. The trousers were made of the same material and were simple cut with two side pockets. There were also a wide miscellany of denim-type, loose-cut, one-piece overalls and boiler suits. Fatigue suits, boiler suits and overalls were German—made or pressed into service from obsolete or captured stocks of various origins. They were easily washable and used

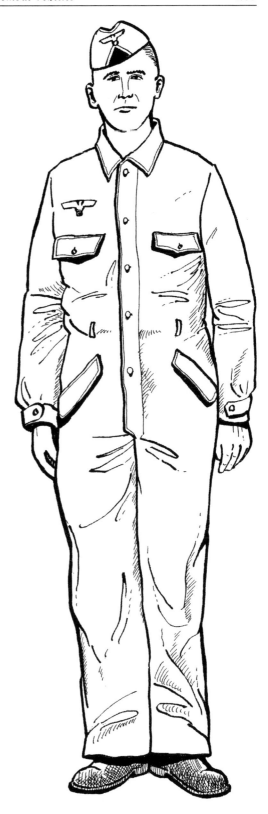

*Mechanic in overalls*

*Panzerkampfwagen Abzeichen. The tank assault badge was awarded to armored personnel (including half-tracks and armored car troops) for three tank engagements on different days. Later versions were instituted for 100, 75, 50 and 25 (shown here) engagements.*

extensively for fatigue duty, dirty jobs in bad weather, work, instruction, training maneuvers, weapon cleaning, motor vehicle maintenance, and so forth. As the war went on, uniforms worn by armored troops and reconnaissance cars crews got much more diversified and adapted to the particularities of the theaters of operation, including light dresses in Northern Africa, thick heavy quilted coats on the Russian front, and various camouflaged tunics. By the end of the war, German logistics got more and more strained, and strict regulations could no longer be observed. In many cases *Drillich* suits were worn as extra or alternative combat outfits instead of or in combination with elements of the official Panzer black suit.

*Waffen SS Untersturmführer (Second Lieutenant) Panzer troop 1944*

On the whole, German World War II uniforms were well designed and well manufactured with a great degree of standardization, combining functionality and a rather smart appearance. However, if troops entered combat zones with regulation dress, the ravages of fighting were hard on uniforms. Replacement supplies from behind the lines were not always forthcoming, and soldiers tended to take what was available and to make do. Soldiers therefore often wore odd mixtures of original issue, items from other friendly troops and occasionally fallen foes and even articles that were stolen or borrowed on the spot. Besides, the unexpected prolongation of the war into 1942 and the effective blockade brought upon Germany resulted in shortage of raw materials and therefore in a need to simplify and use poorer quality cloth by 1943 onwards. The uniforms made from then on had 50 percent or even less wool content mixed with low grade recycled material.

# Conclusion

It is generally believed that the German army was in the forefront of mechanization, as shown by the renowned *Panzer* divisions; the fact was that they were a good deal less advanced in basic military mechanization than most other countries. The German army always suffered from motor vehicle shortages from the start in 1939 until the end in 1945. Although many civilian transport trucks and many enemy captured vehicles were pressed into German service and re-marked, production and replacement were never able to match losses, attrition and destruction of transport vehicles. The fact that motorized *Blitzkrieg* and the German army—at least in the eyes of the public at large—were almost synonymous did not imply that the German soldiers of World War II were equipped with an abundance of tactical-type motor vehicles. The elite armored divisions might have been equipped with high standard and well built equipment, especially for military use vehicles, but these were sophisticated and expensive to elaborate and produce, and their number was sufficient to equip a comparatively small portion, only about 10 percent of Hitler's war machine. The remainder were of a wide variety and became even more disparate as the war continued. As we

have seen, a high proportion of the German forces' transport of troops and supplies was carried out with confiscated, captured or impressed foreign military and civilian vehicles. In spite of the efforts of Göbbels's propaganda department, German armies were by no means totally motorized. Leg-work, bicycles and horsepower continued to predominate over the combustion engine. Horses were used in enormous quantities right throughout the war, not only behind the front lines and in the occupied territories but often in combat zones too. Each 1939 infantry division of 17,200 soldiers included 5,375 horses on its establishment. So far behind were the Germans, as a matter of fact, that the majority of their field artillery went to war in 1939—and even later—behind horse teams. The question why the German Wehrmacht, so forward-looking in many ways, still envisaged a major role for horses at a time when other armies were retiring them of service may be explained by the inadequacy of production versus demand. German automotive production simply could not keep pace with the expansion of the army. The German forces rapidly grew in manpower—from ten divisions in 1933 to 55 divisions in 1939 (of which only 14 were fully motorized), while

*Hf1 transport wagon. The ubiquitous Hf 1 transport wagon was a heavy, four-wheel cart drawn by one or two horses. It weighed 650 kg (1,430 lb.) empty and could carry a load of 750 kg (1,650 lb.). The wagon was generally fitted with a camouflaged, painted canvas cover. The larger Hf 2 needed a four-horse team. It weighed 1,040 kg (2,292 lb.) empty and had a load capacity of 1,720 kg (3,792 lb.). Another standardized horse-drawn wagon was the Hf 7/11 with rubber-tired wheels and steel body. Other carts were used, many of them simply captured, commandeered, looted or "borrowed" from local peasants. The standardized Hf 1 and Hf 2 horse-drawn wagons remained in widespread use until 1945 for transport and heavy loads.*

the capacity of producing combustion vehicles followed a much slower rise. There was thus a continued reliance on the horse in draft roles.

Logistics became increasingly complicated as the tonnage of supplies to be carried multiplied. An army's rapid advance was a supply officer's nightmare; as soldiers and tanks moved farther away from railheads, supplies dwindled. For a 60-mile trip, one tank type Pzkpfw III needed 80 gallons of gasoline, and one Tiger tank consumed 180 gallons of gasoline. An average Panzer division used about 1,000 gallons of fuel per mile (twice this across country). A multitude of supplies such as food, ammunitions or fuel had to be brought and distributed to the front troops. In combat,

casualty evacuation and medical units added more complexities and demanded more vehicles. If some divisions were well equipped, the average German *Versorgungskolonne* (motorized supply column) often looked like a parade of worn-out, used, broken down, pitifully inadequate vehicles. In certain extreme conditions (in northern Africa or on the Russian front, for example), instead of trucks carrying troops, it was the soldiers who were obliged to disembark and push the trucks through loose sand, thick mud or snow. In the North African campaign, shortages of fuel and supply as well as inadequate transport were the reasons of Rommel's failure. In Russia snow and ice, as well as ambushes and sabotages by partisans, made road movement slow and hazardous. In the last two years of the war, all daylight movements were utterly dangerous; the sky was totally dominated by the Allied air forces, and the Germans were under quasi constant bombing and strafing from what they called *Jagdbomber* (*Jabos* in short, fighter-bombers and ground attack airplanes). The Allies were well informed of German moves by the network of agents, radio intercepts and constant aerial reconnaissance. Before they got anywhere near the front, the Germans lost many vehicles, weapons, equipments and men. In June 1944, it took the well-equipped, motorized *2nd Waffen SS Division Das Reich* about two weeks to reach the battlefield of Normandy, 450 miles from Toulouse where it was stationed; the wheeled vehicles proceeded by road and the tracked vehicles and tanks by train. The very slow progression was due to sabotages and ambushes by resistancegroups and Allied air attacks. Having lost many vehicles, weapons and men on the way, *Das Reich* was unable to launch a serious counterattack because of disorganization and lack of fuel for its Panzer. The fate of the hopeless Ardennes Offensive (Battle of the Bulge in winter 1944–1945) was also sealed by lack of fuel, ammunition and supply.

The motorization of the German army started off on very professional lines with high ambitions and great expectations during the 1930s, but it ended in complete shambles. Technical superiority was often bedeviled by administrative muddle, and achievements came often to nothing through inter-service rivalries and an utter lack of vision at the top. World War II was lost by Germany—partly—because the German High Command never fully understood how to master the problem of bringing supplies across oceans and seas that they did not command and across overextended conquered territories. Hitler, a genius of evil and supreme commander in chief of the German army, was greatly responsible for this failure. Although amateurishness was one of his dominant character traits, he considered himself a visionary warlord, the superior of the experts. Unburdened by standard ideas and theories, his quick intelligence and audacity conceived unusual measures that contributed to astonishing victories in the early years of World War II. But as soon as setbacks occurred, his ignorance, incompetence, fanaticism, and rigid stubbornness brought total defeat and downfall. The history of German World War II transport—like that of its *Luftwaffe* (Air Force)—is the story of a tragic failure as the transport force proved itself incapable of meeting the demands placed upon it.

# Bibliography

André, Jean-Patrick, and Jacques Scipion. *Les Uniformes de la Panzertruppe 1934–1942*. Paris: Regi-Arm Publishers, 2003.

Chant, Christopher. *The Nazi War Machine*. London: Tiger Books International, 1996.

*Les Chars Allemands*. n.p.: Musée des Blindés de Saumur, n.d.

Davis, W.J.K. *Wehrmacht Camouflage and Markings 1939–1945*. New Malden: Almark Publishing Co. Ltd., 1972.

Frank, Reinhard. *Lastkraftwagen der Wehrmacht*. Utting: Podzun-Pallas Publishers, n.d.

Frank, Reinhard. *Personenkraftwagen der Wehrmacht*. Utting: Podzun-Pallas Publishers, n.d.

Frank, Reinhard. *Mercedes im Kriege*. Friedberg: Podzun-Pallas Publishers, 1985.

Hogg, Ian, and John Weeks. *Military Vehicles*. London: Quarto Publishing, 1980.

Oswald, Werner. *Kraftfahrzeuge und Panzer der Reichswehr, Wehrmacht und Bundeswehr*. Stuttgard: Motorbuch Verlag Publishers, 1971.

Schulten, C.M., and J. Theil. *Nederlandse Pantservoertuigen*. Bussum: Van Holkema & Warendorf Publishers, n.d.

Senger und Etterlin F.M. *Die deutschen Panzer 1926–1945*. Munich: Lehmann Verlag, 1968.

Spielberger, Walter J. *Militärfahrzeuge von Krauss-Maffei bis 1945*. Koblenz: Wehr & Wissen Publishers, 1980.

*Vehicules Blindés Allemands 1939–1945*. Paris: Hachette Editions, 1978.

Wiersch, Bernd. *VW-Kübelwagen und VW-Schwimmwagen*. Friedberg: Podzun-Pallas Publishers, 1987.

# Index